EUROPEAN HISTORICAL DICTIONARIES
Edited by Jon Woronoff

His Royal Highness, Jean, Grand Duke of Luxembourg and Duke of Nassau. Reprinted with permission from the Press and Information Service, Ministère d'Etat.

Historical Dictionary
of Luxembourg

Harry C. Barteau

European Historical Dictionaries, No. 14

The Scarecrow Press, Inc.
Lanham, Md., and London
1996

SCARECROW PRESS, INC.

Published in the United States of America
by Scarecrow Press, Inc.
4720 Boston Way
Lanham, Maryland 20706

4 Pleydell Gardens, Folkestone
Kent CT20 2DN, England

British Cataloguing-in-Publication Information Available

Library of Congress Cataloging-in-Publication Data
Barteau, Harry C.
Historical dictionary of Luxembourg / by Harry C. Barteau.
p.   cm. — (European historical dictionaries ; no. 14)
Includes bibliographical references.
1. Luxembourg—History—Dictionaries. I. Title. II. Series.
DH908.B37   1996   949.35'003—dc20   95-26325   CIP
ISBN 0–8108–3106–6 (cloth : alk. paper)

To Wallace P. Bishop,
former Professor of History at Northeastern University,
a gentleman, scholar, and friend to all his students,
with my increasing admiration and affection.

Contents

Illustrations

Editor's Foreword

Although one of Europe's smallest countries, Luxembourg has long enjoyed a significance greater than its size might warrant. This can be traced in part to its strategic location that was sometimes an advantage, but all too often a problem. Its present role derives from its enviable position as one of the capitals of the European Union, several of whose key institutions it houses. A shrinking industrial sector has been more than compensated for by the startling growth of its service sector, especially as a financial and banking center. Still, it takes considerable effort and outstanding ability for Luxembourg to maintain the comfortable living standard it has established for its residents. If being a Grand Duchy seems like an anachronism, most other aspects of Luxembourg's economy and financial organization are keen, competent, and up to date.

Despite its important role in the European Union and its prominence in financial circles, Luxembourg is not very well known abroad. Very few outsiders, even those who bank their money there, realize how the broader economy works and how it manages to keep up with the times. Even fewer can imagine what part a Grand Duke plays in a smoothly functioning democracy, and what other institutions of government exist. Thousands of foreigners visit the country every year, but few go out into the countryside to discover what the country, apart from the capital city, is really like.

This *Historical Dictionary of Luxembourg* fills several major gaps, with a broad array of entries about significant persons, places, events, institutions, politics, social conditions, culture, and the economy, as well as an extensive chronology, lists of rulers and prime ministers, maps, photographs, and other items.

Few foreigners know Luxembourg as well as the author, who has lived in the Grand Duchy for the past twenty years, serving, until his recent retirement, as director of the American International School of Luxembourg. He has imparted his knowledge of Luxembourg to his students, their parents, and many visitors, and, through the present book, hopes to make many more people aware of the importance of the Grand Duchy to Europe, past, present, and future. If he can, at the same time, win a few more friends for the nation he considers the greatest little country in Europe, he will feel he has accomplished something worthwhile.

Jon Woronoff
Series Editor

Acknowledgments

My thanks are due to the staff of the National Library (Biblio-thèque National) of Luxembourg, most particularly to René-Charles Bour and Maximilian Laver for their valuable assistance in locating sources. They are also due to Professor Ekkehard Stiller, director of the Miami University John E. Dolibois European Center, for permission to use its library, and to librarian Christine Vankrunkelsven for help in locating materials in its collection.

My debt to Seth H. Ruef, computer coordinator of the American International School of Luxembourg, for expert computer assistance in drawing up the maps in this book is gratefully acknowledged.

I owe my wife, Maryann, a double debt of gratitude, not only for her assistance as librarian at the American International School of Luxembourg, but also because she typed this entire book into our computer. For this, as well as for so many other things, I thank her most gratefully.

A special note of thanks goes to Lawrence G. Elliott, roving editor of the *Reader's Digest*, who suggested that I be selected to write the *Historical Dictionary of Luxembourg*.

Chronology

c. 900–400 B.C.	Celtic tribes from Danube Valley cross Rhine into Gaul, Spain, and the British Isles.
58–52 B.C.	Roman legions led by Julius Caesar conquer Gaul.
54 B.C.	Caesar conquers Treveri, Gallic tribe along the lower Moselle.
52 B.C.–A.D. 450	Gallo-Roman era. Gaul part of Roman empire.
44 B.C.–A.D. 180	Pax Augustorum. Trier becomes important Roman city.
200–300	Rhineland Franks begin raids into northeastern Gaul.
300–450	Rhineland Franks enlisted in Roman armies, permitted to settle among Gallo-Romans in Rhine-Moselle area. Salian Franks settle in lands between lower Rhine and Scheldt.
451	Hunnish raid into northern Gaul, led by Attila.
455	Trier occupied by Rhineland Franks, who settle in large numbers in area between the Rhine, Meuse, and Moselle, later known as Austrasia.
481–511	Conquest of Gaul completed by Salian Franks under Clovis. Frankish rule established over Neustria.
481–752	Merovingian period. Descendants of Clovis reign over lands of the Franks.
628–752	Austrasian mayors of the palace dominate the weak Merovingian rulers.
698	St. Willibrord establishes monastery at Echternach.
752	Pepin the Short elected king of the Franks, deposing last Merovingian ruler. Founds Carolingian dynasty.
768	Charlemagne, son of Pepin the Short, be-

comes king of the Franks. Establishes his capital at Aix-la-Chapelle (Aachen).

800   Charlemagne crowned Roman Emperor in the West by Pope Leo III.

843   Treaty of Verdun. Charlemagne's empire divided among his three grandsons. Lothair I given Middle Kingdom to rule.

855   Death of Lothair I. Lothair II inherits northern part of his kingdom, which becomes known as Lotharingia, or Lorraine.

870   Treaty of Mersen. Lothair II dies without heirs and Lorraine is divided between his uncles, Charles the Bald of France and Louis the German.

925   Henry the Fowler establishes German control over Lorraine.

936   Otto I elected king of the Germans, crowned at Aachen.

950   Sigefroi, son of Wigeric, count of the Ardennes, given Echternach as fief by Otto I.

962   Otto I crowned Holy Roman Emperor by Pope John XII in Rome.

963   Sigefroi begins construction of castle on the Bock.

966   Sigefroi accompanies Otto I on second invasion of Italy.

963–1354   City of Luxembourg grows up under protection of Sigefroi's castle. Sigefroi's successors recognized as counts of Luxembourg. County of Luxembourg becomes important feudal state.

1136   Direct male line of Sigefroi comes to an end with the death of Conrad II. Henry, count of Namur, becomes count of Luxembourg as Henry IV.

1244   Countess Ermesinde grants municipal charter to city of Luxembourg.

1308   Henry VII, count of Luxembourg, elected king of the Romans (Germans). Crowned at Aachen in 1309.

1310–13   Henry VII invades Italy, is crowned king of the Lombards in 1311 and Holy Roman Emperor in 1312.

1310   John, son of Henry VII, becomes count of

	Luxembourg. Marries Elizabeth of Bohemia in 1311.
1312	John crowned king of Bohemia, first of four Luxembourgish kings to rule that country.
1312–40	John fights in several campaigns in Germany, Italy, Lithuania, and Lorraine; loses sight in one eye in second Lithuanian campaign.
1340	John seeks medical treatment in Montpellier, loses sight of other eye. Known thereafter as John the Blind.
1346	Charles, eldest son of John the Blind, elected king of the Romans. John dies fighting on French side at Battle of Crécy. Charles assumes title of count of Luxembourg and is crowned king of the Romans as Charles IV.
1348	Charles IV crowned king of Bohemia as Charles I. Makes Prague capital of the Holy Roman Empire.
1353	Charles IV relinquishes Luxembourg to his half-brother, Wenzel (Wenceslas) I.
1354	Luxembourg raised to status of Duchy, with Wenzel I as its first duke. Wenzel marries Jeanne of Brabant.
1356	Joyeuse Entrée of Wenzel I and Jeanne of Brabant into Brussels, their new capital. Charles IV issues Golden Bull regulating election of Holy Roman Emperors.
1383	Wenzel I dies without heirs. Brabant reverts to wife's family. Duchy of Luxembourg reverts to his nephew, Wenzel (Wenceslas) II, Holy Roman Emperor and king of Bohemia.
1383–1443	Time of troubles. Wenzel II, in need of money, gives Luxembourg as a pawn for repayment of a substantial loan. Luxembourg falls under control of various creditors in turn, ending up under the rule of Wenzel's niece, Elizabeth of Goerlitz. Sigismund, brother of Wenzel I and his successor as Holy Roman Emperor, is unable to repay loan, and leaves Elizabeth in control.
1441	Elizabeth of Goerlitz sells the Duchy of Luxembourg to Philip the Good of Burgundy.
1443	Burgundian armies capture city of Luxembourg in surprise night attack.

1443–1555	Period of Burgundian rule. Duchy of Luxembourg ruled by dukes of Burgundy from their capital at Brussels.
1477	Death of Charles the Bold, duke of Burgundy, at the Battle of Nancy. His daughter Mary becomes regent and marries Maximilian of Austria.
1506	Charles of Ghent, grandson of Mary of Burgundy and Maximilian of Austria, inherits Burgundian possessions, including the Duchy of Luxembourg, at the age of 6.
1516	Charles of Ghent becomes king of Spain as Charles I, heir to Ferdinand and Isabella.
1517	Beginning of Protestant Reformation in Germany.
1519	Charles of Ghent inherits Austria, Bohemia, and Hungary upon the death of his grandfather, Maximilian I. Elected king of the Romans in 1520 as Charles V.
1521	Charles V presides over Imperial Diet at Worms, which condemns the teachings of Martin Luther.
1527	Imperial troops capture Rome, take Pope Clement VII prisoner.
1530	Charles V crowned Holy Roman Emperor by Clement VII in Bologna. (Last Holy Roman Emperor to be crowned by a pope.)
1552–54	Large part of Luxembourg city, including Sigefroi's castle, destroyed while under siege during war between Charles V and Francis I, king of France.
1555	Charles V turns over control of Burgundian possessions in the Netherlands, including Duchy of Luxembourg, to his son Philip.
1556	Philip becomes king of Spain as Philip II.
1559	Philip II returns to Spain, appoints his sister Margaret of Parma regent of the Netherlands.
1559–66	Political and religious strife in the Netherlands.
1566	Iconoclastic Fury causes Margaret to send to Philip II for help.
1567	Philip II sends Spanish army under duke of Alva to restore order and reestablish royal control in the Netherlands. Alva sets up

	Council of Blood, and hangs counts of Egmont and Horn. William the Silent goes into exile in Germany.
1568	William the Silent's first invasion of the Netherlands ends in failure.
1572	William the Silent's second, more successful, invasion of the Netherlands. Aided by the Sea Beggars, he gains control of Holland, Zealand, and Utrecht.
1575	Unpaid Spanish troops in Netherlands mutiny and sack several cities, including Antwerp (Spanish Fury). Southern provinces join northern provinces in revolt.
1577	Don Juan of Austria sent to Netherlands by Philip II as governor. Spanish troops withdrawn. New iconoclastic outbreaks.
1578	Duke of Parma, son of Don Juan, sent to Netherlands with new army to put down rebellion and restore order.
1578–87	Parma reconquers southern Netherlands, including Antwerp.
1581	Seven northern provinces declare their independence, as the United Provinces, with William the Silent as stadholder.
1584	Assassination of William the Silent.
1588	Defeat of the Spanish Armada ends Spanish hopes of reconquering the northern Netherlands.
1609	Spanish sign twelve-year truce with United Provinces.
1618–48	Thirty Years War.
1621	Spain renews war against United Provinces.
1635	Entrance of France into Thirty Years War turns Luxembourg into battleground.
1648	Treaty of Westphalia ends Thirty Years War. Dutch independence recognized.
1648–59	Fighting continues in Spanish Netherlands between Spain and France.
1659	Treaty of the Pyrenees ends war between France and Spain. France annexes part of the Duchy of Luxembourg, including area around Thionville (First Partition of Luxembourg).
1672–78	French war against the United Provinces (Dutch Republic).

1678–84	Louis XIV conquers Duchy of Luxembourg.
1684	Fortress of Luxembourg captured by French armies led by Marshal de Créqui.
1684–97	French rule Luxembourg. Vauban redesigns fortifications of city, makes it into Gibraltar of the North.
1689–97	War of the League of Augsburg. England joins Holland, Austria, Brandenburg, Sweden, and Spain in alliance against Louis XIV.
1697	Treaty of Ryswick. Louis XIV forced to return Luxembourg to Spanish rule.
1700	Charles II of Spain dies, naming Philip of Anjou, grandson of Louis XIV, as his heir.
1701	Louis XIV puts French troops into border forts, including Luxembourg.
1702–13	War of the Spanish Succession. New grand alliance formed against France. Duke of Marlborough and Prince Eugene of Savoy inflict heavy defeats upon French armies in Germany and the Netherlands.
1713	Treaty of Utrecht. Spanish Netherlands transferred to Austrian rule. Louis XIV's grandson confirmed as king of Spain, as Philip V.
1715–95	Austrian Hapsburgs rule over the southern Netherlands, including the Duchy of Luxembourg. Time of peace and relative prosperity.
1789–90	Brabantine Revolution against the reforms of Emperor Joseph II. Put down by Field Marshal von Bender, Austrian governor of Luxembourg.
1795	French revolutionary armies capture fortress of Luxembourg after long siege.
1795–1814	French rule Luxembourg, which becomes the Department of Forests.
1798	*Klöppelkrieg.* (Rising in protest against conscription of Luxembourgers into French army.)
1804	Napoleon I visits Luxembourg, given key to the city.
1815	Napoleon's defeat at Waterloo. Congress of Vienna creates Kingdom of the Netherlands, including Belgium and the former Dutch Republic, under rule of William I (William VI, prince of Orange). Luxembourg becomes a

Grand Duchy under the personal rule of William I, but is joined to the new German Confederation rather than the Kingdom of the Netherlands. Eastern third of Luxembourg annexed by Prussia (Second Partition of Luxembourg). Prussian garrison installed in fortress.

1830 Belgians revolt against Dutch rule and establish their independence. Invite Leopold of Saxe-Coburg-Gotha to be their king.

1830–39 Period of Joint Rule. Luxembourg sends delegates to Belgian Congress, but Prussian troops hold the city of Luxembourg for the Dutch king.

1839 First Treaty of London (Third Partition of Luxembourg) goes into effect. French-speaking western part of the Grand Duchy becomes Belgian province of Luxembourg. Truncated Grand Duchy becomes more or less independent, under continued rule of Dutch kings, and remains part of the German Confederation.

1840 Abdication of William I. William II becomes king of the Netherlands and grand duke of Luxembourg (1840–49).

1841 Large iron ore deposits discovered in the Minette.

1842 Luxembourg joins German customs union, the *Zollverein*.

1848 William II grants the Grand Duchy a liberal constitution.

1849 Accession of William III as king of the Netherlands and grand duke of Luxembourg.

1857 William III imposes reactionary constitution on Luxembourg, strengthening his powers as grand duke.

1859 First Luxembourg railroad opened. Michel Lentz writes *De Feierwon*, a poem in celebration of the great event.

1866–67 Napoleon III tries to purchase Luxembourg from William III.

1867 Second Treaty of London recognizes independence and permanent neutrality of Luxembourg. Prussian garrison withdrawn. Fortifications of Luxembourg to be dismantled.

1868	Liberal constitution of 1848 restored.
1884	Thomas process of removing impurities from iron ore introduced into Luxembourg. Beginning of Luxembourg's rise as a major producer of steel.
1890	William III dies. His daughter Wilhelmina becomes queen of the Netherlands, but Adolf of Nassau-Weilburg becomes grand duke of Luxembourg.
1903	Completion of Pont Adolf joining older and newer parts of Luxembourg city.
1912	Marie-Adelaide, granddaughter of Adolf, becomes grand duchess of Luxembourg.
1914–18	World War I. Luxembourg under German occupation.
1918–19	Peace conference at Versailles. Belgium advances claim to annex Luxembourg. Two American divisions occupy Grand Duchy.
1919	Abdication of Marie-Adelaide in favor of her sister Charlotte. Referendum establishes Luxembourg's overwhelming desire to remain independent under the Nassau-Weilburg dynasty.
1922	Customs and monetary union established with Belgium.
1939	Celebration of 100th anniversary of Luxembourg independence (dating from year First Treaty of London went into effect).
1939–45	World War II.
10 May 1940	German troops occupy Luxembourg. Government and grand ducal family go into exile.
1942	Hitler proclaims Luxembourg part of the Third Reich. Conscription of Luxembourgers into German army begins. General strike in protest put down with great severity.
1944	Governments-in-exile sign Benelux agreement. American 5th Armored Division enters Grand Duchy at Rodange on 9 September and liberates the city of Luxembourg on 10 September.
16 Dec. 1944–	Battle of the Bulge (Rundstedt Offensive).
18 Jan. 1945	German troops reoccupy northern Belgium and Luxembourg. American Third Army under Patton enters Luxembourg and races

	north to defeat the Germans and drive them out of Luxembourg again.
1947	Customs and monetary union with Belgium renewed.
1948	Benelux agreement goes into effect. Luxembourg joins Marshall Plan.
1949	Luxembourg joins NATO.
1951	Luxembourg becomes seat of European Coal and Steel Community (Schuman Plan).
1957	Treaty of Rome. Luxembourg becomes one of the six founding members of the European Economic Community (EEC).
1959	Luxembourg begins process of transforming itself into major financial center.
1963	Luxembourg celebrates the 1000th anniversary of the founding of the city.
1964	Grand Duchess Charlotte abdicates in favor of her eldest son grand duke Jean.
1985	Death of Grand Duchess Charlotte.
1989	Luxembourg celebrates 150th anniversary of its independence.
1992	Treaty of Maastricht goes into effect. Attempts to establish greater sense of unity within the European Community by adopting measures tending toward common economic, financial, social, and foreign policies. Strengthens powers of European Parliament and adopts the name *European Union*. Luxembourg is one of the first states to ratify this treaty.
1994	Celebrations to mark 50th anniversary of liberation of Luxembourg. Jacques Santer named president of the European Commision.
1995	Luxembourg named 1995 European City of Culture.

Acronyms and Special Terms

ADR	Action Committee for Democracy and Pension Reform
ARBED	Luxembourg steel conglomerate
Benelux	Customs union between Belgium, the Netherlands, and Luxembourg
Bon Pays	Southern two-thirds of Luxembourg, the Good Country
casemates	Underground passages connecting the strong points of the Fortress of Luxembourg
CFL	Luxembourg State Railways
Conseil de Gouvernement	The Luxembourg cabinet, made up of the heads of the government departments
Conseil d'Etat	Council of State. Upper chamber of the Luxembourg legislature and final court of appeals
CSV	Christian Social People's Party
DP	Democratic Party
EC	European Community (name by which the European Economic Community was known between 1967 and 1992)
EEC	European Economic Community
E'sleck	Letzebuergesch name for the Oesling (Ardennes)
EU	European Union. (Name by which the European Community has been known since 1992)
Gelle Fra	Golden Lady (Statue of Victory on the World War I and II Monument)
Grund	Site of the original town of Luxembourg
LCGB	Luxembourg Christian Labor Federation

LSAP	Luxembourg Socialist Workers Party
Minette	Mining and industrial district in the South
Ministre de l'Etat	Minister of State (head of the Luxembourg government, the prime minister)
Musée de l'Etat	National Museum
NAMSA	NATO Maintenance and Supply Agency
NATO	North Atlantic Treaty Organization
Octave	Spring festival in honor of the Virgin Mary
OGB-L	Luxembourg Independent Labor Federation
RTL	Radio-Television Luxembourg
SES	European Satellite Society
Vieux Luxembourg	Society for the restoration of the old city, the Grund.
Zollverein	German Customs Union (1834–1918)

REGIONS OF THE GRAND DUCHY

Introduction

The Grand Duchy of Luxembourg is one of the smallest independent nations in Europe, but not the least important. It is the home of one of the world's largest steel companies, it is an important railroad hub, and its capital city is a leading financial center. Its stable government, favorable economic climate, and freedom from industrial strife make it an attractive haven for foreign investment, as witnessed by the large number of companies that have made the Grand Duchy their European headquarters in recent years.

The Grand Duchy is the most prosperous country in Europe today, if not in the world. Its employees are paid the highest wages and enjoy the most comprehensive system of social benefits, it has the lowest rate of unemployment of any industrial nation, and it maintains a stable currency and a favorable balance of payments.

Luxembourg has played an important part in the movement toward European unity. It is a member of Benelux, the customs union between Belgium, the Netherlands, and Luxembourg; it was the first capital of the European Coal and Steel Community; it was one of the six founding members of the European Economic Community (EEC), and it is one of the three capitals of the EEC (now known as the European Union).

Luxembourg has also had an interesting history. From small beginnings it grew to be one of the most important feudal states in western Europe. Four of its rulers became kings of Bohemia, and four became Holy Roman Emperors (five if Charles V is included). After four centuries of independence, it came under foreign rulers for another four hundred years, reemerging as an independent state in the nineteenth century. Its history is entangled with that of most of the other nations of western and central Europe. It has been, at one time or another, part of the Holy Roman Empire, the Burgundian Circle, the Spanish and Austrian Netherlands, the first French Republic and Empire, the German Confederation, and the Zollverein, the German customs union.

It has been occupied by Burgundians, Spaniards, Frenchmen, Austrians and Prussians, and twice during the twentieth century by Germans.

Luxembourg's fortress has been besieged and captured many times, and foreign troops of many nationalities have ravaged its peaceful farmlands. The country has been partitioned three times since 1659. Through all their trials, however, its people have retained a sense of their own identity, centered on pride in their native language and traditions.

Luxembourg has special links with the United States, although many Americans are unaware of this. Over seventy thousand Luxembourgers emigrated to the United States during the nineteenth and early twentieth centuries, and most of them have kept up their ties with their native land. American troops occupied the Grand Duchy briefly after the First World War and liberated it from the Germans during the Second World War. The bodies of over five thousand American troops who fell in the Battle of the Bulge are buried in the American Military Cemetery in Hamm, and the grave of their former commander, General George S. Patton, Jr., is located there as well. Fifty years after their liberation, Luxembourgers still remember their liberators.

After World War II, the Grand Duchy was one of the first nations to join the Marshall Plan, and it was one of the first to join NATO as well. There is no country in Europe, and perhaps no country in the world, where Americans find a friendlier welcome.

There is much for visitors to see in Luxembourg. To begin with, there is the beautiful scenery—the forest-covered hills of the Ardennes, the swift streams and rocky cliffs of Little Switzerland, and the vine-covered slopes of the Moselle, for instance. Then there are the castles—the ruins of more than a hundred feudal castles, including the eleventh century fortress at Vianden, may be found within the present boundaries of the Grand Duchy, as well as medieval towns such as Echternach, Esch-sur-Sûre, and Clervaux. The city of Luxembourg, capital of the Grand Duchy, is worth not one but many visits, with its historic buildings, interesting public squares, and splendid view over the gorges of the Alzette and the Petrusse. The country calls itself the Green Heart of Europe, and the reality corresponds to the name.

Geography

The Grand Duchy of Luxembourg is a small nation with a total land area of 2586 square kilometers (998 square miles). Its greatest length north to south is 82 kilometers (51 miles) and its greatest width 57 kilometers (35 miles). Its neighbors are France to the south, Germany to the east, and Belgium to the north and west. (All three of these nations have annexed parts of it at one time or another and have tried to annex the whole.)

The country is divided into two major regions, the Ardennes in the north and the Bon Pays (Good Lands) in the south. The Ardennes are the remains of a once mighty mountain chain, worn down by the glaciers of the four Ice Ages into a range of low, heavily forested hills cut through by deep, narrow valleys, which stretches from northern France across Belgium and Luxembourg into Germany, where it is known as the Eifel. The Ardennes make up approximately a third of the total land area of Luxembourg.

The Bon Pays, the southern part of Luxembourg, is part of the upper Lorraine plain and has a different geologic history. During the interglacial periods it has been covered four times by shallow inland seas. The sedimentary deposits left behind by the seas have decayed into a light, mineral-rich soil, highly suitable for farming. Fossils of marine life are found everywhere, and the area has abundant ground water. In the extreme south it once had rich deposits of iron ore, but these have been mined out; the last iron mine was closed in 1981.

There are no navigable rivers in Luxembourg except for the Moselle, which forms the border with Germany for a short distance. The Moselle has been canalized since the Second World War and carries a heavy volume of freight; Luxembourg's river port at Mertert handles over a million tons a year currently and is expected to double its capacity within a short time.

The political geography of Luxembourg does not correspond exactly to its physical geography. Although separated from Belgium and the Netherlands to the west and north by the Ardennes, it has frequently been joined to them politically, as part of the Burgundian Circle, the Spanish and Austrian Netherlands, and more recently Benelux. On the other hand, as part of the border lands between France and Germany, Luxembourg has been subject to political, economic, and cultural influences from both nations, and has been occupied by both German and French armies at various times in its history.

The People

The people of Luxembourg are descended in part from the Treveri, a Gallic tribe who lived along the lower Moselle in pre-

GRAND DUCHY OF
LUXEMBOURG

BELGIUM

Liège

Troisvierges

Clervaux

Clervé R.

Our R.

Bastogne

GERMANY

Wiltz R.   Wiltz

Vianden

Sûre R.

Esch/Sûre

Diekirch

Ettelbrück

Sûre R.

Berg

Echternach

Redange

Attert R.

Mersch

Wasserbillig

Septfontaines

• Junglinster   Mertert

Arlon

Grevenmacher

Trier

Eisch R.

BELGIUM

LUXEMBOURG

Moselle River

Mamer R.

Ehnen

Remich

Paris

Esch/Alzette   *Alzette R.*

Mondorf Les Bains

Metz

FRANCE

Dudelange

Thionville •

Roman times, and in part from the Rhineland Franks who moved into the area between the fourth and sixth centuries of the present era. The Treveri were part of the Celtic migration into western Europe that began about 900 B.C.; the Franks were part of the Germanic invasion that followed the Celtic one. Since this part of Europe has always been a European crossroads, many other elements have entered into the population, but the core remains the Gallo-Frankish mixture formed during the early Middle Ages.

The Romans added something to the mixture: when the lands of the Treveri were part of Roman Gaul, soldiers, traders, and officials from every part of the empire came and went, and some of them stayed. Saxons were added when Charlemagne settled small groups of them from east of the Rhine among the Franks. Huns, Magyars, and Northmen raided the area, but left few traces of their passage other than a trail of destruction. Burgundians, Spaniards, Austrians, and Frenchmen came in small numbers over the centuries. Louis XIV, having practically depopulated the capital city during his famous siege of the fortress in 1683–84, introduced a number of French tradesmen and artisans into the city, and other Frenchmen came during the era of the French revolution and Napoleonic empire. None of these invaders changed the basic nature of the population. Large numbers of Germans and Italians, attracted by opportunities for employment in the growing steel industry, moved into Luxembourg during the late nineteenth and early twentieth centuries, but this migration has largely been absorbed. Since the Second World War, large numbers of Portuguese have migrated to the Grand Duchy, and they form the largest group of foreigners in Luxembourg today. Unlike the Germans and Italians, who settled mainly in the Minette, the Portuguese have spread throughout the entire country, and have not yet been absorbed into the general population.

The Grand Duchy is unique among the nations of western Europe in that 30 percent of its small population is made up of foreigners. Many of these are employees of the European Union or of the foreign banks and other companies that have set up branches in recent years. These may be considered temporary residents, but a few have purchased homes here and may stay. In time, the population problem will be solved as foreigners adopt Luxembourg nationality and are absorbed into the general population, but at the moment some Luxembourgers fear that they are in danger of becoming a minority in their own country.

The population of the Grand Duchy at the end of 1995 was estimated to be 406,600, of whom about 72,000 lived in the capital city. The next largest city, Esch-sur-Alzette, the largest town in the industrial south, had a population of approximately 24,000.

Languages

The native language of most Luxembourgers is Letzebuergesch, a language descended from the dialect spoken by the Rhineland Franks who moved into the area between the fourth and sixth centuries. It was once widely spoken in the area between the Rhine, the Meuse, and the Moselle, but its use is now confined to the Grand Duchy and the border areas of Germany, France, and Belgium that once belonged to Luxembourg. Its nearest relatives are Dutch, Flemish, and the Plattdeutsch dialects still spoken in the Rhineland. It is not derived from High German, the literary language of Germany since the sixteenth century, but both languages have a common ancestry in the remote past.

There are very few words of Celtic derivation in Letzebuergesch today, but both the name of the country and its language are derived from one Celtic word, *Lucilinburhuc*, a word meaning "Little fortress on the hill", referring to an earlier fort built on or near the hill on which Sigefroi built his castle in 963.

Letzebuergesch did not become a written language until the nineteenth century. During the early Middle Ages most documents were written in Latin, the language of the Catholic Church; later French replaced Latin in official documents and in the courts. Some French words and phrases have made their way into Letzebuergesch, but there has been no amalgamation between French and Letzebuergesch as there was, for instance, between the Anglo-Saxon spoken by the common people in England and the Norman French spoken by their eleventh century conquerors. Letzebuergesch has remained the language of the people of Luxembourg throughout their history and French has continued to be a foreign language.

Since 1830, both French and German have been legal languages in Luxembourg; Letzebuergesch was declared to be the official language of the country as recently as 1984. French is still employed in the law courts, although evidence may be given and depositions taken in Letzebuergesch. Members of the Chamber of Deputies may address that body in French, German, or Letzebuergesch and their speeches are printed in the official proceedings in the language each was speaking. Official notices are sent out in both French and German, but in the villages notices of local events may be written in Letzebuergesch.

Very little Letzebuergesch is taught in the schools; it is learned at home in the family. Both German and French are taught in the primary schools, and most adult Luxembourgers are trilingual. In the secondary schools, certain subjects are taught in French and certain in German so that students retain their mastery of both languages. The majority of students also study English in secondary school, and most adults can speak and understand English.

Most Luxembourgers read a German-language newspaper, either the *Luxemburger Wort* or the *Tageblatt*, although both contain articles and stories in French and, in recent days, Portuguese as well. According to surveys, most Luxembourgers watch German-language television and listen to German-language radio, although they tune in to any program offered in Letzebuergesch.

Letzebuergesch remains the language closest to the hearts of native Luxembourgers, because its continued use strengthens their claim to a separate national existence. When the Germans occupied Luxembourg during the Second World War, they conducted a survey in which they asked the the people whether they considered themselves to be basically French- or basically German-speaking. Letzebuergesch was not offered as a choice, but 97 percent of the people surveyed crossed out both German and French and wrote in the word Letzebuergesch instead.

Religion

Most native Luxembourgers (about 95 percent) are Catholics. The country is divided into 13 deaneries and 265 parishes, the whole of the country forming a single diocese. Since 1870 Luxembourg has had its own bishop. On the occasion of Pope John Paul II's visit to Luxembourg in 1988 the country was raised to the rank of an archdiocese, and the incumbent bishop became an archbishop.

Religious orders established a great number of convents and monasteries over the centuries, but only a few of them still exist. One of the best-known is the Benedictine Abbey at Clervaux. Another is the monastery of the White Fathers (Pères Blancs) at Marienthal, where priests were trained to become missionaries in Africa, but the order closed this monastery in 1974.

Protestant churches were founded in Luxembourg in the early years of the Reformation, but were suppressed by the Spanish when they controlled the country during the sixteenth century. During the reign of Emperor Joseph II in the eighteenth century a policy of complete religious tolerance was announced, but Protestantism was not recognized as a legal religion until 1894.

Luxembourg has had a small Jewish community for centuries,

although the status of Judaism was not officially recognized until 1808, during the reign of Emperor Napoleon I.

There is complete religious tolerance in Luxembourg today and the foreigners who make up 30 percent of the population belong to every variety of church and religion. A Russian Orthodox church opened its doors in 1983 and the Baha'i sect has a place of worship, although no mosques have been built as yet.

Government and Political Parties

Luxembourg is a constitutional monarchy ruled by a hereditary grand duke. The present dynasty has ruled Luxembourg since 1890, when Adolf of Nassau-Weilburg became its fourth grand duke. Grand Duke Jean, the present ruler, inherited the throne in 1964 upon the abdication of his mother, Grand Duchess Charlotte, who had ruled the country since 1919. His eldest son, Prince Henry, is heir apparent. The principal residence of the family is their castle in Colmar-Berg.

Luxembourg is also a parliamentary democracy, and all men and women eighteen years of age and older have the right to vote. The nation's laws are made by an elected Chamber of Deputies and the country is governed by a Council of Ministers headed by a prime minister. A Council of State appointed by the grand duke reviews all proposed laws and amendments to existing laws, and justice is administered by an independent judiciary.

There are three major political parties in the Grand Duchy and several smaller ones. The two largest ones are the CSV (Christian Social People's Party) and the LSAP (Luxembourg Socialist Workers Party). The third major party is the DP (Democratic Party). Since members of the Chamber of Deputies are elected by a system of proportional representation, no single party ever has a majority of the seats, and governments are formed by a coalition of two major parties. Since 1984, the country has been governed by a coalition of the CSV and the LSAP. The prime minister, Jean-Claude Juncker, is a Christian Democrat, but several members of his cabinet belong to the LSAP.

Local Government

Luxembourg is divided into three administrative districts and twelve cantons. Each canton is made up of one or more communes, consisting of a central town and the surrounding villages.

Each commune has its own elected council, which, like the central government, is controlled by a coalition of two or more political parties. The mayor is the head of the political party that controls the highest number of seats on the council. Luxembourg city, for instance, is governed by a coalition between the Democratic Party and the Christian Social People's Party, and the mayor is a Democrat.

Education

Luxembourg has free public education; every child attends a local primary school and goes on to some type of secondary school. The primary schools are under the direction of the local governments, but the secondary schools are controlled by the Ministry of National Education.

Until 1994 most children spent a single year in kindergarten, entering at the age of five, but a new law requires children to spend two years in kindergarten in future, entering at age four. This law went into effect in 1995. Children enter primary school when they are six.

There are six grades in primary school. Children begin studying German in the first grade and French in the second. Letzebuergesch is used in kindergarten and continues in use throughout primary school, but little formal instruction is given in the language, and classes are taught in German or French, depending upon the subject.

There are several types of secondary school in the Grand Duchy. The most highly regarded are the athenées and the lycées, which offer a seven-year program of study leading to the baccalaureate, required for entrance to higher education. Entrance to the athenées and lycées is by examination, and not every pupil can pass the examination. Those who fail the entrance examinations or elect not to take them must enter some other kind of secondary school. Of those who gain admission to an athenée or lycée, many find the work too hard, and are forced to drop out to enroll in another type of school. (There is no essential difference between the athenées and the lycées at present, but during the nineteenth century an athenée offered both Latin and Greek as classical languages, whereas a lycée offered only Latin.)

There are lycées or athenées in most of the principal towns, and Luxembourg city has four. The oldest and most prestigious is the Athenée Grand-Ducal, successor to a school founded by the Jesuits in 1603. For a long time this was the only secondary school in the country. It was operated by the Jesuits until Empress Maria Theresa suppressed the order in 1773, after which it became a state school. It took its present name in 1817. For a long time it was strictly a boys' school, but it became coeducational after World War II. For the past twenty years it has been located in a modern set of buildings on a campus in Merl. Its former buildings, among the most beautiful in Luxembourg, now house the National Library.

Students who are not admitted to a lycée or do not want to attend one may enter one of the lycées techniques, formerly known as middle schools, which they may attend until they are sixteen or seventeen, following which they must attend classes part-time until they are eighteen. The lycée technique offers a normal academic education but does not prepare students for the baccalaureate.

Luxembourg has many special schools—an agricultural college in Ettelbruck, vocational schools, a teacher-training college, and a special school to train students for positions in banks and commercial companies. It also has excellent music conservatories. The conservatory in Luxembourg city, formerly housed in the retreat house of the abbey of Orval in the center of the city, is now housed in a magnificent new building on a campus in Merl, close to the Athenée Grand-Ducal and the Lycée Michel Rodange.

A few secondary schools operated by the Catholic Church offer parents an alternative to the state schools for their children. There are also schools primarily for foreigners. Children whose parents are employed by the European Union may attend the European School, located on the Kirchberg, which has sections taught in each of the major languages of the member nations. Other foreign children, and a few Luxembourgers as well, attend the American International School of Luxembourg, which offers a complete program of primary and secondary studies following the American curriculum. There is also a French secondary school, the Collège Vauban, and an English primary school, St. George's.

Luxembourg has no university, and graduates of the Luxembourg lycées must study at foreign universities in France, Belgium, Switzerland, Germany, or elsewhere. Because of the high cost, very few attend American universities, although some do go on to study at American graduate schools.

Luxembourg does have a university center, where students may follow a course of studies corresponding to the program normally offered during the first year at university. Since it is becoming increasingly difficult to gain entrance to a foreign university, the government has embarked upon a major program to expand the university center.

The History of Luxembourg

Prehistory to the Fifteenth Century

People have lived in Luxembourg and the surrounding regions since long before history began. Archaeologists have found evidence of human habitation dating well back into the Old Stone Age, when Neanderthals roamed western Europe, and as recently as the Aurignacian period, when more modern types of humans had replaced the Neanderthals. More plentiful remains date from the Middle Stone Age and from the New Stone Age, when people had learned to farm and had settled down to live in villages. Several sites dating from the New Stone Age have been discovered in Luxembourg, some quite recently, as well as sites from the Bronze and Iron Ages.

We know very little about the earlier inhabitants of Luxembourg, but about three thousand years ago Celts from the Danube Valley crossed the Rhine into western Europe, bringing with them their iron tools and weapons, horses and cattle, and we know a great deal more about them.

The Celtic tribes who settled in the lands between the Rhine and the Atlantic were called Gauls by the Romans, and the country they lived in was called Gaul. They were a prosperous people who grew grain, raised horses and cattle, coined money, and made beautiful ornaments out of gold and silver. They were divided into a number of tribes and confederations who waged war against each other and against their neighbors to the east, the Germans. Their disunity invited invasion, and between 58 and 52 B.C. they were conquered by the disciplined Roman legions commanded by Julius Caesar. For about five hundred years, Gaul was part of the Roman Empire.

At the time of the Roman conquest, Luxembourg and the surrounding parts of northeastern Gaul were inhabited by the Treveri, a warlike Belgic tribe. Conquered by the Romans, they settled down peacefully under Roman rule after two brief uprisings. Many of them enlisted in the Roman army, and a few rose to high military positions.

Gaul prospered under Roman rule, particularly during the two hundred years of peace that began with the reign of Augustus, the first Roman emperor. Wars were fought along the frontiers, where Roman walls and Roman garrisons protected the empire against invasions by barbarian tribes, but within the empire there was peace. Trade flourished and large cities were founded. The Romans built roads, bridges, and aqueducts, as well as temples, basilicas, and other public buildings. Wealthy Romans and Gauls built villas on their country estates, and took the waters at well-known spas.

In Roman times two major roads passed through what is now Luxembourg, one from the west, which passed through Arlon, and another from the south which passed through Metz. The two roads joined in Luxembourg and continued to Trier, an important Roman military base, and still further to Cologne, the most important Roman city on the Rhine. A third Roman road cut across the northwest part of the country from Reims directly to Cologne.

Luxembourg abounds in Roman artifacts although there were no major Roman towns within the the territory of the present Grand Duchy. The nearest important Roman town was Trier (Civitas Augusta Treverorum), where the Romans maintained a large garrison. A small Roman fort or watchtower was built in what is now the city of Luxembourg and there were many small Roman settlements in the southern part of the country and even a few in the north. The ruins of several villas have been excavated, including large ones in Mersch and Echternach. Archaeologists have discovered many Roman sites in the last hundred years; one of their most recent discoveries is a small Roman theater in Dalheim and another is a large mosaic in Vichten. Important collections of Roman artifacts can be found in the National Museum in Luxembourg, as well as in museums in Arlon and Trier.

The centuries of Roman peace came to an end with a series of invasions by German tribes during the fourth and fifth centuries A.D. Frankish tribes living along the middle Rhine moved into the area of the Meuse, the Moselle, and the Rhine, a region that came to be called Austrasia. Other Frankish tribes from the lower Rhine, the Salian Franks, conquered Belgium and eventually the rest of Gaul. The Rhineland Franks brought their language to Luxembourg, where they settled in large numbers, mingling with the Gallo-Romans who already lived there.

Northern Gaul had become partly Christianized in Roman times, but the Franks were pagans who worshipped the Teutonic gods. They destroyed or plundered many of the churches, and

Christianity died out during the early centuries of their rule. Anglo-Saxon missionaries from England undertook the task of reconverting northern and central Europe during the seventh century. One of these missionaries, St. Willibrord, founded a Benedictine monastery in Echternach in A.D. 698, and this became an important center for the spread of Christianity.

The Salian Franks who conquered southern Gaul encountered a much larger Christian population, still living in the Roman towns and led by active bishops. Whether from policy or conviction, they adopted Catholic Christianity and became the strongest allies of the Roman Church. Their king, Clovis, was one of the earliest and most prominent converts. He was the first to unite all of Gaul, including Austrasia, under Frankish rule, and his descendents, the Merovingian kings, ruled for almost two centuries.

As time went on, the Merovingians declined in ability and power and came to be dominated by a strong line of Austrasian mayors of the palace. One of these, Pepin the Short, deposed the last Merovingian king in 752, and was elected king of the Franks. His election was confirmed by the pope, whom Pepin repaid by helping fight his enemies, the Lombards of Northern Italy. Pepin's son Charles the Great (Charlemagne) continued the alliance with the papacy and was rewarded by being crowned Roman Emperor in the West by the pope on Christmas Day 800. He led the Frankish armies into Italy, Germany, and Spain, where he campaigned for years against the Lombards, Saxons, and Moors. At the time of his death, Charlemagne ruled an empire extending from Hungary in the east to the Atlantic Ocean in the west, which he governed from his capital at Aix-la-Chapelle (Aachen), about a hundred kilometers north of the present Luxembourg border.

Charlemagne's empire did not long survive his death in 814. By the Treaty of Verdun, signed in 843, it was divided among his three grandsons. The western kingdom, given to Charles the Bald, eventually became France. The eastern kingdom, awarded to Louis the German, developed into Germany. The third kingdom, a strip of territory between the other two, was awarded to the eldest grandson, Lothair I, but never developed into a single nation. It was divided again upon the death of Lothair I, with the northern section going to his son Lothair II. This section, known as Lotharingia, and later Lorraine, was divided again in 870 between Charles the Bald and Louis the German, but by 925 it had fallen entirely into the German sphere of influence. Several feudal states grew up in this area, and one of them was Luxembourg.

In 963 Sigefroi, son of the count of the Ardennes, purchased a small piece of land from the Abbey of St. Maximin in Trier and built a castle on a rocky outcrop known as the Bock. Around this castle a small city grew up, and from this center Sigefroi and his successors created a small feudal state that came to include a large part of upper and lower Lorraine. In the eleventh century the rulers of this state were recognized as counts of Luxembourg, a title they passed on to their descendents.

As Luxembourg grew in size and power, the counts of Luxembourg began to play an important part in European affairs. In 1308 one of them, Henry VII, was elected king of the Romans, a preliminary to his being crowned Holy Roman Emperor in 1312. (The Holy Roman Empire, founded by Otto the Great in 962, included Germany, some of the Slavic lands to the east, and northern Italy.) Henry's son John was crowned king of Bohemia in 1312, and during the next hundred years three of the rulers of Luxembourg became both kings of Bohemia and Holy Roman Emperors. Increasingly, the interests of the ruling family became centered in their eastern possessions and Luxembourg itself became less important to them. In 1353 it was given to Wenzel I, half brother to the ruling emperor, Charles IV. The next year it was elevated to the status of a Duchy and Wenzel I became its first duke. Under Wenzel I, Luxembourg reached its greatest extent, about four times the size of the present Grand Duchy.

Burgundian and Spanish Rule (1443–1714)

Wenzel I died in 1383 without leaving a direct heir, and the title of duke of Luxembourg reverted to his nephew Wenzel (Wenceslas) II, king of Bohemia and Holy Roman Emperor. Needing money, Wenzel II pawned the Duchy, which was ruled for the next fifty-eight years by a series of temporary sovereigns trying to get their money back by taxing the Luxembourgers. In 1441, it was purchased from the residual heiress, Elizabeth of Goerlitz, niece of the emperors Wenceslas and Sigismund, by Philip the Good, duke of Burgundy. Since Elizabeth had already promised to sell it to William of Saxony, Philip had to fight for his new possession. A Burgundian army captured the city of Luxembourg in 1443, putting an end to almost four hundred years of Luxembourg independence. For the next four hundred years Luxembourg was under some form of foreign rule, although it managed to keep a sense of nationality throughout this period by the continued use of the Letzebuergesch language.

Beginning in 1443 Luxembourg was ruled by the Burgundians

from their capital at Brussels. The dukes of Burgundy, having acquired most of the Netherlands by purchase or marriage, sought to make their scattered territories into an independent kingdom, but their attempt came to an end with the death of Charles the Bold, son of Philip the Good, in a battle against a Swiss army at Nancy in 1477. His daughter, Mary of Burgundy, married Maximilian of Austria, a Hapsburg, who later became Holy Roman Emperor. In 1506 their possessions in the Netherlands, including the Duchy of Luxembourg, were inherited by their six-year-old grandson, Charles of Ghent, son of Philip of Hapsburg and Joanna of Castile.

Charles of Ghent became king of Spain in 1516 and Holy Roman Emperor in 1520 as Charles V, the name by which he is best known in history. The empire he came to rule over was larger than Charlemagne's. To his possessions in the Netherlands, eastern France, Spain, Italy, and the New World were added the Austrian lands, including Bohemia and Hungary, as well as nominal rule over all of Germany. In inheriting these vast territories, however, Charles V had acquired a religious problem.

In 1517 Martin Luther published a set of 95 theses, arguments against various practices that had grown up in the Catholic Church that he believed were contrary to the Scriptures and the teachings of the early church fathers. Summoned before the Imperial Diet at Worms in 1521, Luther refused to recant the beliefs contained in his writings and public statements, and was declared a heretic and an outlaw. Under the protection of the elector of Saxony, however, Luther went on with his writing and teaching, translating the New Testament into German and becoming the leader of the Protestant Reformation.

Charles V, who had presided over the Diet at Worms that condemned Martin Luther, tried unsuccessfully to maintain the unity of the Catholic faith in his domains. Wars against the Ottoman Turks, who threatened his Austrian possessions, and against the French who coveted his lands in Italy and the Netherlands, prevented him from giving his full attention to religious matters. The rulers of the north German states, who had converted to the new faith, successfully defended their right to maintain Protestant churches in their realms, and Charles was not able to prevent large numbers of his own subjects in the Netherlands from becoming Protestants. He even found it necessary to employ Protestant troops in his wars against the Turks and the French. Charles had quarrels with the popes as well, and Protestants were included in the imperial armies that captured Rome in 1527 and took Pope Clement VII prisoner.

In 1555, Charles V, worn out by his efforts to maintain political and religious unity in his vast domains, turned over his possessions in Italy and the Netherlands to his son Philip, and in 1556 he relinquished his lands in eastern Europe to his brother Ferdinand. Retiring to Spain, Charles abdicated all his titles in 1558 and died the following year.

Charles's son Philip (Philip II of Spain) inherited his father's possessions in Spain, Italy, the Netherlands, and the New World. When he conquered Portugal in 1580, he added that country and its extensive overseas empire to his own. During his reign, he was unquestionably the most powerful ruler in Europe.

Philip II was determined to maintain religious and political unity in the Netherlands, but his harsh methods provoked a revolt against Spanish rule, which began in 1568 and lasted for the next eighty years. Spanish armies reconquered the ten southern provinces including the Duchy of Luxembourg, which had not joined the revolt in the first place, but failed to conquer the seven northern provinces, which declared their independence in 1581 and became known as the United Provinces or Dutch Republic. Although the Spanish continued their efforts to reconquer the United Provinces, they were unsuccessful. A twelve-year truce was declared in 1609 and Dutch independence was finally recognized in 1648.

Luxembourg and the other southern provinces continued under Spanish rule until 1714, during which time they were known as the Spanish Netherlands. Protestantism was banned in the Spanish Netherlands, and the Catholic Church became once again the only authorized church. During this time, many Protestants and Catholics, whose livelihoods had been destroyed by the continual warfare, fled north into the United Provinces, where their industry contributed to the rise of Dutch prosperity and strength. Amsterdam replaced Antwerp as the principal seaport in the Netherlands, and Holland replaced Flanders as the most prosperous province.

Under Spanish rule, Luxembourg was far from prosperous. The period was one of constant warfare, and hostile armies continually invaded Luxembourg territory, destroying property and crops.

Spanish power in Europe, at its height under Philip II, declined steadily during the seventeenth century. France, reunited under the Bourbon kings after a century of civil war between Catholics and Protestants, steadily increased in wealth and power and challenged Spanish rule in the countries along its borders. The greatest of the French kings, Louis XIV, who ruled from 1643 until 1715, attempted to expand France to the Rhine, its "natural boundary." This called for the conquest of the Spanish Netherlands and their annexation to France, and the French armies attempted to accomplish their king's goal in a series of wars and campaigns.

Louis XIV's attempt to conquer the Spanish Netherlands, as well as the German territories along the Rhine, alarmed the other European powers, and they formed a coalition against him, the League of Augsburg, which included Spain, Austria, Brandenburg, and the Dutch Republic. When William III of Orange, stadholder of the Netherlands, became king of England in 1689, he added England to the coalition, and French expansion was brought to a halt. Louis XIV failed to conquer and hold the Spanish Netherlands in the end, but he did achieve some success. In 1659, France annexed the region around Thionville and additional territories belonging to the Duchy of Luxembourg, and between 1678 and 1684 French armies conquered the rest of the Duchy. In 1684 the French, after a long siege, captured the fortress of Luxembourg itself.

Luxembourg remained under French rule for the next thirteen years (1684–97). During this time Vauban, the great French military engineer, completely redesigned the fortifications of the capital city, turning it into the strongest fortress in northern Europe, the "Gibraltar of the North." Some of the barracks and other buildings he constructed are still in use as public buildings today.

French rule over Luxembourg came to an end in 1697 with the Treaty of Ryswick, which ended the War of the League of Augsburg and forced Louis XIV to give up most of his conquests in the Netherlands. Shortly thereafter, however, the death of the last Hapsburg king of Spain gave Louis XIV the chance to accomplish at a single stroke the goal for which his armies had been struggling for half a century. Louis succeeded in having one of his grandsons, Philip of Anjou, placed on the Spanish throne, so that Bourbon kings now ruled over France, Spain, and all the Spanish possessions in Europe. Spain, formerly France's enemy, became her closest ally, and the combined power of France and Spain threatened to upset the balance of power.

The other nations of Europe refused to accept this situation, and a new Grand Alliance was formed against Louis XIV. During the ensuing War of the Spanish Succession, the allied armies led by the famous duke of Marlborough and Prince Eugene of Savoy won a series of victories that forced the French to sue for peace. By the Treaty of Utrecht, which ended this war, Louis XIV's grandson was allowed to keep the crown of Spain, but the French were forced to agree that the Spanish crown would remain separate from the French crown. The Spanish Netherlands, including Luxembourg, were transferred to Austrian rule.

Austrian and French Rule (1715–1814)

Under Austrian rule, Luxembourg enjoyed a period of relative tranquillity and prosperity, especially during the reign of Maria Theresa and her son Emperor Joseph II, famous as "enlightened despots." Some of the most attractive buildings in Luxembourg were built during the period of Austrian rule. Roads were built connecting Luxembourg with Trier and Brussels, a regular postal service was established, and commerce flourished. Most welcome to the farmers was the absence of war, which enabled them to till their fields in peace.

This period of peace and tranquillity came to an end with the French Revolution of 1789. The French first attempted to set up a constitutional monarchy under Louis XVI. Later, when Louis XVI tried to flee the country, they deposed him and set up a republic. The Austrians—alarmed by the threat not only to the French king but also to his queen, Marie-Antoinette, an Austrian archduchess—formed a coalition of the other European monarchies against the French revolutionaries. An allied army marched through Luxembourg to invade France and restore the king and queen to power. Turned back by the French at the Battle of Valmy, the allied army retreated, having brought about what they most wanted to prevent—the execution of the king and queen. Another result was to make revolutionary France an enemy, and to make the Austrian Netherlands a natural target for the French armies, which proceeded to conquer and annex them.

After a long siege, the fortress of Luxembourg was captured by the armies of the French republic in 1795 and Luxembourg became part first of the French republic and then of the French empire under Napoleon I. When France was redivided into departments, Luxembourg became the Department of Forests. An attempt to conscript Luxembourgers into the French army, however, led to an uprising against them, the famous Klöppelkrieg, the War of the Clubs, but since the peasants were poorly armed the uprising was quickly put down and the leaders executed. Thousands of Luxembourgers were conscripted into the French armies and fewer than half of them ever returned.

One positive aspect of the French occupation was the introduction of the Code Napoléon, which became the basis of the Luxembourg legal system.

Dutch Rule (1815–90)

After the downfall of Napoleon, the Congress of Vienna elevated Luxembourg into a Grand Duchy and put it under the rule of William I, king of the Netherlands. At the same time the eastern third of the country was separated from the Grand Duchy and annexed by Prussia. The rest of the Austrian Netherlands, now Belgium, was joined to Holland as the Kingdom of the Netherlands, to be ruled by William I.

The Grand Duchy, strictly speaking, was not part of the Kingdom of the Netherlands but a separate possession of William I as grand duke. Although under Dutch rule, it was made part of the new German Confederation established by the Congress of Vienna in 1815. As protection against a possible French attempt at reconquest, a Prussian garrison was put into the fortress and remained there until 1867.

Both Belgium and Luxembourg were unhappy under Dutch rule, and in 1830 the Belgians revolted and set up a separate nation, inviting Leopold of Saxe-Coburg-Gotha to become their king. A Dutch army was sent to Belgium to put down the revolt, but the French sent in an army of fifty thousand men, which forced the Dutch army to retire.

Between 1830 and 1839 Luxembourg sent representatives to the Belgian Congress in Brussels, but the Prussian garrison kept the capital city loyal to William I. In 1839, by the First Treaty of London, Luxembourg was divided: the French-speaking western part, more than half the remaining area of the Grand Duchy, became part of Belgium as the Province of Luxembourg. The smaller Letzebuergesch-speaking part remained under Dutch rule, kept its Prussian garrison, and continued to be part of the German Confederation. In 1842, it became a member of the German customs union, the Zollverein.

After the abdication of William I in 1840 and the succession of William II, the Dutch relaxed their direct rule over Luxembourg, permitting the Grand Duchy an increasing degree of autonomy and self-government. William II granted Luxembourg a liberal constitution in 1848, which created an elected Chamber of Deputies with the power to pass laws. Increased control over their own destiny gave Luxembourgers a greater degree of self-confidence and a stronger sense of national identity.

Membership in the German customs union brought about a

certain amount of commercial development and prosperity. Railroads, roads, bridges, and schools were built, and new industries developed. The Rising German economic influence was matched by an increase in French cultural influence and by a determined attempt to make Letzebuergesch into a written language. Poetry, novels, plays, and songs were written in Letzebuergesch, and a new sense of national pride developed.

A crisis arose in 1866–67 when Napoleon III attempted to purchase the Grand Duchy from William III. The Dutch king was willing to sell and a purchase price was agreed upon, but the Prussians objected. The crisis might have led to war, but was solved instead by a Great Power conference in London in 1867. By the Second Treaty of London, signed at that conference, the Grand Duchy was to remain under the sovereignty of the House of Orange-Nassau, but was to become a perpetually neutral state, its neutrality guaranteed by the powers that signed the Treaty. The Prussian garrison was to be withdrawn and the fortifications dismantled. The last two provisions were carried out, although the guarantee of neutrality proved, in the end, worthless.

During the last part of the nineteenth century, Luxembourg went through a period of extensive economic development. The introduction of a new process of steel manufacture developed by an Englishman, Sidney Gilchrist Thomas, which made it possible to remove impurities from the ore mined in Luxembourg, led to the development of a major steel industry. A by-product of the Thomas process, a new fertilizer rich in phosphorus and other minerals, greatly improved the productivity of agriculture in the Oesling.

Independence (1890–1996)

Luxembourgers themselves consider their national independence to have begun in 1839 when the First Treaty of London separated the French-speaking provinces from the Grand Duchy and gave them to Belgium, leaving the Letzebuergesch-speaking provinces to carry on alone. A case may also be made for 1867, when the Second Treaty of London guaranteed Luxembourg's neutrality and moved the Prussian garrison out of its fortress. After 1890, however, when Luxembourg got its own ruling dynasty, there can be no question about its independence.

William III died in 1890 leaving no son to succeed him. His daughter Wilhelmina became queen of the Netherlands, but Luxembourg, governed by the terms of the Nassau Family compact of 1783, passed to Adolf of Nassau-Weilburg, head of another branch of the Orange-Nassau family, who became grand duke in 1890 and founded the present line of rulers. He was followed on the Luxembourg throne by his son William IV in 1905 and by his granddaughter Marie-Adelaide in 1912.

During World War I Luxembourg was occupied by German troops in violation of the terms of the Second Treaty of London. The German occupation was highly unpopular, and over three thousand Luxembourgers who found themselves in France at the outbreak of the war, enlisted in the French army and fought on the Allied side. After the German defeat, Luxembourg regained its independence, but Marie-Adelaide, accused of having been pro-German during the war, was forced to abdicate as grand duchess in 1919 in favor of her sister Charlotte. Two American divisions occupied the Grand Duchy briefly after the war.

In 1922 Luxembourg entered a customs and monetary union with Belgium, which replaced the customs union it had belonged to with Germany before the war. Luxembourg remained relatively prosperous during the 1920s and 1930s. Although it was hurt, like the rest of the world, by the great depression of the 1930s, Luxembourg was able to limit unemployment by restricting immigration and by sending many foreign workers home, but this did not completely solve its problems.

Luxembourg declared its neutrality when World War II began in 1939; nevertheless the German army occupied the Grand Duchy again when they invaded Belgium, the Netherlands, and France in May 1940. The Luxembourg government, including the grand ducal family, left the country just ahead of the German invaders and went into exile. A government-in-exile was formed in London, and Prince Jean, the present grand duke, and his father Prince Felix joined the British army. Prince Jean joined the Irish Guards, a regiment in which he served throughout the rest of the war.

During the German occupation, Luxembourg was placed first under German military administration, then under a civil administration headed by Gustav Simon, the gauleiter of Koblenz-Trier, who speedily became the most hated man in Luxembourg. In 1942 Hitler declared Luxembourg part of the German Reich and began conscripting Luxembourgers into the German army and the Labor Service. A general strike protesting both measures was declared throughout Luxembourg, but it was put down with great severity; a number of strikers were shot by firing squads and their families were deported to Germany, where most of them were interned in concentration camps. Thousands of Luxembourg youths fled into the Ardennes to avoid conscription and joined the Belgium resistance. Thousands of other Luxembourgers enlisted in the Allied armies or joined the French resistance. At least five resistance groups were formed within the Grand Duchy itself, and they did their best to sabotage the German war effort.

Many clergymen were arrested and deported and most of the remaining religious orders were dissolved. Monasteries and other church buildings were taken over for the use of the German storm troopers (the S.A.) and the German security services (the S.S.). Synagogues were destroyed, Jewish property was confiscated, and Jews were arrested and sent to concentration camps. The Gestapo set up headquarters in the Villa Pauly and the Germans took over the police. Policemen who refused to join the Nazi Party were dismissed and deported to Germany.

German became the sole official language and the sole language of instruction in the schools. French-language newspapers were forbidden, and use of the French language in public was banned. Nazi doctrines were taught in schools and textbooks were replaced by German ones. Teachers under fifty years of age were sent to Germany for reeducation. Hitler Youth and German Girls organizations were set up and all young people between the ages of sixteen and nineteen were required to attend Hitler Youth training camps.

In all, 12 percent of the Luxembourg population was deported during the war, and thousands of others forced to serve in the German army or labor corps. Liberation from the hated Nazi yoke was eagerly awaited.

On 9 September 1944, American troops of the 5th Armored Division entered the Grand Duchy and on 10 September they liberated Luxembourg city. Prince Felix entered the city with the American troops, and Prince Jean was hastily sent for to share in the public demonstrations of gratitude and affection. After this, he returned to his brigade, in which he served until the war was over and Germany finally defeated. The following April, Grand Duchess Charlotte returned from exile amid scenes of great jubilation.

After World War II, Luxembourg entered the most prosperous period of its history. In 1948 the Grand Duchy joined the fifteen nations participating in the European Recovery Program (the Marshall Plan). Luxembourg abandoned her traditional policy of neutrality and joined the North Atlantic Treaty Organization (NATO) in 1949. Its customs and monetary union with Belgium was renewed in 1947, and the customs union was widened to include the Netherlands in 1948. This new economic grouping took the name Benelux. In 1950 the Grand Duchy joined and became the first seat of the European Coal and Steel Community, the forerunner of the Common Market, sometimes known as the Schuman Plan after its founder Robert Schuman, a native Luxembourger who became a member of the French cabinet. In 1957 Luxembourg became one of the six founding members of the European Economic Community (EEC) and one of its three capitals. (The EEC has now changed its name to the European Union.)

Both before and after World War II, steel was Luxembourg's largest industry, but since the war Luxembourg has made a major attempt to diversify its industrial base, welcoming foreign investment and encouraging the construction of new factories to produce a wide variety of goods. This diversification has become increasingly important since the worldwide decline in the steel industry that began in 1975. With the help of the government, the Luxembourg steel industry has cut down and streamlined steel production to make its steel products more competitive in the world market. In the course of doing this, thousands of workers in the steel industry have lost their jobs, but the government provided temporary work for the redundant workers on various projects including roadwork and the restoration of ruined castles during an interim period, and the new industries the government attracted to Luxembourg provided more permanent positions for them in the long run. Since 1951, over two hundred new firms have been established in Luxembourg, providing employment for over twelve thousand workers.

In addition, Luxembourg has made itself into a major financial center. Over two hundred foreign banks and over one hundred reinsurance companies have established branches in Luxembourg, providing thousands of jobs. The money the Grand Duchy derives from financial services enables it to maintain a favorable balance of payments and underpins the entire economy. The country's future economic prosperity seems reasonably well assured.

In the modern world, no country can be completely independent. Luxembourg's economic prosperity and its national existence are increasingly linked to its membership in such international organizations as Benelux, the European Union, and the United Nations. However important its ties to other nations, though, Luxembourg hopes to retain its own national soul. This hope is embodied in its national slogan, *Mir wölle bleiwe wat mir sin!* (We want to stay what we are).

The Dictionary

ABBEY OF ALTMUNSTER. Located on the banks of the AL-ZETTE below the castle on the BOCK. Founded as a Benedictine abbey in 1083 by Conrad I, count of Luxembourg from 1056 to 1086. The abbey was destroyed by CHARLES V in 1543 during his wars with Francis I. Restored by the monks, it was again destroyed during the French siege of Luxembourg in 1684. The abbey was rebuilt between 1688 and 1721, and these buildings are still standing today. After the rebuilding, it was known as the Abbey of Neumunster, causing a certain amount of confusion among historians.

When Luxembourg was captured by the armies of the French Revolution in 1795, the French authorities closed the abbey and attempted to sell the buildings off because they were too expensive to maintain, but the French could not find a buyer. The buildings became an orphanage in 1807 and were used as a prison from 1869 to 1977, when a new prison was constructed in Schrassig. Within the past few years, a project has been launched to make the old abbey buildings into a museum.

ABBEY OF ECHTERNACH. Founded by ST. WILLIBRORD in A.D. 698, the Benedictine Abbey of Echternach is the oldest in Luxembourg. Since there were no secular clergy in the area at that time, the abbey created parishes and appointed priests, following in the Irish monastic tradition. The abbey became an important center for the production of illuminated manuscripts in the eighth and the eleventh centuries.

From 847 to 971, the Abbey of Echternach was ruled by secular canons, who elected their own abbot. SIGEFROI, who received ECHTERNACH as a fief from OTTO I in 950, placed the Abbey of Echternach under the jurisdiction of the ABBEY OF ST. MAXIMIN IN TRIER in 971, which thereafter ap-

Cross-references appear in capital letters.

pointed the abbots and brought the abbey under strict Benedictine rule.

The abbey was a center for learning in northern Europe. It was visited several times by ALCUIN OF YORK, the Anglo-Saxon monk and advisor to CHARLEMAGNE who led the movement called the Carolingian Renaissance. Alcuin wrote the first biography of St. Willibrord.

The most famous of the illuminated manuscripts produced at Echternach was an edition of the Gospels called the *Codex Aureus*, THE GOLDEN BOOK OF ECHTERNACH.

During the early eighteenth century, the monks tore down the original monastery and built a new one in the baroque-rococo style of the eighteenth century. These buildings, adjoining the basilica, are still standing, as is the *Orangerie* built as a residence for its abbots. Following the French Revolution, the monastery was sacked in 1794 by a band of *sans-culottes* (a rabble inspired by revolutionary principles) and the monks driven into exile. (They carried the *Codex Aureus* with them.) The buildings became national property and were sold to various private owners.

During the nineteenth century the Luxembourg state assumed proprietorship of the abbey and became responsible for the maintenance of the buildings. Today they house the Lycée Classique of Echternach, a well-known secondary school with a number of illustrious graduates. (*See also* BASILICA OF ECHTERNACH, ECHTERNACH, and ST. WILLIBRORD)

ABBEY OF ORVAL. A Benedictine monastery that became a center of culture and learning in Luxembourg during the Middle Ages. It had an extensive library and was a scriptorium for the production of illuminated manuscripts. PIERRE REDOUTE, a celebrated painter of flowers, received his early training as a painter from one of the monks at the abbey.

The abbey was located in the French-speaking part of the Duchy of Luxembourg, separated from the Grand Duchy in 1839 by the FIRST TREATY OF LONDON, but had already been destroyed by the armies of the French Revolution in 1795.

ABBEY OF ST. MAURICE AND ST. MAUR. Founded in 1909 by a small group of Benedictine monks from Glanfeuil in France seeking refuge from the anticlerical attitude of the French government of the day, the abbey stands upon a hill above CLERVAUX. Monks from several countries live at the abbey under the strict rule of St. Benedict, dividing their time between labor and prayer. They hold regular retreats for laymen who need respite from the stress of modern life, substitute for diocesan priests in the vicinity when needed, and dispense the sacraments of the church.

During WORLD WAR II, the abbey was taken over by the Nazis, who used it as a training center for Hitler Youth, but after the war the monks returned and resumed their regular functions.

The abbey is highly respected in Luxembourg, and receives frequent visits from groups interested in learning about monastic life.

ABBEY OF ST. MAXIMIN IN TRIER. One of the oldest Benedictine monasteries in Germany, the Abbey of St. Maximin, founded in 633, accumulated great wealth and power during the Middle Ages. SIGEFROI was lay advocate for the abbey, managing its lands and estates. In an agreement reached in 963, Sigefroi gave up certain lands he held along the SURE near Ettelbruck in return for a grant by the abbey of a small piece of land they owned along the banks of the ALZETTE, which became the nucleus of Luxembourg. He built a castle upon a hill called the BOCK beneath which a small town grew up. Sigefroi showed his gratitude for the grant by placing the ABBEY OF ECHTERNACH, granted him as a royal fief in 950, which he ruled as lay abbot, under the jurisdiction of the Abbey of St. Maximin in 971.

Sigefroi and his wife were buried, in accordance with the terms of his will, before the altar of St. Clement in the Abbey of St. Maximin. (*See also* BOCK, LUCILINBURHUC, and SIGEFROI.)

ACTION COMMITTEE FOR DEMOCRACY AND PENSION REFORM (ADR). Running on a single issue (pension reform) in 1989 the "⅚ Action Committee," as it was then known, won four seats in the CHAMBER OF DEPUTIES. The committee has since changed its name and adopted positions on a number of other issues. Its first aim continues to be greater equalization of old-age pensions, but it also calls for action against unemployment, greater justice in the tax system, an independent and more efficient judicial system, improvement of education, better planning for the future of agriculture and forestry, recognition of the role of women in business, more respect and better care for older citizens, and closer European integration.

The ADR's policies are, in many respects, the opposite of those favored by the NATIONAL MOVEMENT.

The ADR believes that under the present political system there is not much difference between the policies of the three major parties that have dominated the government for the past forty years and wants to offer the voters a real choice. Their best-known candidate, Ferdinand Rau, a former member of the CHRISTIAN SOCIAL PEOPLES PARTY, died in a road accident on 2 June 1994, ten days before the 1994 national elections. Despite the loss of their principal vote-getter, the ADR gained a seat in the elections, and has five members in the new Chamber of Deputies. (*See also* ELECTIONS OF 1994)

ADOLF OF NASSAU-WEILBURG. Grand duke of Luxembourg, 1890–1905. Founder of the present dynasty, who came to the throne at the age of 73. Adolf was a member of the senior branch of the HOUSE OF ORANGE-NASSAU which ruled various lands in Germany, including the small duchy of Nassau-Weilburg north of Frankfort am Main. Adolf was deprived of this duchy by the Prussians for having sided with the Austrians in the Austro-Prussian War of 1866, although he was allowed to keep his ancestral castle and his personal lands, including extensive estates in Bavaria. He spent most of the next twenty-four years in exile in Vienna.

The junior branch of the Orange-Nassau family established itself in the Netherlands, where they became stadholders (hereditary governors) of Holland and several other provinces. In 1814–15, the CONGRESS OF VIENNA created a new Kingdom of the Netherlands, which included not only the present-day Netherlands but also Belgium. The reigning stadholder, William VI, who had been driven into exile by NAPOLEON I, was named king of the Netherlands as WILLIAM I. In addition, he was given Luxembourg and became its first grand duke, as compensation for having ceded certain family lands in Germany to the Kingdom of Prussia.

By the terms of the Orange-Nassau family compact of 1783, the head of the senior branch of the family was to inherit all the family lands in Germany if the junior branch failed to produce a male heir. (In compensation, the senior branch gave up its claim to the Dutch province of Limburg.) When WILLIAM III died in 1890 without a male heir, his daughter Wilhelmina became queen of the Netherlands, but Adolf of Nassau-Weilburg became grand duke of Luxembourg. He arrived in Luxembourg by train with his wife on 23 July 1890 and was greeted at the station by a delegation of prominent citizens led by PAUL EYSCHEN, the prime minister.

Despite his advanced age, Grand Duke Adolf was an active ruler and initiated many projects, including the PONT ADOLF, which spanned the gorge between the old town of Luxembourg and the new area around the railroad station. He continued to spend a part of every year at one of his various family estates in Germany, and continued to make his home at one of his Bavarian castles until his new grand ducal residence, the Castle Berg in Colmar, was ready for him. When he died in 1905, he was succeeded as grand duke by his son, WILLIAM IV.

ADVOCATE. During the Middle Ages, an advocate was a lay person who managed the estates of a monastery or bishopric. The position could be a lucrative one, and the appointment was not always controlled by the abbey or bishopric concerned. SIGEFROI, the founder of Luxembourg, was advocate for both the ABBEY OF ST. MAXIMIN IN TRIER and the ABBEY OF ECHTERNACH, largely through the influence of the Saxon kings of Germany, with whom he was closely allied.

The term *advocate* today means merely an attorney licensed to appear before the law courts.

AETIUS, FLAVIUS. Roman general who defeated ATTILA the Hun at the Battle of the Catalaunian Fields (Chalons) in A.D. 451. Franks, as well as Visigoths and Burgundians, served under his command in this battle. (*See also* ATTILA and HUNS)

AGRICULTURE. Luxembourg traditionally has been a country of small farms, where farmers worked hard to earn a decent living for their families. The soil in the Oesling, the AR-DENNES district in the north of the country, was particularly unsuitable for farming, since it lacked phosphates and lime. Even in the BON PAYS, the southern two-thirds of the country, the land is unsuitable for large-scale farming, although the soil is richer in minerals. The south is hilly and heavily forested, although less so than the north, and farming is possible only in the river valleys, which broaden out at places into wide fields and meadowlands.

The land-holding system also militated against large farms. The CODE NAPOLEON, introduced during the French occupation (1795–1815), called for the equal division of property among heirs, which tended to reduce the size of farms from generation to generation. A shortage of arable land, in fact, led to a heavy migration of Luxembourgers to other countries, including the United States, during the nineteenth century.

The growth of industry, particularly the steel industry, during the latter part of the nineteenth century changed this pattern. The slag produced by a new steel-making process developed by SIDNEY GILCHRIST THOMAS, introduced in 1884, turned out to be a valuable fertilizer. Mixed with melted chalk, it became the famous "Thomas Scoria", which, applied to the mineral-poor soil of the Ardennes, made it possible to plant crops in land previously unsuitable. The new jobs provided in the steel mills and other factories also provided alternative careers for the children of farmers, so that fewer people had to earn a living from the land. (*See* IRON AND STEEL MANUFACTURE.)

The number of farms in Luxembourg decreased from 11,556 in 1958 to 3,945 in 1989, and the average size of farms increased from 14.5 hectares (about 35.8 acres) in 1958 to 37.2 hectares (about 93 acres) in 1989. With larger farms, farmers can raise larger crops and more livestock and can use more labor-saving machinery. At the same time, the percentage of Luxembourgers engaged in agriculture dropped from 13 percent in 1970 to 6 percent in 1989. These changes, along with the formation of farmer cooperatives, have led to a great increase in farm income. In general, farmers in Luxembourg are doing pretty well today.

In recent years, farmers in the Grand Duchy have shifted production away from arable crops toward dairy farming. The amount of acreage devoted to raising cereals and similar crops has been almost halved since 1958, whereas the land devoted to forage crops and pasture lands has almost doubled. The number of cattle has increased by 64 percent, and milk, butter, and cheese production have increased by the same percentage.

One cloud hovers on the horizon. Luxembourg, like other countries in western Europe, depends heavily upon the agricultural subsidies provided by the EUROPEAN UNION to keep prices up. With the signing of the GATT (General Agreement on Trade and Tariffs) and aggressive action by the United States to get its principal rivals to lower agricultural subsidies, the European Union may be forced to eliminate or greatly reduce farm subsidies. France, a nation with many small farms, has taken the lead in fighting the proposed reductions, but the effect of eliminating subsidies would have at least as great an effect upon farm income in Luxembourg, a country smaller and less able to stand up to heavy agricultural competition than France. (*See also* WINE MAKING)

ALBERT AND ISABELLA. Shortly before his death, PHILIP II of Spain carried out a project originally conceived by his father, CHARLES V, and made the Netherlands into a separate kingdom ruled by his daughter Isabella, who had married Archduke Albert of Austria. At this point, the Spanish Netherlands consisted of the ten southern provinces, including the Duchy of Luxembourg. The seven northern provinces that had declared their independence in 1579 continued to reject Spanish rule.

The Duchy of Luxembourg, although it had consistently remained loyal to its Spanish rulers, refused to be assimilated into the new kingdom, voting to supply the new sovereigns with a payment of three hundred thousand florins instead, provided their privileges were respected. Albert accepted the payment and agreed to respect the attached reservations.

During the reign of the "Archdukes," as Albert and Isabella were known, the war against the Dutch was carried on. The Dutch responded to Spanish attacks and in turn made frequent raids into the southern Netherlands. In 1604, Dutch armies pillaged St. Vith, Bastogne, ARLON, and MERSCH, all at that time part of the Duchy of Luxembourg.

To halt these incursions, Albert negotiated a twelve-year truce with the United Provinces from 1609 to 1621. The sovereigns used the truce to repair some of the damage suffered by the southern provinces during the long war, revive agriculture and industry, restore the damaged churches, and revise the law code. They also encouraged education, welcoming the Jesuit order into their domains to found schools.

In another significant development, Albert and Isabella encouraged the migration of Huguenots from the southern provinces to the Dutch republic, suspending the persecution inaugurated under Charles V and Philip II long enough for this migration to take place. The movement to the north had begun during the early years of the Spanish invasion, but the sanction given it by the archdukes swelled the migration to a flood as thousands of Protestants, and even many Catholics, fled to the more tolerant northern provinces. The refugees proved a lasting benefit to the United Provinces, since they included skilled workers from the cloth factories of Ghent and Bruges, diamond cutters from Antwerp, merchants, and educated people of all professions. The southern provinces were simultaneously deprived of the very people who might have revived commerce and industry in the ravaged south, and the economic decline into which the south had fallen was accelerated. Amsterdam replaced Antwerp as the principal seaport of the Netherlands, and an age of Dutch prosperity and overseas expansion began.

When Archduke Albert died in 1621, leaving no male heir, the southern Netherlands reverted to the direct rule of the Spanish crown. Isabella continued to administer the Spanish Netherlands as governor-general in the name of her nephew, Philip IV of Spain.

ALCUIN OF YORK. Chief scholar at the court of the Emperor CHARLEMAGNE, and one of the founders of the Carolingian Renaissance. He conducted palace schools at Charlemagne's summer capital at Aachen and his winter court at THION-VILLE, and eventually became the abbot of St. Martin at Tours.

Alcuin paid several visits to the ABBEY OF ECHTER-NACH founded by ST. WILLIBRORD, and wrote the first biography of St. Willibrord.

ALVA, DUKE OF (FERNANDO ALVAREZ DE TOLEDO). An advisor to both CHARLES V and PHILIP II, the duke of Alva was sent with an army of ten thousand troops in 1567 to crush resistance to Philip's rule in the Netherlands. His army marched north from Italy along the Spanish Road, a strip of territory along the eastern borders of France under control of the Spanish and their allies. Alva, establishing his headquarters in Brussels, put down resistance with great severity. He executed the counts of Egmont and Horn, but failed to capture WILLIAM THE SILENT (William I of Orange), who became the focus of resistance to Spanish rule thereafter.

Alva attempted to restore the supremacy of the Catholic Church in the Netherlands, establishing new bishoprics and persecuting heretics, in line with the policy of his royal master, Philip II. His harsh policies inspired the Netherlands to further revolt.

Luxembourg played no part in the rebellion of the Netherlands against Spanish rule, serving principally as a base to which the Spanish army could retire in time of trouble.

ALZETTE. A river rising in France that flows north across the Luxembourg border, past the city of Luxembourg, where it is joined by the PETRUSSE, and on north until it joins the MAMER and the Eisch at MERSCH. The combined rivers flow north again until they join the SURE at Ettelbruck. The Alzette is not very large at any point, but over the millennia it cut a deep gorge around the eastern part of Luxembourg through the porous sandstone upon which the city is built, helping make the city a natural fortress.

AMERICAN INTERNATIONAL SCHOOL OF LUXEMBOURG. Founded in 1962 as the DuPont School. Later, managed by Goodyear, it became the English-speaking School of Luxembourg. In 1972, it was reorganized as a non-profit association, taking the name American School of Luxembourg. Still later, it added the word "International" to its name.

The American International School offers an American curriculum to pupils from kindergarten through high school. (In 1993, it added a preschool program for three-year-olds.) A half-day kindergarten program is offered for four-year-olds, and a full-day program for five-year-olds. Six years of primary education are offered in the lower school and six years of secondary education in the upper school. Honors courses are offered in grades nine through twelve and Advanced Placement courses are offered in several subjects. Most graduates go on to college or university in the United States, but many attend universities in other countries.

The school is open to pupils of all nationalities, races, and religions, although the majority are from countries outside the EUROPEAN UNION. Enrollment has grown steadily from 75 in 1975–76 to 510 in the 1991–92 school year, although it has declined slightly since then. In January 1996, 476 pupils of 35 different nationalities were attending the school, with Americans making up 25 percent of the student body, Japanese 14 percent, and Swedes 13 percent. The faculty is composed of teachers from eleven nations.

The school has been located in a set of buildings in Limpertsberg, formerly known as the Institut St. Joseph, for the past eighteen years. In 1987 the government proposed moving the school to new facilities, to be built at government expense on a campus located on the *Geesseknäppchen* in Merl, close to the ATHENEE GRAND-DUCAL, the *Lycée Michel Rodange*, the *Lycée Technique du Commerce et de Gestion*, and the *Conservatoire*, but the proposal aroused a considerable amount of local opposition, not only because of its cost, but also because there are already three thousand secondary students in schools on the site and traffic congestion is high in the area. The government initially proposed to move the COLLEGE VAUBAN to the same site, but in 1995 it announced a new plan to build another Luxembourg lycée on the campus instead. The CHAMBER OF DEPUTIES passed legislation in January 1996 to authorize the proposed new campus development, but there is still opposition based on the high cost and the inconvenience to residents of the area, and there are still some procedures to be followed before construction can actually begin. New buildings for the American International School will be the last to be constructed, and there is some doubt that the school will ever be moved there.

AMERICAN LUXEMBOURG SOCIETY. A society formed after WORLD WAR II to commemorate and carry on the spirit of cooperation between Americans and Luxembourgers that began during the Second World War. The society sponsors a number of events during the year. In 1992–93, following severe floods in the United States, it raised more than U.S. $400,000 for the victims of these floods.

AMERICAN MILITARY CEMETERY IN HAMM. In Hamm, a small town to the southeast of Luxembourg city, the American War Graves Commission maintains a beautiful cemetery for the American soldiers who died fighting for the liberation of Luxembourg during WORLD WAR II. Not all the soldiers who died in the fighting are buried at Hamm, since their families were given the option of bringing their bodies back to the United States for burial, but the families of over five thousand of the soldiers elected to have them remain in Luxembourg. In addition to the graves, marked by white crosses and Stars of David, the cemetery includes a memorial chapel and panels with maps showing the progress of Allied forces during the liberation of Europe. GENERAL GEORGE S. PATTON, JR., commander of the American Third Army, is buried in the cemetery at the head of his troops. Originally, at his own wish, Patton was buried among his troops, whose graves were laid out in alphabetical order, but visitors wore out so much of the grass around Patton's and neighboring graves that he had to be reburied in a special plot at the head of the cemetery.

Services are held in the cemetery every year on or close to the day celebrated as the American Memorial Day in May, and every year veterans of the fighting in Luxembourg visit the cemetery with their families. A special ceremony honoring

Patton, attended by the grand duke, was held at the cemetery in December 1995.

ARBED (ACIERS REUNIE DE BURBACH-EICH-DIFFER-DANGE). A large international conglomerate with its headquarters in Luxembourg, which owns and mines iron ore deposits and operates steel plants in Luxembourg, France, Belgium, Germany, South Korea, and Brazil. It is the fourth largest steel company in Europe and the sixth in the world.

Faced with the world-wide surplus of steel, ARBED has taken steps to rationalize the manufacture of steel in its plants, concentrating on its most productive lines and closing its least profitable. Many of its operations have been computerized, and its work force has been steadily reduced through early retirement and layoffs. The government has helped ARBED by providing temporary employment for redundant workers and subsidizing their salaries. ARBED showed a net loss of 5.7 billion Luxembourg francs (about U.S. $178 million) in its world-wide operations in 1993, and a somewhat smaller loss in 1994, but showed a net profit for the first half of 1995.

Since steel manufacture has been Luxembourg's largest industry since the the last decades of the nineteenth century, further declines in steel manufacture might threaten Luxembourg's prosperity. However, the government's success in attracting foreign investment to Luxembourg in other lines of manufacturing and, above all, the transformation of Luxembourg into a major banking center, has helped offset the decline in steel production. ARBED has recently introduced the latest electric-arc process of steel-making in its plants and hopes to improve its competitive position with the new technology.

ARDENNES. A hilly, forested region stretching from northwestern France across southeastern Belgium and northern Luxembourg into eastern Germany, where it is known as the Eifel. It covers the northern third of Luxembourg, where it is also known as the Oesling or the E'sleck.

The Ardennes was once a mountain range higher than the present-day Alps. Geologists believe that it was formed by the coming together of two tectonic plates, one sliding beneath the other to raise it into a vast mountain range.

The Ardennes were covered by ice sheets during the four Ice Ages, which ground them down to their present relatively low elevation. Although the hills are not high, the valleys between them are steep and narrow, and they are traversed by many small swift streams. The rocks that underlie the Ardennes are volcanic in origin and include slates and quartzites. The topsoil formed by the weathering of the rocks in the Inter–Ice Ages was largely scraped off by the glaciers and deposited further south on the BON PAYS and the plains of northern France. Historically, the Ardennes region has not been considered good farming land. A fertilizer rich in lime and in phosphates, formed as a by-product of the steel-making process, has made it possible to farm the fields of the Ardennes, but dairy farming and logging are still staples of the Ardennes economy. Herds of wild boar and deer roam the hillsides, and the region offers excellent hunting.

ARLON. A town in the southern part of the Belgium province of Luxembourg, a few kilometers from the border of the Grand Duchy. In Gallo-Roman times, Arlon was a more important town than any now within the borders of the present Grand Duchy, and it abounds in Gallo-Roman remains, many of them preserved in its small but excellent museum. Many of the inhabitants of the southwestern part of Luxembourg do their shopping in Arlon, where LETZEBUERGESCH is still spoken by many of the older people.

An important Roman road from Reims to TRIER passed through Arlon, along the line still followed by the "route d'Arlon" which links Arlon to Luxembourg.

ATHENEE GRAND-DUCAL. The Athenée Grand-Ducal is the descendent of the Jesuit college founded in 1603. For a long time this was the only secondary school in Luxembourg. The French closed the college in 1795, but reopened it almost immediately as the Central School. In 1816 it became a Luxembourg state school and in 1817 it was elevated to the status of an athenée, becoming the Athenée Grand-Ducal, and providing a classical education.

Until WORLD WAR II the Athenée Grand-Ducal was a boys school; it did not become coeducational until after the war. From 1816 to 1964 it occupied the buildings constructed by the Jesuits during the seventeenth and eighteenth centuries, but in 1964 it moved into a new set of buildings especially built for it in Merl, a western suburb of the city. In 1973, the NATIONAL LIBRARY moved into the former buildings of the Athenée Grand-Ducal, considered among the most beautiful in Luxembourg.

For generations the leaders of Luxembourg government and

business were trained at the Athenée Grand-Ducal, among them ROBERT SCHUMAN, later the French foreign minister and one of the chief promoters of the EUROPEAN COAL AND STEEL COMMUNITY, who stood first in his class.

ATTILA. Ruler of the HUNS from approximately 443 until his death in 453. Led a mixed army of Huns and Germans on a large-scale raid into Gaul in 451, which crossed what later became Luxembourg territory. The place at which his army crossed the SURE River is still called ETTELBRUCK, Attila's Bridge.

On their way south the Huns looted and burned many towns, including TRIER and MERSCH, on or close to the lands that comprise the present-day Grand Duchy. Attila was finally stopped by a mixed army of Burgundians, Visigoths, Franks, and Romans led by the Roman general FLAVIUS AETIUS at the battle of the Catalaunian Fields near present-day Chalons. The Huns were defeated in the battle but not destroyed; they retreated to their lands north and east of the Danube, only to reappear in northern Italy the following year.

AUSTRASIA. The part of northeastern Gaul lying between the Meuse, the MOSELLE, and the Rhine occupied by the RHINELAND FRANKS, tribes who originally occupied lands along the middle stretches of the Rhine. Enough Franks settled in Austrasia so that the German language prevailed there over the Gallo-Roman dialect which developed into French in other lands conquered by the Franks.

Austrasia, at several times during the early Middle Ages, formed a separate kingdom, distinct from NEUSTRIA, the "new lands" conquered by the SALIAN FRANKS where French became the common language.

CLOVIS conquered Austrasia, but his descendants, the Merovingian kings, lost power during the eighth century to a line of Austrasian mayors of the palace, descended from PEPIN OF HERSTAL.

Austrasia eventually became part of LOTHARINGIA, the Middle Kingdom inherited by Lothair II, son of LOTHAIR I, eldest grandson of CHARLEMAGNE. This middle kingdom rapidly disintegrated, and Luxembourg was one of the successor states, eventually coming to comprise a substantial part of the former Austrasia.

AUTOMOBILE MANUFACTURING. The Grand Duchy has over two hundred thousand automobiles on its roads for a population of only slightly over four hundred thousand people. The only automobile manufacturer in Luxembourg is Renault, which has built a plant in the new development zone in Gasperich. Cars are imported from most other member countries of the EUROPEAN UNION, however, and even from countries that are not yet members.

Japanese automobiles, many manufactured in plants in neighboring countries, now hold a major position in the Luxembourg market, especially cars produced by Nissan, Subaru, and Toyota.

BALDWIN, Archbishop of Trier. Baldwin was the younger brother of HENRY VII, count of Luxembourg, who became Holy Roman Emperor in 1313. Baldwin, like Henry, was educated in Paris. He became a canon in Trier at an early age and was elected archbishop of Trier in 1307 at the age of 22. Although an ecclesiastic, Baldwin was an excellent soldier. As one of the imperial electors, he joined PETER OF ASPELT in seeking the imperial throne for his brother Henry. Baldwin was one of Henry's chief supporters, joining him in his invasion of Italy in 1311, where he took part in the fighting, splitting the helmet and head of Count Orsini with a single blow during the capture of Rome.

Baldwin was also one of the principal supporters of his nephew, JOHN THE BLIND, fighting several campaigns in Germany as well as in Lorraine on his behalf. While absent during his various wars, John left Baldwin in charge of Luxembourg and later of Bohemia. When Baldwin was captured and imprisoned by Loretta of Stakenberg, John paid his ransom. In return, Baldwin helped secure the election of John's son, CHARLES IV, as emperor, and supported him on his throne, lending him considerable sums of money from the revenues of his archbishopric. Baldwin died in 1354, after serving forty-seven years as archbishop of Trier.

BANKING. Within the past twenty-five years Luxembourg has transformed itself into one of the world's leading banking centers. Approximately 6 percent of the world's overseas investments in 1993 ended up in Luxembourg. In 1993 alone, the number of banks in Luxembourg increased from 213 to 224.

Among the largest banks operating in Luxembourg is the Deutsche Bank, a subsidiary of the Deutsche Bank of Frankfurt, whose net profits in 1993 amounted to 8.2 billion Luxembourg francs, considerably more than the net loss of 5.7 billion francs incurred by ARBED, the Luxembourg steel giant. The net profit of the 98 largest banks amounted in 1993 to 48 billion Luxembourg francs, and the entire banking sector paid between 48 and 50 billion francs in taxes to the Luxembourg government.

Other major banks showing excellent profits on their Luxembourg operations include the Kredietbank Luxembourg, the Banque Internationale à Luxembourg, the Banque Générale du Luxembourg, the Crédit Européen (acquired by Belgium's Banque Bruxelles Lambert in 1987), the Banque UCL, and the Banque de Luxembourg.

Banking has now become Luxembourg's major industry, employing about 17,000 workers, and bringing in a large part of the government's tax revenues. These banks continue to flourish even in a period of recession and major unemployment in Europe, probably because of Luxembourg's liberal banking laws.

BASILICA OF ECHTERNACH. Originally the church of the Benedictine ABBEY OF ECHTERNACH. ST. WILLIBRORD built the first abbey church on land given him by abbess Irmina of Oeron. A later church replaced it in Carolingian times (c. 800). After a fire destroyed the Carolingian church in 1016, the monks built a new one in the Romanesque style; it was completed in 1031. Modifications in the Gothic style were made in the new church in the fourteenth century, although the changes were removed during later restorations. The interior has a distinctive style of architecture, with the arches supported by alternating square and round columns. The crypt of the original Merovingian church was preserved and lies under the main altar. The remains of St. Willibrord are preserved there, as well as wall drawings from the eleventh century. The original Merovingian baptismal font is also located in the crypt. Pilgrims dance down into the crypt during the annual DANCING PROCESSION.

The present church has been destroyed and rebuilt several times. During the nineteenth century, after the French Revolution, it was turned into an iron works for a time. Demolition was proposed at one point, but through the efforts of the Archaeological Society the church was restored instead. It became a papal basilica in 1939. The church was destroyed again in 1944 by German artillery fire during the BATTLE OF THE BULGE but was restored after WORLD WAR II between 1949 and 1952. (*See also* ABBEY OF ECHTERNACH,

DANCING PROCESSION AT ECHTERNACH, and ST. WILLIBRORD)

BATTLE OF THE BULGE. On 16 December 1944, German armored divisions struck suddenly through the ARDENNES across the northern part of Luxembourg and Belgium, catching the American defenders by surprise and inflicting heavy casualties and damage. The ultimate goal of the German drive was Antwerp, the recently liberated Belgian port through which supplies were flowing to enable the Allies to make their final invasion of Germany. The Germans scored some impressive initial successes. They cut off the American 101st Airborne division at Bastogne, just west of the Luxembourg border, and raced on toward the Meuse and Antwerp. This attack was known to the Germans as the Rundstedt Offensive and to the Allies as the Battle of the Bulge.

All Allied forces north of the Bulge were put under the command of Field Marshal Bernard Montgomery, and American, British, and Canadian units under his command swung south to bring pressure against the northern edge of the German salient. Units of the American Third Army swung north from the fighting in Lorraine at the same time to hit the Germans from the south. The Germans had hoped to capture enough fuel to keep their tanks moving west, but failed and were forced to retreat. This was the last major German attack in the west during WORLD WAR II, and used up the last of the German reserves. Luxembourg had suffered little damage during the war up to this point, but the final offensive destroyed many of the towns in the Ardennes as well as ECHTERNACH. (*See also* CLERVAUX; PATTON, GENERAL GEORGE S., JR.; WILTZ; and WORLD WAR II)

BAUMBUSCH. A belt of forest belonging to the city of Luxembourg, which borders the city to the north. Translated literally it means "tree woods". The Baumbusch has hiking trails, a "fitness parcours" (a trail through the woods along which fitness buffs stop at indicated points and perform certain physical exercises) and various other recreational facilities. It suffered heavily from three major wind-storms that hit this part of Europe during the winter of 1989–90. The storms cut wide swaths through the forest, uprooting trees in some places but leaving the forest standing on either side. Not all the damage has been repaired yet (January 1996) and the work of clearing fallen timber and replanting goes on. Most of the newly planted trees are evergreens, although most of the original trees in Luxembourg were deciduous, including elms, beeches and oaks, among others. The evergreens grow more quickly and can be harvested sooner, but ecologists question whether they should continue to be planted instead of the deciduous varieties that originally covered most of the country.

BECH, JOSEPH (1887–1975). One of Luxembourg's leading twentieth century statesmen. He entered politics as a member of the Catholic Party during the 1920s, became minister of foreign affairs in 1926 (a position he held until 1959) and then prime minister in 1927 after forming a coalition with the Liberals. His government, worried by what it saw as a communist threat during the Great Depression, passed a "Muzzling Act" in 1937 aimed against the communist press. This act was rejected in a public referendum, which led to the resignation of Bech's government. A new coalition government that included Catholics, Socialists, and Liberals was formed under PIERRE DUPONG, minister of finance in the old government. Joseph Bech remained minister of foreign affairs, a position he held from 1937 until his retirement in 1959. In 1940, when the Germans invaded the Grand Duchy, Joseph Bech left Luxembourg with other members of the government, becoming minister of foreign affairs of the government-in-exile. After the war he played a leading part in renewing the CUSTOMS AND MONETARY UNION WITH BELGIUM, the formation of BENELUX, in Luxembourg's adherence to the MARSHALL PLAN and to NATO, and to the formation of the EUROPEAN COAL AND STEEL COMMUNITY and the European Economic Community. (*See* EUROPEAN UNION)

While holding the post of foreign minister and prime minister during the 1920s and 1930s, Bech was also minister of viticulture, and as such presided over the transformation of the Luxembourg wine industry. (*See also* WINE MAKING) He resumed the viticulture portfolio after WORLD WAR II, prompting a comment from Winston Churchill that if all foreign ministers were also ministers of viticulture, world affairs would be run better.

Bech served as prime minister for five years again (1953–1958) after WORLD WAR II.

BECK, JEAN. Born in the GRUND at Luxembourg in 1588, he entered the Austrian service as a volunteer at an early age, and took part in the THIRTY YEARS WAR from its beginning.

Serving under General Wallenstein, he rose rapidly in rank, and was ennobled by Emperor Ferdinand III in 1637. He was made governor of Luxembourg in 1642 and helped defend it against the invasions of the French army. He was mortally wounded at the battle of Lens in 1648 and died shortly thereafter.

BELGIAN REVOLUTION OF 1830. Belgians, joined to the Dutch in the Kingdom of the Netherlands in 1815, considered themselves treated unfairly by their Dutch rulers. They rose against them in 1830 and declared their independence. Most Luxembourgers supported the uprising, and Luxembourg even sent delegates to a Belgian National Congress in Brussels. The presence of the Prussian garrison, however, prevented the capital city of Luxembourg from joining the uprising.

Although Belgium effectively ruled itself after 1830, with Leopold of Saxe-Coburg-Gotha as its king, its independence was not recognized by other nations for some time. Finally, in the FIRST TREATY OF LONDON accepted by WILLIAM I in 1839, Belgian independence and neutrality were recognized by the Great Powers. The French-speaking part of the Grand Duchy (amounting to over half its territory) was separated from the LETZEBUERGESCH-speaking part and joined to Belgium as the province of Luxembourg. The rest of the truncated Grand Duchy continued under Dutch rule, with the same borders it enjoys today, and remained a part of the GERMAN CONFEDERATION.

The Grand Duchy considers 1839 the year it gained its independence, despite the continued rule of the Dutch king, its membership in the German Confederation, and the continued presence of a Prussian garrison. The explanation lies in its formal separation from Belgium in that year, and the increased tendency of the Dutch rulers after that date to allow Luxembourgers to run their own affairs under their own laws. (*See also* JOINT RULE, 1830–1839)

BENDER, FIELD MARSHAL VON. Austrian field marshal, governor of the fortress of Luxemburg, who put down the BRABANTINE REVOLUTION in Belgium in 1790. Bender later defended the fortress of Luxembourg against a siege by the troops of the French Revolution that lasted from 21 November 1794 until 7 June 1795. The first French commander, General René Moreau, died during the siege and was succeeded by General Hatry, to whom Bender surrendered the city and fortress. Marshal von Bender was eighty years old at the time, but he held out until famine forced his army to capitulate. He did not surrender unconditionally, but signed a convention that guaranteed the lives and goods of the Luxembourg citizens and allowed the Austrian army to march out with all the honors of war.

BENEDICTINES. The Benedictines, founded during the sixth century by St. Benedict, are the oldest monastic order in the Roman Catholic Church and were for centuries the most important. They wore black gowns and, in the early years of their existence, performed most of the labor on their own monastic estates. The order spread from its original abbey at Monte Cassino in Italy over all of western and central Europe and became very wealthy. The Benedictines helped preserve learning in western Europe during the Dark Ages, maintained scriptoriums for the copying of manuscripts, and produced educated men to serve the new national states as clerks, scholars, bishops, abbots, and even royal chancellors. It was from the Benedictine ABBEY OF ST. MAXIMIN IN TRIER that SIGEFROI, the founder of Luxembourg, purchased the land upon which he built his castle in 963.

A number of Benedictine abbeys were founded on Luxembourg lands, including the ABBEY OF ALTMUNSTER in the GRUND, founded by Conrad I in 1083, and more recently the ABBEY OF ST. MAURICE AND ST. MAUR in Clervaux, built in 1909–10. A good many of the abbeys were closed during the reforms of JOSEPH II and during the French occupation of 1795–1815. Others suffered considerable damage at the hands of the Germans during WORLD WAR II. (The Nazis turned some of the abbeys, including the Abbey of St. Maurice and St. Maur in Clervaux, into Hitler Youth Hostels)

In general, the successors of Sigefroi tried to stay on good terms with the principal Benedictine abbey in the vicinity, the Abbey of St. Maximin in Trier, and were successful in getting some members of their family appointed abbots of St. Maximin and even archbishops of Trier. Some of the counts quarreled with the abbey and with the archbishops, however, frequently over river tolls the counts collected on the MOSELLE. (*See also* HENRY VII)

BENELUX. A customs union between Belgium, Luxembourg, and the Netherlands, formally signed in 1948, by which the three countries agreed to establish common tariffs on the importation of goods into the three member states and to abolish customs duties on items traded among them, with certain exceptions such as duties on alcohol, wine, beer, and tobacco. The Benelux agreement grew out of a customs convention signed by the governments-in-exile on 5 September 1944 when the three countries were still under German occupation.

The Benelux agreement has been superseded in part by later, more inclusive agreements, but it was the first treaty since WORLD WAR II to provide for relatively free movement of people and goods between a group of European nations. Until recently, Luxembourgers still had to show their passports when they crossed into France and Germany. They have not been required to do so when crossing into Belgium or the Netherlands for decades.

BITBURG. Bitburg was the principal city in the part of Luxembourg annexed by Prussia in 1815, following the Napoleonic Wars. The annexed area reduced Luxembourg's size by about a third. Many of the inhabitants of the former Luxembourg lands in Germany still speak LETZEBUERGESCH, and many of them still take part in the annual pilgrimage and dancing procession in honor of ST. WILLIBRORD in ECHTERNACH on Whit-Tuesday.

Bitburg is better known today as the site of an important American air force base and of a military cemetery honored by a visit from American president Ronald Reagan during his term in office. Since a number of the German soldiers buried there were members of an S.S. unit that had murdered American prisoners of war during the BATTLE OF THE BULGE, this was not the most politic visit Reagan might have made. (*See also* DANCING PROCESSION AT ECHTERNACH and THREE PARTITIONS OF LUXEMBOURG)

BOCK. A hill on the eastern side of the present city of Luxembourg. In 963 SIGEFROI purchased the Bock and a small tract of land adjoining it from the ABBEY OF ST. MAXIMIN IN TRIER. Sigefroi built a castle on the Bock, from which he ruled the lands he inherited from his father, WIGERIC, count of the Ardennes. The Romans had built a small fort on the Bock, and either from that or from the Roman watchtower on the present site of the FISHMARKET, Sigefroi's castle derived the name LUCILINBURHUC which meant in Celtic "little fort on a hill". The name came in time to be applied not only to the castle but also to the town and county which grew up around it. In the Frankish dialect, this name was corrupted into "Letzebuerg", which is what Luxembourg is still called today in its native language.

Sigefroi's castle served as the seat of his successors and of later rulers of Luxembourg until it was destroyed by an explosion and fire in 1554, during the reign of CHARLES V in the course of his war with Francis I of France. VAUBAN built a new fort on the foundations of the castle in 1685, and this served as an integral part of the city's fortifications until they were dismantled in 1867 under the terms of the SECOND TREATY OF LONDON. Excavations conducted on the Bock before 1963 uncovered some of the foundations of Sigefroi's castle, and new walls were built on these foundations in 1963, in connection with the city's celebration of the thousandth anniversary of its foundation. The bridge linking the Bock with the upper city, built during the period of Burgundian and Spanish rule, is still standing.

BON PAYS. The southern two-thirds of Luxembourg, called in German the "Gutland", in English the "Good Country". The Bon Pays consists largely of the southern and eastern parts of the country, since the ARDENNES divide Luxembourg from west-south-west to east-north-east. It is covered with a good layer of alluvial soil, the weathered remains of limestone and sandstone deposits laid down during the four interglacial periods when southern Luxembourg, as well as most of northern and eastern France, was covered by a shallow inland sea.

The fossilized remains of various forms of undersea life, including crustaceans and fish, can be found throughout southern Luxembourg. A good collection of these fossils is on display at the NATIONAL MUSEUM.

Southern Luxembourg is hilly, although not nearly so hilly as the Ardennes to the north. Most of the hills are formed of lateral and terminal moraine from the glaciers that covered northern Europe during the Ice Ages.

There is little to distinguish southern Luxembourg geologically from northeastern France—no natural barriers divide Luxembourg from France to the south and Germany to the south and east. The present borders are not natural but historical ones and have changed frequently over the centuries.

BOUFFLERS, LOUIS FRANCOIS, DUC DE. One of LOUIS XIV's generals who played a prominent part in the

French-Dutch war of 1672–1678 as a commander of dragoons. Between 1676 and 1684 he campaigned in Luxembourg, battering most of Luxembourg's castles into submission with his artillery train, destroying many of them in the process. Some were restored, but most of them survived only as ruins after that time.

BRABANTINE REVOLUTION. A revolt that took place in the Austrian Netherlands in 1789 against certain reforms introduced by EMPEROR JOSEPH II without the consent of the provinces. The Duchy of Luxembourg did not take part in this revolt, which was put down in 1790 by troops under FIELD MARSHAL VON BENDER, governor of Luxembourg.

BREWING AND BREWERIES. Beer has been brewed in Luxembourg from at least Celtic times and continued to be brewed during Roman and Frankish times. The monks of the ABBEY OF ALTMUNSTER, founded in 1083, brewed their own beer, growing their own hops and milling their own grain. Outside the monasteries, most of the beer brewed in medieval and modern times was produced in small family-owned breweries, but during the nineteenth century a new process was imported from Germany, and Luxembourg began brewing lager beer on a larger scale and exporting it to France and Belgium.

As the breweries grew in size, their number decreased. In 1840 there were twenty-four breweries in Luxembourg; by 1900 their number had decreased to twelve, and at the present day there are only four. The largest is the Brasseries Réunies located along the ALZETTE in Clausen, below the city of Luxembourg. The Brasseries Réunies incorporates three formerly independent breweries, of which the Clausen brewery, dating back to 1563 when COUNT MANSFELD, governor of Luxembourg, built his own brewery on his own estate, is the oldest. The other two breweries incorporated in the Brasseries Réunies are the Mousel brewery which goes back to 1825, and the Henri Funck brewery, which it absorbed in 1982.

Other noted breweries in Luxembourg are the Bofferding brewery (Brasserie National) in Bascharge, the Diekirch brewery in the town of the same name, and the Simon brewery in WILTZ. Most of the beer produced in the Grand Duchy is the blond, pilsener type. In addition to their excellent standard brands, each of the breweries produces a special high-quality beer. The Brasseries Réunies, for instance, produce not only Mousel and Henri Funck beers, but also a Royal Altmunster, the Brasserie de Diekirch produces not only Diekirch beer, but also a Diekirch Reserve and a Diekirch Grand Reserve, and the Simon brewery produces not only Simon Pils, but also a Simon Regal, with an alcoholic content above five percent. On special occasions, they brew a dark beer, such as the Henri Funck Easterbrew and a Christmas Brew.

The beers brewed in Luxembourg are as high in quality and as excellent in taste as any brewed in Europe, although they are not as well known as some of the more famous brands such as Heineken and Carlsberg. About 37 percent of the Grand Duchy's production is exported, mainly to France, Belgium, and the United Kingdom. Another large part of its production is consumed by weekend tourists who drive their cars across the borders on Sunday, fill their gasoline tanks with Luxembourg's lower-priced gasoline, buy a few cartons of Luxembourg's lower-priced cigarettes, and buy a case or two of Luxembourg beer or wine.

BRONZE AGE. The Bronze Age was preceded in western Europe by an intermediate stage when copper was used. Bronze is an amalgam of copper and tin, and tools and weapons made from bronze are harder and more durable than tools and weapons made from copper alone. Like other discoveries, the use of bronze seems to have reached western Europe from the Danube Valley, brought either by the Celts or their immediate predecessors. The Bronze Age lasted from about 1800 B.C. until 700 B.C. in western Europe, and was followed by the Iron Age, which overlapped it.

Many Bronze Age artifacts have been found in Luxembourg. In this area the Hallstadt culture (late Bronze Age) which ended about 700 B.C. seems to have overlapped with the La Tène culture (early Iron Age) which began about 750 B.C.

CAPUCHINS. A mendicant and missionary order dedicated to poverty and hard work that set up a cloister and church in Luxembourg in the early seventeenth century. Among their activities was the sending of missionaries to Louisiana. During the reign of MARIA THERESA (1740–1786) many of the monasteries in Luxembourg, including the Capuchins, were suppressed. A street named the rue des Capucins still extends from the PLACE D'ARMES to the Grand Rue, the principal shopping street in Luxembourg city. The old municipal theatre, the Theatre des Capucins, actually stands on the site of the former monastery.

CARGOLUX. Europe's largest all-cargo airline, which operates from Luxembourg's FINDEL Airport and flies cargoes to destinations all around the world. Its cargo terminal is new, large, and cost-efficient. It contains 14,000 square meters of storage space and operates 24 hours a day, 365 days a year. In 1990 it handled over 116,000 tons of air freight.

CASEMATES. A system of underground passages excavated through the soft sandstone underlying the upper city during late medieval and early modern times. These passages were an important part of the city's fortifications; food, supplies, and ammunition were stored there, and troops could be moved along them from one part of the city's defenses to another.

The casemates at their greatest extent were about twenty-four kilometers (fourteen miles) in length. They last served a practical use during WORLD WAR II, as a place where the Luxembourgers took shelter during British air raids. Most of the casemates have now been closed off, but small sections have been kept open as a tourist attraction. There are two entrances to the casemates, one near the BOCK and one at the PLACE DE LA CONSTITUTION on the southern side of the old city.

CASTLE OF VIANDEN. The *chateau fort* at Vianden is an excellent example of the feudal castles that dominated western Europe during the period from the tenth through the fourteenth centuries. Similar castles were built throughout northern France, Germany, the southern parts of the Netherlands and other countries. The castles built by the crusaders in the Holy Lands were of the same type—huge, menacing fortresses, with thick stone walls and turrets, designed to withstand a long siege and impervious to capture by any foe not equipped with heavy siege engines.

The castle of Vianden, once the seat of the COUNTS OF VIANDEN, dominated the lower valley of the Our River in northeastern Luxembourg. A small town grew up under its walls and an outer wall with watchtowers was built around this town as a first line of defense. Part of this wall still stands.

The castle was built on a small steep hill overlooking the Our. Archaeological excavations have discovered that a small Roman fort stood on the site during the centuries of Roman rule, and Roman coins of the first century A.D. have been discovered there. A Frankish fort was built on the ruins of the Roman fort during the ninth century, and the COUNTS OF

VIANDEN built their castle on the site of the Frankish fort during the High Middle Ages (eleventh through fourteenth centuries).

No major architectural changes were made after 1264, although improvements were made in the living quarters to make them more comfortable. The counts of Vianden continued to live in the castle until 1417, when the title and the castle were inherited by the Nassau family. After that, the castle became the residence of the bailiffs who administered the Vianden estates in the name of the counts of Nassau-Vianden, who made their residences elsewhere. The castle was abandoned during the wars of the seventeenth century, and gradually fell into ruins. MARSHAL BOUFFLERS shelled the castle for three days in 1678, after which it was no longer habitable.

In 1820 WILLIAM I, who inherited the castle in 1815 when he became grand duke of Luxembourg, sold it to a wealthy citizen of Vianden, who stripped it of everything salable, including the remaining furniture, the lead from the roofs, and some of the stones from the towers. The castle was repurchased by WILLIAM II who succeeded his father as grand duke in 1840, and sporadic attempts were made at restoration during the next few reigns.

ADOLF OF NASSAU-WEILBURG, who became grand duke in 1890, purchased the castle of Vianden from the Dutch royal family during the early years of his reign. In 1977, the Luxembourg state acquired the castle, and began a major work of restoration, which reached completion in 1995. The castle has been restored to its seventeenth-century appearance. However, anachronisms such as plastered interior walls and radiators have been installed so that the rooms may be used for public functions.

In its ruined state, the castle of Vianden was more impressive twenty years ago than it is today after its restoration, but the massive structure rising above the town still dominates the landscape and is visited by thousands of people every year.

CATHEDRAL OF NOTRE DAME OF LUXEMBOURG. In 1870, when Luxembourg was made a diocese, the country had no cathedral. A seventeenth century Jesuit church, which had become a parish church after the suppression of the Jesuit order under JOSEPH II, was chosen to become the cathedral and renamed the Cathedral of Notre Dame of Luxembourg.

Between 1935 and 1938 the cathedral was enlarged by the addition of a new choir on the southern side with beautiful stained-glass windows. At the same time, new towers were built over the choir and a new portal, designed by AUGUST TREMONT, was installed to give access to the cathedral from the south.

In the crypt are buried the bones of JOHN THE BLIND, which were returned to Luxembourg in 1946 from the chapel of Kastel, which had been created for them at Mettlach in the Saar by Frederick-William IV of Prussia in 1838, and of CHARLOTTE, reigning grand duchess of Luxembourg from 1919 to 1964.

CATHOLIC CHURCH. Most native Luxembourgers (about 95 percent) are Roman Catholics, although the foreign population (30 percent of the total population) belong to a variety of churches and religions. Despite the overwhelming preponderance of Roman Catholics, there is almost no evidence of religious bigotry. Judaism was recognized as an official religion in 1808, when Luxembourg was part of the First French Empire, and Protestantism was recognized as an official religion only in 1894, although the three Dutch grand dukes and the first two German grand dukes were all Protestants.

Protestant churches were, in fact, founded in both Luxembourg and Belgium in the early years of the Reformation but were later suppressed.

The principal religious differences in Luxembourg in recent years have not been between the churches but, as in many Catholic countries, between the clericals and the anticlericals. The anticlericals (the Liberals and the Socialists) were particularly strong in the years before WORLD WAR I, when they succeeded in passing laws in the CHAMBER OF DEPUTIES secularizing education and removing it from religious control. This conflict has largely died down today. The church still maintains secondary schools, and part of the teachers' salaries are paid by the state, although the vast majority of Luxembourg children attend secular public schools.

Luxembourg today is divided into thirteen Catholic deaneries and 265 parishes. It did not have a bishop of its own until 1870, when Monsignor Nicholas Adames, the vicar apostolic, was made its first bishop. Monsignor Adames did not take office until 1873, however, after WILLIAM III had given his consent.

In 1988, in connection with the visit of Pope John Paul II, Luxembourg was raised to the status of an archdiocese, and

Jean Hentgen, bishop of Luxembourg since 1971, was made the first archbishop.

Léon Lommel, who served as bishop co-adjutor and then bishop of Luxembourg from 1948 to 1969, was much beloved for his kindness and friendliness. He was born on his father's farm at Schleiderhof in 1893 and, according to his sister, had a book in his hands even when he was herding the family cows. He studied philosophy and theology at the University of Rome, but kept up his family ties even after he became bishop.

CATTENOM. The location of a nuclear reactor just across the Luxembourg border in France. Its proximity to Luxembourg has aroused a considerable amount of consternation, not only among the Greens but also among ordinary Luxembourg citizens, since a major accident, even one far smaller than the Chernobyl disaster in the Ukraine, would spread radioactive fallout over most of southern Luxembourg. The Luxembourg government's plans for coping with such an emergency are largely confined to advising citizens to get in their cars and drive rapidly to the north.

The actual odds for or against a nuclear accident at Cattenom are unknown. GREENPEACE has been fighting the location and operation of the plant on the Luxembourg border for years without a great deal of success.

CELTS. A people speaking one of the eight major branches of the Indo-European language who migrated into western Europe between approximately the years 900–500 B.C., from their earlier homes in the Danube River valley, where they had learned to farm, forge iron, and make iron tools and weapons. They conquered and mingled with the earlier Neolithic and Bronze Age people who had settled western Europe in sufficient numbers so that Celtic languages came to be spoken in most of the lands the Celts conquered. At the height of their expansion Celtic tribes settled in and controlled large parts of southern and western Germany, Helvetia (Switzerland), northern Italy, Belgium, France, Spain, and the British Isles, including Ireland. One group of Celtic tribes even moved southeast and settled in central Anatolia, in the area where the modern city of Ankara is located. (These are the people referred to in the Bible as the Galatians.)

The Celts were organized into tribes and never joined together into larger kingdoms or established central governments. They were eventually conquered by the Romans, the

Germans, and the Moors, among others. Celtic languages are still spoken in parts of Brittany, Wales, western Scotland, and western Ireland.

The Romans called the Celtic tribes with whom they came into closest contact GAULS.

CENTRAL RAILROAD STATION (GARE CENTRALE). Located across the gorge of the PETRUSSE from the old city at the southern end of the avenue de la Liberté. The first station, a wooden building, was built on the site in 1859, the year the first railroad was inaugurated. It was replaced between 1908 and 1912 by a cathedral-like building with a vast hall and a high clock tower.

CENTRE UNIVERSITAIRE (UNIVERSITY CENTER). Located in LIMPERTSBERG, the Centre Universitaire offers Luxembourg students a one-year program equivalent to the first year in a European university. The Centre Universitaire is also open to foreign residents of Luxembourg. It has no dormitories but almost all of its students live at home, and their only expenses are a small registration fee and the cost of their books. The center added an American studies program in 1990 , and some of its classes are conducted in English.

The Centre Universitaire is currently being expanded. An attractive new classroom building was opened in 1993, and the center plans to add two-year programs in certain fields in the near future. (*See also* EDUCATION and HIGHER EDUCATION)

CERCLE MUNICIPAL. A modern building on the PLACE D'ARMES completed in 1907, which has meeting rooms, conference halls, and space for art and photographic exhibits. The frieze of the building shows COUNTESS ERMESINDE granting a municipal charter to the city of Luxembourg in 1244. A tourist office (Syndicat d'Initiative) is located in one corner, and the entrance to the MODEL OF THE FORTRESS is located on one side.

The *Cercle Municipal* carries that name because a literary society met in an earlier building on the site from 1826 on.

CHAMBER OF DEPUTIES. The Chamber of Deputies, Luxembourg's single-house legislature, is elected by a combination of proportional representation and single-member voting by all men and women eighteen years of age or older. The chamber is composed of sixty deputies, elected from the country's four electoral districts—North, East, Central, and South. Members of the Chamber of Deputies hold office for five years. Voting is compulsory for Luxembourg citizens, and failure to vote can be punished by a fine.

Political parties prepare lists of candidates in each of the four electoral districts. The number of names on each list may not exceed the number of deputies to which that district is entitled by its population, and each voter in that district has a number of votes equal to the number of deputies to be elected. Voters may, by making a cross in the appropriate box, cast all their votes for the list presented by a single political party, or may divide their votes among individual candidates and parties, casting one or two votes for each candidate selected. The total number of votes cast by a voter may not exceed the number of deputies to be elected, or the ballot becomes invalid.

Since election is by weighted proportional representation, none of the political parties has had a majority of the seats in the Chamber of Deputies for the past fifty years, and governments are coalitions of two or more political parties with enough seats among them to command a majority in the Chamber of Deputies. In the ELECTION OF 1994 five political parties won seats in the chamber, but eight others failed to win any. A coalition government between the CHRISTIAN SOCIAL PEOPLE'S PARTY (CSV) and the LUXEMBOURG SOCIALIST WORKERS PARTY (LSAP), holding twenty-one and seventeen seats respectively, was renewed, with the DEMOCRATIC PARTY (DP), holding twelve seats, forming the principal opposition. (*See also* POLITICAL PARTIES)

The present Chamber of Deputies has the following political line-up.

Party	Members
Christian Social People's Party (CSV)	21
Luxembourg Social Workers Party (LSAP)	17
Democratic Party (DP)	12
Green Alliance (GLEI-GAP)	5
Action Committee for Democracy and Pension Reform (ADR)	5
Total	**60**

CHAPEL OF ST. QUIRIN. A small chapel built into the rock of the city walls, which supposedly contained the relics of St.

Quirin before they were transferred to Neuss in Germany. The chapel was built close to a well and is thought to have been a site sacred to the worship of the pagan gods in pre-Christian times.

CHARLEMAGNE. Charles the Great, grandson of CHARLES MARTEL and son of PEPIN THE SHORT who became king of the FRANKS in 752. When Pepin died in 768, he divided his kingdom between his two sons, Carloman and Charles. Charles was given AUSTRASIA, NEUSTRIA, and Aquitaine, and Carloman became ruler of a domain in eastern France, the former Burgundian kingdom. Charles established his capital at Aachen (Aix-la-Chapelle) in Austrasia, near where the Belgian and German borders now meet. When Carloman died in 771, Charles seized his lands and added them to his own kingdom.

In 773, in response to an appeal from Pope Adrian I, Charlemagne invaded Italy, crushed the Lombards, and assumed the IRON CROWN OF THE LOMBARDS, ending the existence of a separate Lombard kingdom.

Charlemagne reaffirmed the DONATION OF PEPIN which had given the pope temporal rule over central Italy. Appealed to by a later pope, Leo III, whose subjects had risen against him, Charlemagne invaded Italy again in 799, restored Leo III to power, and was in return crowned Roman Emperor in the West by the pope on Christmas Day 800.

Charlemagne spent most of his reign establishing his rule over the German tribes to the east of the Rhine, including the Saxons. This done, he took on the burden of defending the eastern frontiers of the empire against the Slavs and Avars. He also invaded Spain twice. On the first occasion, his armies were unsuccessful and had to retreat across the Pyrenees. His second invasion was more successful, and he established a Spanish march south of the Pyrenees.

Although he was illiterate, Charlemagne sponsored a revival of learning in western Europe that has come to be known as the Carolingian Renaissance. He invited noted scholars, among them ALCUIN OF YORK, to his court, and he set up a palace school for his children and those of his courtiers.

When Charlemagne ruled the Franks, Luxembourg had not yet come into existence, but the future Grand Duchy was strategically placed between Charlemagne's summer capital at Aachen and his winter capital at THIONVILLE. The Frankish tribesmen of Austrasia served in Charlemagne's army, paid taxes into his treasury and when his empire broke up during the reigns of his grandsons, set up a number of feudal states in the northern lands he had once ruled. One of these became the County of Luxembourg, later the Duchy of Luxembourg, and still later the Grand Duchy of Luxembourg.

CHARLES IV. Eldest son of JOHN THE BLIND by his first wife, Elizabeth of Bohemia. He was educated in Paris, where his tutor was the future Pope Clement VI. At the age of fourteen he accompanied his father on an expedition to Italy and was left in charge of the army when his father returned to Germany. After the failure of the Italian expedition, his father made him marquis of Moravia and governor of Bohemia for a two-year period, where he was more successful as a ruler than his father had been.

In 1346 John succeeded in having Charles chosen KING OF THE ROMANS by the German electors, with the strong support of his great-uncle ARCHBISHOP BALDWIN OF TRIER and the archbishop of Mainz, and aided by huge payments to the pope and cardinals to secure their approval.

Following his election as king of the Romans, Charles accompanied his father to the BATTLE OF CRECY where John died. Charles was wounded, but survived. After the battle, although John had declared WENZEL I, his son by a second marriage, heir to Luxembourg, Charles seized the county and ruled it in his own name for seven years, appropriating its revenues for his own purposes. He was crowned Holy Roman Emperor in Bonn in 1346 and king of Bohemia in Prague in 1348. In 1355 he went to Italy, where he received the IRON CROWN OF THE LOMBARDS.

During Charles's administration of Luxembourg the Black Death struck, which within the next 150 years killed half the population of Europe. In Luxembourg alone, sixty thousand people died of the plague during its first outbreak, in 1349–50.

Charles IV was popular in Bohemia, which his wise measures made peaceful and prosperous. In 1348 he founded the University of Prague, which soon became one of the leading universities in Europe. He took little further interest in the affairs of Luxembourg after he left it to be ruled by his half brother WENZEL I in 1353.

As emperor, Charles IV concentrated on building up a Germano-Slav empire in central Europe with its capital at Prague, abandoning the old idea of a Holy Roman Empire uniting Germany and Italy, with its capital at Rome. In 1356, he issued the famous GOLDEN BULL, which regulated the succession to the throne of the Holy Roman Empire, and in 1376 he succeeded in having his son WENZEL II elected king of the Romans to succeed him as emperor.

CHARLES V. Known originally as Charles of Ghent (Ghent is the city in Flanders where he was born in 1500), Charles became ruler of the Burgundian possessions in the Netherlands, including Luxembourg, at the age of six, following the early death of his father, PHILIP THE FAIR. His aunt, Margaret of Austria, served as regent until Charles was declared of age in 1515.

Through his mother, Joanna the Mad, Charles inherited a claim to the throne of Spain. In 1516, upon the death of Ferdinand of Aragon, he became king of Spain with the title of Charles I, although formal recognition was delayed until his visit to Spain in 1518. His mother Joanna was made joint ruler with him but her mental condition prevented her from sharing in his rule. One of the provisions of his accession to the Spanish throne was that Charles had to learn Spanish. Another was that his eldest son PHILIP II was to be raised as a Spanish prince, a provision that caused Philip difficulties in the Netherlands, which came to regard him as a foreign ruler rather than a native prince as his father Charles had been.

Charles inherited the Hapsburg possessions in Austria, Bohemia, Germany, and Hungary in 1519 upon the death of MAXIMILIAN, his paternal grandfather. He was elected Holy Roman Emperor the same year, and crowned at Aachen (Aix-la-Chapelle) in 1520 as Charles V.

Charles V, the name he is best known by, ruled Spain and the Spanish colonies in the New World, the Hapsburg possessions in Austria, Bohemia, Germany, and Hungary, Franche-Comté in France, and the Burgundian possessions in the Netherlands. With his vast territories he also inherited great problems. One was the threat from the Ottoman Turks, who invaded his Hungarian lands and threatened Vienna; another was his struggle with Francis I of France, who tried to break through the ring of Hapsburg lands that surrounded his kingdom of France; and the third was the Protestant Reformation, which began in Germany in 1517 when Martin Luther posted his 95 theses on the church door at Wittenberg. The Reformation spread rapidly through North Germany, Scandinavia, Bohemia (where it had been preceded a century earlier by a similar movement under the leadership of John Hus), and even in the Netherlands, not to mention England, France, and Scotland.

During Charles's reign, Francis I invaded the Low Countries, overthrowing the Prince Bishop of Liège with the help of Robert de la Marck, the famous "Wild Boar of the Ardennes" (known in English literature chiefly through his portrayal in Walter Scott's novel *Quentin Durward*).

In 1542, a French army under the duke of Orleans seized the fortress of Luxembourg, but it was recaptured nine days later by imperial forces under René of Nassau. French armies again captured the fortress in 1543, but in 1544 it was retaken by the imperial forces. During these battles for Luxembourg the castle built by SIGEFROI in 963 and the ABBEY OF ALTMUNSTER were destroyed.

In 1545, Charles appointed COUNT PETER ERNEST VON MANSFELD as governor of Luxembourg, a position he held until his death in 1604, although he was captured by the French in 1587, during his defense of Ivoix, and held prisoner at Vincennes until he was ransomed.

In 1548, Charles promulgated a Pragmatic Sanction by which his Netherlands provinces became, in effect, an independent kingdom with its capital at Brussels, and no longer a part of the Holy Roman Empire. He also tried to reform the church in the Netherlands, controlled up until that time by a small number of large ecclesiastical sees, by creating fourteen new bishoprics. This plan was rejected by the reigning pope, to the eventual distress of the church. Under Charles, a native of the Netherlands, it would have been a popular measure, but when his son, Philip II of Spain, sought to carry it out, it was regarded as an instance of Spanish tyranny.

Charles V has sometimes been depicted as a religious bigot whose prime aim was to restore Catholicism throughout Europe. His record in that respect is somewhat mixed, however. He made alliances with Protestant princes in Germany, and Protestant soldiers served in the imperial army which besieged Rome and captured Pope Clement VII in 1527 and in the armies with which Charles fought the Turks. In Spain and Italy, he restrained the powers of the Inquisition, and his tendency was to issue edicts against Protestantism but suspend their operation for a definite number of years or pending the meeting of a church council. His edicts against Protestantism in the Netherlands were severe enough, but seldom enforced.

Charles was successful in his wars against Francis I in Italy and the Netherlands, and in his wars against the Turks, but less successful in restoring religious or even political unity to his German domains. In 1555, worn out by his struggles, he gave control over his possessions in the Netherlands to his son PHILIP II, and in 1556 he abdicated his Spanish crown, making Philip ruler over Spain and the Spanish possessions overseas, as well as most of Italy and Franche-Comté. His brother Frederick was given authority over the Hapsburg possessions in Austria, Bohemia, Germany, and Hungary in 1555, although Charles's formal abdication as Holy Roman Emperor was delayed until 1558. Charles died in Spain in 1589.

CHARLES VI. Archduke of Austria and Holy Roman Emperor (1711–1740), who became duke of Luxembourg and ruler of the rest of the former Spanish Netherlands in 1715 under the terms of the TREATY OF UTRECHT. During his reign and that of his Austrian successors, Belgium and Luxembourg were known as the Austrian Netherlands.

Luxembourg prospered under the rule of Charles VI, largely because it was at peace during his reign but also because of the measures Charles took to encourage commerce, agriculture, and education. A great highway, the first since Roman times, was built linking Trier and Luxembourg with Brussels and Ostend. The postal service, first established in 1704 under Philip V, was improved and a regular mail service, using specially constructed coaches, was inaugurated between Luxembourg and Brussels in 1722. Potato cultivation was introduced in 1720, greatly increasing the food supply of ordinary Luxembourgers. The fortifications of the city of Luxembourg were enlarged and strengthened, to provide greater protection in case of war.

When Charles VI died, he left no male heirs. To secure the succession to his daughter, MARIA THERESA, he prepared a new law of succession to the Hapsburg lands, the Pragmatic Sanction of 1723, which was signed by the other great powers of Europe, as well as by the estates of his own dominions. The Estates of the Duchy of Luxembourg ratified the Pragmatic Sanction in 1723, the same year it was promulgated. In spite of the agreement the other powers had signed, however, Maria Theresa's right of inheritance was challenged immediately upon her father's death.

CHARLES THE BOLD. Son of PHILIP THE GOOD, duke of Burgundy and Luxembourg, count of Charolais, and ruler of several other principalities from 1467 to 1477. He quarreled with his father during his lifetime but was reconciled with him before his death.

Charles inherited from his father some of the wealthiest provinces in western Europe, and with a little patience and diplomacy he might have succeeded in uniting them into a single kingdom of the Netherlands. He was eager to win military glory, however, and waged a series of wars against his neighbors, including Louis XI of France, his most bitter foe. He succeeded in adding Gelderland to his domains, but nothing else. In 1477, attempting to gain control of Lorraine, which lay between his provinces in Burgundy and in the Netherlands, he fell in battle against a Swiss army in Nancy. He was buried in Nancy, but later his remains were transported to Luxembourg, then to Bruges where he was finally interred next to his daughter MARY OF BURGUNDY.

After his death, some of Charles's possessions in France were taken over by Louis XI and became the property of the French crown. His daughter Mary, with the aid of her husband MAXIMILIAN OF AUSTRIA, succeeded in holding his possessions in the Netherlands and some of his French lands.

CHARLES MARTEL. Illegitimate son of PEPIN OF HERSTAL, mayor of the palace (majordomo) who had united AUSTRASIA and NEUSTRIA. When Pepin died in 714, Charles was imprisoned by Pepin's wife, who saw him as a threat to her own grandsons. After some difficulty, Charles won his freedom, defeated the Neustrians in battle, and spent ten years consolidating his power as mayor of the palace of the entire Frankish realm. In 732, when the Moors of Spain invaded Aquitaine, Charles assembled an army against them and defeated them at the Battle of Tours, winning himself the sobriquet of Charles Martel, Charles the Hammer. He was succeeded by his sons Carloman and Pepin in 741. In 747, Carloman retired to a monastery and his brother, known as PEPIN THE SHORT, became sole mayor of the palace in the Frankish lands.

CHARLOTTE, Grand Duchess of Luxembourg, 1919–1964. Charlotte, the second daughter of WILLIAM IV became grand duchess of Luxembourg in January 1919 upon the abdication of her elder sister MARIE-ADELAIDE following the end of WORLD WAR I. Almost immediately, the Belgian government put in a claim at the Peace Conference at Versailles for the Grand Duchy to be annexed to Belgium. In a plebiscite held on 28 September 1919, after the signing of the Treaty of Versailles, 77 percent of the voters of Luxembourg voted in favor of the continuation of the Grand Duchy as an independent monarchy under the rule of Grand Duchess Charlotte. Another 17 percent voted for the establishment of a republic. The plebiscite confirmed that the Grand Duchy would continue to be an independent state.

By her prudent and wise conduct, Charlotte reestablished the ruling dynasty as the popular symbol of the Luxembourg people and their national independence. During Charlotte's reign, the constitution was amended to give every citizen twenty-one years of age and older, including women, the right to vote. The customs union with Germany, dissolved by the German defeat in World War I, was replaced by a CUSTOMS AND MONETARY UNION with Belgium, agreed upon in 1921 and ratified in 1922. Given the attempted annexation of the Grand Duchy by Belgium in 1919, this union was not a wildly popular agreement, but the French government had refused to enter into an economic agreement with the Grand Duchy and a new agreement with Germany was ruled out by the immense unpopularity of the Germans because of their occupation of Luxembourg during World War I.

A number of social reforms were introduced during Charlotte's reign, including a comprehensive system of social insurance, the eight-hour working day, and the right of the worker to fair dismissal. A system of retirement pensions, unemployment insurance, workmen's compensation for industrial accidents, and health insurance was established. (Luxembourg's health insurance system, set up between the two world wars, is, indeed, one of the fairest and most efficiently run of any in the world.)

Grand Duchess Charlotte did not repeat the mistakes of her elder sister Marie-Adelaide during World War I. When German troops invaded the Grand Duchy on 10 May 1940, the grand ducal family left the country immediately to avoid capture by the Germans. The family spent most of WORLD WAR II in exile, in the United States, Canada, and Great Britain. A Luxembourg government-in-exile was set up in London, which cooperated with the Allied powers in World War II and became one of the founding members of the United Nations in 1945. Charlotte's husband, PRINCE FELIX OF BOURBON-PARMA, and her son, Prince Jean, the hereditary grand duke, served in the British army during the war, and returned to Luxembourg on 10 September 1944 when the country was liberated by American troops. The grand duchess returned from exile a few months later.

The dynasty emerged from World War II with enhanced

popularity and dignity. During the war, they had represented the hope of the nation for its eventual freedom and the reestablishment of its independence. After the war, they led the country in the reestablishment of its financial prosperity and in the movement towards a united Europe.

In 1964, after a reign of forty-five years, Grand Duchess Charlotte abdicated in favor of her eldest son and heir, JEAN, the present grand duke. She continued to live for another twenty-one years after her abdication, and became an increasingly honored and respected symbol of the nation.

CHIMAY, COUNT OF. Governor of Luxembourg who surrendered Luxembourg to the French in 1684 after the city had sustained a bombardment that destroyed all but ten of the 450 houses in the city.

CHRISTIAN SOCIAL PEOPLE'S PARTY (CSV). This party has a solid basis of support in the rural regions, as well as the support of the CATHOLIC CHURCH and a majority of the business community. It can be compared in some respects with the German Christian Democratic Party. It is conservative and slightly to the right of center. With the built-in support it enjoys, the CSV normally emerges from each national election with the greatest number of votes and the largest number of seats in the CHAMBER OF DEPUTIES, although never with an absolute majority. It thus finds it necessary to form an alliance with either the LUXEMBOURG SOCIALIST WORKERS PARTY or the DEMOCRATIC PARTY in order to form a government.

The CSV has the support of a large and aggressive labor federation, the LUXEMBOURG CHRISTIAN LABOR FEDERATION (LCGB), which fights vigorously for workers rights and thus adds something to the party's strength, particularly among newly naturalized citizens.

In the ELECTIONS OF 1994, the CSV lost one seat in the Chamber of Deputies but remained the largest single party, holding twenty-one seats out of sixty. It formed its third national coalition in a row with the LSAP, with most of the cabinet, headed by Prime Minister JACQUES SANTER, retaining their positions. When Santer became president of the EUROPEAN COMMISSION in January 1995, he was succeeded as prime minister by JEAN-CLAUDE JUNCKER.

The CSV is normally referred to in ordinary conversation and in writing as the Christian Social Party (in French the Parti

Christian Social) rather than by its full name as the Christian Social People's Party.

CHURCH OF ST. MICHAEL. The oldest church in the city of Luxembourg, dating from 987 and included within the first city walls. The church has been damaged, destroyed, and rebuilt several times over the centuries. It was heavily damaged by cannon fire during the siege of the fortress by the MARSHAL DE CREQUI in 1683–84, but rebuilt by LOUIS XIV, who added the church's onion-shaped dome. When the French revolutionary army captured the city in 1795, the church was left undisturbed because of a statue of St. Michael, wearing a Phrygian cap, which stood in a niche outside the wall. The Phrygian cap, adopted by the French revolutionaries as a "liberty cap", convinced the French that St. Michael was a supporter of the revolution.

CINEMATEQUE MUNCIPALE. The city of Luxembourg has an extensive collection of French, German, British, and American classic films, which are shown on a regular basis at the Cinéma-tèque Municipale, a small, recently renovated moving picture theater on the Place du Théâtre in Luxembourg city.

CLERVAUX. A small town in the Luxembourg ARDENNES with a long history. Traces of Celtic settlements and a Roman fort have been found there. A castle, parts of which date from the twelfth century, still dominates the town. The castle was enlarged during the period of Burgundian rule in the fifteenth century, and became, by marriage, one of the possessions of the de Lannoi family in 1631. In 1634 Claude de Lannoi built the north wing. New additions to the castle continued to be made until 1887, when parts of it were torn down by the count de Berlaymont to use in building a new mansion house.

The castle was largely destroyed during the BATTLE OF THE BULGE on 6 December 1944, but was restored after the war. It now houses a collection of models of various feudal castles that once flourished in Luxembourg lands, as well as a small museum of the Battle of the Ardennes (1944–45). In addition, the famous collection of photographs assembled by EDWARD STEICHEN known as "The Family of Man" is housed in the castle.

Local legend has it that the Delanos of Fairhaven, Massachusetts, including Sarah Delano, the mother of President Franklin Delano Roosevelt, are descended from the counts de Lannoi who owned the castle at Clervaux. However, PHILIPPE DE LANNOI, of French Huguenot descent, arrived in Plymouth aboard the *Fortune* in 1621, and the de Lannoi family did not acquire the castle at Clervaux until 1631, so Philippe de Lannoi could not be directly descended from them, although he may have been a distant relation.

CLOVIS. King of the Salian Franks from 481–511, Clovis began his reign at the Salian capital in Tournai. Using that as a base, he seized the Gallo-Roman kingdom of Soissons, controlled by a Roman named Syagrius, in 486. Using Soissons as a new base, he next defeated the Alemanni, who had made the mistake of invading his kingdom in 498. Having conquered the Alemanni he next turned on the Burgundians, whom he defeated in 500, in a battle near Dijon. In 507 he overcame the Visigoths and occupied their kingdom in southwestern Gaul. Thwarted momentarily by Theodoric, king of the Ostrogoths, who led an army from northern Italy into southern Gaul, Clovis turned north and absorbed the Frankish kingdom of AUSTRASIA, finally establishing himself as king of all the Franks.

Clovis was undoubtedly helped in his conquest of Gaul by his conversion to Catholic Christianity in 496, which gained him the support of the Catholic population of southern Gaul and its influential bishops. (Most of the earlier German invaders of Gaul had been Arian Christians.) The Franks had been pagans before their invasion of Gaul, and remained so for some time. Clovis's baptism at Reims in 496 gained him the support of most of the Gallo-Roman population of Gaul, who regarded the Arians as worse than pagans.

After Clovis's death in 511, his territories were divided among his four sons, which effectively brought an end to the first Frankish kingdom. His descendants, called Merovingians after Clovis's grandfather Merovech, fought among themselves as well as against outsiders and gradually declined in strength. Eventually, their power was taken over by their Austrasian mayors of the palace, who succeeded in reuniting the Frankish kingdom under their own rule.

CODE NAPOLEON. Code of civil law drawn up by a distinguished committee of jurists and legal scholars which became the basis of civil law in France under Emperor NAPOLEON I. This was speedily followed by a code of criminal law, and both these codes were introduced into Luxembourg, then part of France, where they remain the basis of the legal system today.

COLLEGE VAUBAN. An independent French secondary school founded a few years ago to prepare students for the French baccalaureate examinations. The school is housed in the buildings in Limpertsberg that formerly served the *école professionel* and is badly in need of new facilities. At one time the government planned to move it to the proposed new international campus on the Geesseknäppchen in Merl, but now plans to build another Luxembourg lycée there instead.

The Collège Vauban follows a French curriculum entirely and aims to prepare its students for entrance to the French universities. Not all of its students are French; students of other nationalities are also admitted. The school exists mainly, however, for children of the French business community in Luxembourg who are not eligible for entrance to the French-language stream of the EUROPEAN SCHOOL. Its advantage over the Luxembourg system is that all major subjects are taught in French, and its students do not need to have the degree of fluency in German that would enable them to survive in a good Luxembourg athenée or lyceé.

COLMAR-BERG. Colmar-Berg is the home of the grand ducal family, in the castle of Berg. When the family is in residence the grand ducal flag flies from the castle.

Colmar-Berg is also the location of Goodyear (Luxembourg) S.A., the largest integrated tire factory in Europe, which provides employment to almost four thousand workers, including many who commute daily from across the Belgian border. The Goodyear Technical Center, which does research on the production of better, safer tires, is also located in Colmar-Berg. Somewhat to the surprise of the American managers who set up the Technical Center, they found that most European tires surpassed American tires in quality and performance. Five decades of research and testing however, have enabled Goodyear to make tires to equal, if not surpass, tires manufactured by the traditional European firms.

Goodyear has recently emerged the victor in a dispute about operating its assembly lines seven days a week. Although the workers voted against this by a two-thirds majority, the government gave Goodyear permission to operate on Sundays, moved by the company's threat to move some of its operations to other countries, which would have resulted in the loss of several hundred jobs. Goodyear promised in return to fill most of the new positions that will be created with workers on the government's unemployment register, and has already started hiring and training these new workers.

Colmar-Berg is located just off the main road between MERSCH and ETTELBRUCK, the two principal towns in the center of the Grand Duchy.

CONGRESS OF VIENNA (1814–15). Called by the Great Powers to redraw the borders of Europe and restore stability after the defeat of NAPOLEON I. Austria, Prussia, Russia, and Great Britain dominated the congress, but France, represented by its astute foreign minister, Talleyrand, was included in its deliberations despite Napoleon's defeat. Talleyrand was able to use his negotiating skill to exploit the differences between the other powers and to secure the interests of France and the restored Bourbon dynasty.

The powers assembled at the Congress of Vienna had difficulty agreeing among themselves about the proper way to reorganize Europe, but did their job well enough so that almost a hundred years passed before the next major European war, although there were plenty of minor wars during this century of peace.

One of the decisions of the congress was to incorporate the nine provinces of Belgium and the seven provinces of the northern Netherlands under the rule of Prince William VI of Orange, stadholder (governor) of Holland, who in 1815 became WILLIAM I, king of the Netherlands. Another decision was to set up Luxembourg as a separate state under the rule of William I as grand duke of Luxembourg. In 1815, the Grand Duchy of Luxembourg was more than double its present size, despite having lost a third of its territory in the east to Prussia. BITBURG and PRUM were the principal cities lost to Luxembourg.

The reestablishment of Luxembourg as an independent principality under Dutch rule was not greeted with great enthusiasm by most Luxembourgers, whose preference would have been to recreate the Austrian Netherlands by reuniting with the Belgium provinces in a larger state ruled over by an Austrian prince. Austria had no interest in reestablishing its rule in the southern Netherlands, either directly or indirectly, so this option was not available.

CORNICHE. Sometimes called "the balcony with the most splendid view in Europe," the Corniche is a promenade along the top of the ancient fortifications of the city of Luxembourg, extending from the BOCK, the hill upon which SIGEFROI built his castle, to the Bastion of the Holy Spirit, one of the strongest forts which defended the city. The Corniche overlooks the valley of the ALZETTE upon whose banks, under the protection of the castle, the original town of Luxembourg arose. It also looks across the valley to the PLATEAU DU RHAM to which the city's fortifications were later extended, including the WALL OF WENCESLAS as well as the barracks designed by VAUBAN during the French occupation of 1684 to 1697.

COUNCIL OF GOVERNMENT (CONSEIL DE GOUVERNE-MENT). The cabinet, consisting of the ministers who head the various governmental departments and the secretaries of state, presided over by the Minister of State (prime minister), appointed by the grand duke. The cabinet is responsible to the CHAMBER OF DEPUTIES which may turn it out of office by voting against it on a major measure, such as the budget. This has not happened in the past fifty years. (*See also* GOVERN-MENT, NATIONAL)

COUNCIL OF STATE (CONSEIL D'ETAT). The Council of State has administrative, legislative, and judicial functions. It examines proposed laws and proposed amendments to laws, and it serves as a court of appeals in certain cases, including disputes between administrative bodies and cases in which individuals allege that government officials or public bodies have acted incompetently, exceeded their powers, acted out of self-interest, violated the law, or not followed procedures established by law.

The Council of State is also called upon to advise the grand duke on any matters he refers to it. In certain cases decisions may be made by the government only with the advice and consent of the Council of State.

The Council of State has twenty-five members, not including those members of the reigning family who may take part in its deliberations. Its members are appointed by the grand duke, who names them either directly or upon the recommendation of the CHAMBER OF DEPUTIES or the Council of State. One-third of the members are appointed directly by the grand duke, one-third upon recommendation of the Chamber of Deputies, and one-third upon the recommendation of the Council of State. In the latter two cases, the grand duke makes his appointments from a list of three nominees submitted by the chamber or the council. Members of the grand-ducal family who sit with the Council of State are appointed directly by the grand duke.

Members of the Council of State must be Luxembourgers, must not have been deprived by law of their civil or political rights, must reside in Luxembourg, and must be at least thirty years old. They may not be members of the current government or of the current Chambers of Deputies. They must retire when they reach the age of seventy-two.

The Council of State is an ongoing body. Individual members may resign or may be dismissed by the grand duke, but only after the reasons for dismissing the member have been discussed by the council. The grand duke also has the right to dissolve the Council of State if he feels it necessary to change its membership substantially.

The Council of State meets as a whole when exercising its legislative functions or when called upon to give its advice to the government or the grand duke. It elects a president to preside over its sessions, and a vice-president to preside when the president is absent. The grand duke may take part in its meetings if he chooses; when he is present he presides over the meeting. Members of the government may also attend sessions of the Council of State and take part in its deliberations, but may not vote.

The judicial functions of the Council of State are exercised by a committee of eleven of its members appointed by the grand duke. They must be doctors of law or possess equivalent qualifications. The committee's sessions are normally presided over by the president of the Council of State, unless he declines to do so or fails to possess the necessary qualifications, in which case the vice-president of the council presides with the same reservations. In case neither the president nor the vice-president qualify to preside over the judicial committee, the grand duke appoints some other qualified person to preside over its meetings. Members of the government may attend meetings of the judicial committee, it being understood that any remarks they may make are not part of the official proceedings.

The legislative functions performed by the Council of State are particularly important, and in some respects it resembles the upper house in nations that have a bicameral legislature. It may initiate legislation, proposing new laws or amendments to existing laws for the Chamber of Deputies to consider. A proposed law may not be submitted to either the grand duke or the Chamber of Deputies until the Council of State has given its advice upon it, except in matters the government considers urgent, in which case the government may submit a proposed law directly to the Chamber of Deputies. In such a case, however, the Chamber of Deputies may submit the proposed law to the Council of State before discussing it, and in any case the advice of the Council of State must be submitted to the Chamber of Deputies before final action is taken upon the proposed law. The Council of State may not veto a proposed law, but it may delay the final vote in the Chamber of Deputies upon such a law for up to three months.

COUNTS OF VIANDEN. The counts of Vianden were originally lords of a small fief on the banks of the Our River in what is now northeastern Luxembourg, where they built a strong castle during the eleventh through the fourteenth centuries. (*See* CASTLE OF VIANDEN) The counts held their fief directly from the German emperor (the Holy Roman Emperor) and enjoyed good relations with the imperial court. They reached the height of their power during the early thirteenth century when they held lordship over two hundred estates and were rivals of the counts of Luxembourg. In 1264, however, Count Philip I, who had deposed his nephew, the rightful heir, became vassal to Henry V, count of Luxembourg, in return for Henry's support of his right to rule Vianden.

The first count of Vianden mentioned in the records is Bertolphe, who held the title in 1090. Frederick I became count of Vianden in 1129, and his descendents held the title until 1417, when it passed to Englebert I, a member of the younger branch of the Nassau family and grandnephew of Elizabeth, countess of Vianden, who died without leaving a direct heir. Englebert I took the title of count of Nassau-Vianden, and the title remained in his family until the death in 1544 of René de Châlon, count of Nassau-Vianden and prince of Orange.

With the death of René de Châlon, the title of count of Nassau-Vianden passed to his cousin WILLIAM THE SILENT (Prince William I of Orange), who led the revolt of the Netherlands against Spanish rule during the reign of PHILIP II of Spain. Philip II confiscated the lands William held as count of Vianden in 1566, and placed them under the control of COUNT MANSFELD, governor of Luxembourg. William the Silent was assassinated in 1584, but his lands were restored to his son and heir, Philip-William of Orange, in 1604.

The title of count of Vianden stayed in the Orange-Nassau

family until 1890, although they were deprived of their Vianden estates from 1693 to 1697, and again from 1702 to 1759. One of the most famous counts of Vianden was WILLIAM III OF ENGLAND, prince of Orange and stadholder of the Netherlands from 1650–1702, who became king of England in 1689, and held the crown until his death in 1702. William III was the principal opponent of LOUIS XIV of France during the WAR OF THE LEAGUE OF AUGSBURG (1689–1697). He died childless in 1702, leaving his lands in the Netherlands and Luxembourg (Vianden and its dependencies) to a distant relative, but the Vianden part of the inheritance was not recovered by the Orange-Nassau family until 1759.

WILLIAM I, who became king of the Netherlands and grand duke of Luxembourg in 1815, inherited the title of count of Vianden in 1795, but Vianden, along with the rest of Luxembourg, was under French rule from 1795 until 1815. William I passed on the title to his son and grandson, but the title of count of Vianden was allowed to lapse upon the death of WILLIAM III in 1890, and the accession of ADOLF OF NASSAU-WEILBURG to the throne of Luxembourg as Grand Duke Adolf I.

COURTS AND TRIBUNALS. The courts and tribunals of Luxembourg are independent, conforming to the doctrine of separation of powers, but limited in their jurisdiction by the Constitution. Judges are appointed by the grand duke. They must be at least twenty-five years of age, must possess a doctorate of laws, and must have received probationary training as judges. Various other qualifications are attached to higher positions in the judiciary. They may not hold other offices in the government, such as cabinet member, head of a government department, or member of the CHAMBER OF DEPUTIES. Judges in the lower courts may be appointed directly by the Grand Duke, but in filling the higher ranks of the judiciary, he must act upon the advice of the Superior Court of Justice, the highest court of review.

Judges hold office for life or until they retire and may be suspended or removed from office only in case of misconduct or by a decree of the Superior Court, meeting in council. Their salaries are fixed by law. They may not accept other positions in the government to which a salary is attached, and they may not maintain a private law practice, serve as officers in the military, be in holy orders, or hold office in local government.

They are also forbidden to engage in commercial activities in their own name or through agents.

Trials are public, except where the publicity attending them may threaten public order or morals. Judgments are delivered in open court. Decisions of lower courts may be appealed to higher courts. Courts must follow regular orders of procedure, established by law. They may also rule on the legality of the acts of the central government and local governments; they do not have the power to declare laws unconstitutional, but if two laws conflict, one a statute passed by the legislature and the other a law established by the Constitution, they render their decision in accordance with the constitutional law.

Within the Luxembourg court system, there are courts with ordinary jurisdiction and courts with special jurisdiction. Courts with ordinary jurisdiction include courts presided over by justices of the peace, district courts, and the Superior Court of Justice. One section of the Superior Court functions as a sort of grand jury, to determine whether laws have been broken and whether prosecutions should be brought. Another section acts as a final court of appeals. These courts have both civil and criminal jurisdiction, within certain limits.

The Court of Assizes meets once a month and deals with major crimes. Luxembourg has no system of trial juries, but the six judges of the Court of Assizes function as a jury and may find an accused person guilty only by unanimous decision.

Various special courts and tribunals have jurisdiction over employer-employee relations, act as courts of arbitration, serve as children's courts, or deal with political crimes. There is a special war-crimes court.

The criminal justice system in Luxembourg includes a corps of magistrates charged with investigating and prosecuting violations of the law. They represent the government in cases that appear before the courts and are sometimes called standing magistrates, since they appear on their feet in court to conduct cases, as opposed to the sitting magistrates, who preside over the courts. There are also judges of instruction whose primary function is to investigate the facts and circumstances involved when someone is accused of a crime. They report the results of their investigations weekly to a court consisting of three judges. This council decides upon the further disposition of cases. They may decide that the evidence does not warrant a prosecution or may refer a case to a lower or higher tribunal, according to the nature of the offense with which an accused person is charged, and whether it may or may not be punishable by a prison sentence.

There are various lower-ranking officers of the courts including clerks of the court, bailiffs, process servers, and notaries. The legal system also includes advocates (attorneys who have been admitted to the bar and may represent clients before any of the courts) and *agréés* (lawyers of lower rank who may represent clients only before lower courts).

There is only one penitentiary in Luxembourg, located in Schrassig. Before this was built, prisoners were held in the buildings of the former ABBEY OF ALTMUNSTER which served as a prison from 1869 to 1984.

CRECY, BATTLE OF (1346). This battle in Picardy occurred during the first attempt by Edward III of England to establish his right of succession to the crown of France and to extend the English domains in France. Edward's invasion marked the beginning of the first Hundred Years War between France and England. The English victory in the battle demonstrated the superiority of the English longbow to the mailed knight, although the lesson had to be taught again at Poitiers (1356) and Agincourt (1415).

JOHN THE BLIND, count of Luxembourg (1316–1346) and king of Bohemia, led a force of five hundred knights from his Luxembourgish and Bohemian domains to assist his ally, Philip VI of France, against the English invasion. When it appeared that the battle had been lost by the French, John the Blind, flanked by two of his knights who entwined their horses' bridles with his, led a last desperate charge against the English in which he fell.

According to tradition, Edward the Black Prince, son of Edward III, adopted the crest (three ostrich feathers) and the motto ("Ich dien") of John the Blind as his own after the battle, and it still forms the crest of the prince of Wales, heir to the throne of England.

CREQUI, FRANCOIS. Marshal de Créqui commanded the French forces that laid siege to the fortress of Luxembourg in 1683 and 1684. Aided by the renowned French military engineer, Marshal VAUBAN, he captured the fortress on 7 June 1684, beginning a French occupation that lasted until 1697.

CRISIS OF 1866–67. In 1866, NAPOLEON III of France attempted to gain some form of compensation for his neutrality in the Austro-Prussian War. His preferred compensation would have been the acquisition of certain German territories on the left bank of the Rhine that had been under French control from the early years of the first French republic until the downfall of NAPOLEON I. Bismarck blocked these proposed French annexations, despite having agreed to them in the first place. Napoleon then proposed French annexation of Belgium and Luxembourg, to which Bismarck gave his consent, provided that his agreement not be made public, since he feared reactions from other European powers, particularly England, as well as from German public opinion. In the end, Bismarck agreed to support French purchase of the Grand Duchy of Luxembourg from WILLIAM III, king of the Netherlands. For reasons of his own, which included a strong desire to keep the Duchy of Limburg out of Bismarck's new North German Federation, William III agreed to the sale of Luxembourg to France. A price of 5 million florins was agreed upon and, according to some accounts, paid.

At this point, some of Bismarck's secret agreements with the south German states, as well as the proposed purchase by France of Luxembourg, were published in the newspapers. Bismarck, despite having earlier agreed to the sale, was forced to take a public position opposing it. Napoleon naturally felt cheated, and the resulting crisis could have led to a Franco-Prussian War in 1867, three years before it actually broke out over another issue. Bismarck considered going to war in 1867, but, because he believed that Prussia was not quite ready and that international opinion might not support such a war, did not. The crisis was settled by a meeting of the Great Powers in London. (*See also* SECOND TREATY OF LONDON, 1867)

CRISIS OF 1919. When the armistice ended the fighting in WORLD WAR I, the future status of Luxembourg was in some doubt. The reigning grand duchess, MARIE-ADELAIDE, was considered by a substantial part of the population to have been pro-German during the war. A vote in the CHAMBER OF DEPUTIES for the deposition of the grand duchess failed by the narrow margin of twenty-one to nineteen, with three abstentions.

Marie-Adelaide offered to submit the question of the future form of government to a referendum, and the CHAMBER OF DEPUTIES voted twenty-eight to twenty to hold such a referendum.

A small group of communists had proclaimed a Communist Republic on 10 November 1918 when German troops were in retreat, but this movement had almost no support. A slightly larger group, calling itself the *Action Républicaine*, agitated in favor of a republic and staged a noisy demonstration in the PLACE GUILLAUME and the PLACE D'ARMES on 9 January 1919. That demonstration was easily broken up by a platoon of American military police. (Two American divisions, the 5th and the 33rd, had occupied the Grand Duchy, at the invitation of the government, immediately after the armistice.) This demonstration, however easily broken up, convinced Marie-Adelaide that she should abdicate, and she did so at once in favor of her sister CHARLOTTE.

The Grand Duchy was also having difficulties in its foreign relations. In December 1918, the French foreign minister had refused to receive a delegation led by EMILE REUTER, the Luxembourg prime minister, which had been sent to reestablish diplomatic relations with the French government. Other Allied governments refused or failed to exchange ambassadors with the Grand Duchy as well. At the Paris Peace Conference, Belgium put forward a claim to the Grand Duchy, and it was with some difficulty that the Luxembourg government persuaded the peace conference to await the results of the national referendum scheduled for September 1919 on the future form of the Luxembourg government.

The referendum, when held, proved decisive. Seventy-seven percent of the voters voted for a continuation of the monarchy under GRAND DUCHESS CHARLOTTE. Only seventeen percent voted in favor of the establishment of a republic. Smaller percentages voted in favor of the continuation of the monarchy under Marie-Adelaide or in favor of a union with France or Belgium. The results of the referendum were accepted by the peace conference, ending the crisis.

CUNEGONDE. Daughter of SIGEFROI, who married Henry II of Germany and was crowned with her husband as joint ruler of the Holy Roman Empire in 1014. After her husband's death, she was made regent along with her brothers Thierry of Metz and Henry of Bavaria and helped hold the empire together.

Cunegonde and her husband used her dowry to build the cathedral at Bamberg, in which they were later buried. Because of this, and their liberality toward other churches and monasteries, they were both canonized, Henry II in 1167 and Cunegonde in 1200.

CUSTOMS AND MONETARY UNION WITH BELGIUM, 1922. The German occupation of Luxembourg during WORLD

WAR I, and Germany's subsequent defeat, put an end to Luxembourg's membership in the ZOLLVEREIN, the German customs union. A majority of Luxembourg voters, in a referendum held in September 1919 voted for closer economic ties with France, but the French government was not interested, and so Luxembourg entered into a customs and monetary union with Belgium instead. An agreement was signed on 25 July 1921, but not ratified by the Luxembourg CHAMBER OF DEPUTIES until 1922. By the terms of the monetary union, the Belgian and Luxembourg francs are held at the same value and the currency of one country is equally valid in the other. In practice, although Belgian currency is accepted anywhere in Luxembourg, Luxembourg currency is accepted only in the border regions of Belgium adjoining Luxembourg. Ironically, Luxembourg has a far stronger economy than Belgium and its currency would be worth more than the Belgian currency if the monetary union were to be terminated.

After the interruption of WORLD WAR II, when Luxembourg was incorporated into the Third Reich and forced to adopt the Reichsmark as its currency, Luxembourg renewed its customs and monetary union with Belgium in 1947. In 1948 the customs union was extended to the Netherlands which, however, retained its own currency.

The original customs and monetary union with Belgium was not very popular in Luxembourg because Belgium had advanced a claim at the Paris Peace Conference to be allowed to annex the Grand Duchy. Moreover, Belgium's agricultural and industrial products were in competition with those of Luxembourg rather than complementary. Over the years, however, the union has worked out well.

DALHEIM. Site of a Roman settlement where many archaeological finds have been made. Several temples with statues of Jupiter and Minerva have been excavated there, as well as a Roman bath and an amphitheatre seating 3500 spectators.

DANCING PROCESSION AT ECHTERNACH. A festival unique to Luxembourg. On the first Tuesday after Pentecost every year, a dancing procession is held in honor of ST. WILLIBRORD, who founded the ABBEY OF ECHTERNACH in 698. Preceded by bands playing a lilting tune heard only upon this special occasion, groups of men and women linked by white handkerchiefs dance through the streets of ECHTERNACH. Periodically they stop dancing and walk, chanting in praise of the Virgin Mary and St. Willibrord, before taking up their dance again. The procession enters by one door of the BASILICA OF ECHTERNACH, dances down the aisle and down a set of steps into the crypt, past the tomb of St. Willlibrord, then up the steps on the other side of the altar, down the other aisle, and out the other door, and continues through the streets. Some groups go through the entire procession two or three times.

The dancing procession probably had its origin in pagan times, although the first reference to it in literature dates to the fifteenth century. A legend traces its origin to a citizen of Echternach, a fiddler named Veit, who was about to be hanged for the murder of his wife. He carried his violin to the scaffold and asked permission to play on it one last time. Granted permission, he played a tune that set all the people dancing. Still playing this tune, Veit descended from the scaffold and walked out of the town, but the people of the town were unable to stop dancing until St. Willibrord appeared and prayed for them. They were finally able to stop dancing through the intercession of the saint, but many dropped from exhaustion. The affliction from which they were supposedly cured by the saint is Saint Vitus's Dance. (There are other legends connected with the procession as well.)

People from all over the Grand Duchy, neighboring parts of Germany, northern France, and Belgium make the pilgrimage to Echternach each year to join in the dancing procession. Many of them come from the parts of Germany, including BITBURG and PRUM, annexed by the Prussians in 1815, and some come from Utrecht, of which city St. Willibrord was once bishop. Members of the higher clergy once condemned the procession, but now play a major part in it.

D-DAY. Although Luxembourg had no organized armed forces during WORLD WAR II, thousands of Luxembourgers served in the French and Belgian resistance, and in the various Allied armies. In 1994, GRAND DUKE JEAN honored three surviving Luxembourg D-Day veterans; one of these landed with the 4th Commando Battalion (Franco-British), one with the 29th U.S. Infantry Division, and one served in the Royal Air Force. Grand Duke Jean himself, then heir to the throne, landed in Normandy on 11 June with the Guards Armored Division, in which he served during the entire battle for the liberation of Europe.

DE LANNOI, PHILIPPE. Born in 1602 in Tournai, which was then part of the Spanish Netherlands, Philippe de Lannoi was taken to Leiden by his parents in 1604. There he and his family met the Pilgrim congregation from Scrooby who had taken refuge in Holland from religous persecution in England. Some of the Pilgrims emigrated to the New World in 1620 aboard the *Mayflower*, founding the Plymouth Colony. Philippe de Lannoi joined them in 1621 aboard the *Fortune*, which carried a second contingent of Pilgrims to Plymouth.

Attempts have been made to trace the ancestry of Philippe de Lannoi, whose family became known in America as the Delanos, to the counts of Lannoi who held the castle at CLERVAUX from 1631 to 1884, but it is impossible to establish a direct connection.

DEMOCRATIC PARTY (DP). The Democratic Party draws the support of many professional people, intellectuals, owners of small businesses, teachers, and government employees. It has been the third-largest party in the CHAMBER OF DEPUTIES since 1954 and has entered into the government several times as a member of a coalition. From 1974 to 1979 the DP governed the country in coalition with the LUXEMBOURG SOCIALIST WORKERS PARTY (LSAP) and from 1979 to 1984 in coalition with the CHRISTIAN SOCIAL PEOPLE'S PARTY (CSV).

The DP won only eleven seats in the Chamber of Deputies 1989 elections and twelve in the 1994 elections. Faced by the "Great Coalition" of the CSV and the LSAP, it finds it difficult to form an effective opposition. Like the British Liberal Democratic Party it resembles, the DP tends to do better in local than in national elections, although even in local elections it does not garner as many votes as the CSV or the LSAP. Like the Liberal Democrats, the DP has trouble formulating a policy that clearly distinguishes it from other major parties.

The DP holds a majority in the Luxembourg city government at present (January 1996) where they are in coalition with the CSV. The Luxembourg mayor, LYDIE WURTH-POLFER, is the most prominent figure in the Democratic Party at the present time, having been elected party leader after the 1994 elections. Other major figures in the DP include GASTON THORN, once prime minister, later president of the EUROPEAN COMMISSION, now chairman of the Board of Directors of the Banque Internationale à Luxembourg, and CO-

LETTE FLESCH, former mayor of Luxembourg and former deputy prime minister.

In the ELECTIONS OF 1994 the Democratic Party gained one seat in the Chamber of Deputies, raising its representation to twelve, but was left out of the government again when the CSV-LSAP coalition was renewed.

DEPARTMENT OF FORESTS. Name given to Luxembourg when it was incorporated into France during the French occupation under the First Republic and First Empire (1795–1815). The name was chosen because most of Luxembourg was heavily forested at that time. Even today, forests cover 34.3 percent of the land area of Luxembourg.

DOLIBOIS, JOHN E. Born in Bonnevoie, John Dolibois attended a Luxembourg school then moved to Ohio with his parents where he completed high school and attended Miami University. Joining the faculty at Miami, he rose to become vice president for university relations and alumni affairs. He was also extremely capable as a fund raiser for the Republican Party, and in 1981 he was appointed American ambassador to Luxembourg by President Ronald Reagan. He served in that capacity until 1985.

Ambassador Dolibois was very popular in Luxembourg, not only because he was friendly and capable, but also because he was the first American ambassador who had been born in Luxembourg and spoke LETZEBUERGESCH. While vice president of Miami University he was instrumental in having the MIAMI UNIVERSITY EUROPEAN CENTER located in Luxembourg, and it was renamed the John E. Dolibois Center in his honor in 1986.

DON JUAN OF AUSTRIA. Victor of the Battle of Lepanto against the Turks and hero of Byron's poem, Don Juan was the bastard son of CHARLES V and half brother of PHILIP II. Don Juan was sent to the Netherlands in 1576 with full power to make concessions to restore peace. His mission succeeded at first, and the Netherlands appeared to have been pacified, but in 1577 trouble broke out again, and his son, the duke of PARMA had to be sent to restore order.

DUPONG, PIERRE. Prime minister from 1937 to 1953, including the years when the government was in exile during WORLD WAR II. A member of the CHRISTIAN SOCIAL PEOPLE'S

PARTY, Mr. Dupong was conservative, but not excessively so. He headed a government formed of a coalition between the CSV and the LUXEMBOURG SOCIALIST WORKERS PARTY (LSAP) from 1947 to 1951. His next government, formed in 1951, was a coalition between the CSV and the DEMOCRATIC PARTY (DP). During his administration the constitutional reforms of 1948 were carried out and the Grand Duchy joined BENELUX, the MARSHALL PLAN, NATO, and the EUROPEAN COAL AND STEEL COMMUNITY.

ECHTERNACH. A town on a bend in the SURE River in the eastern part of Luxembourg, opposite Germany. Echternach has been inhabited since prehistoric times. The remains of a settlement of Ligurians from northern Italy going back to the tenth century B.C. have been found there, as well as a Roman villa dating from 50 B.C. large enough to be called a palace. Echternach's present fame dates from the abbey founded there in 698 by ST. WILLIBRORD, an Anglo-Saxon missionary from Northumbria. St. Willibrord was buried under the altar of the abbey church after his death in 739.

Echternach was once a walled city, and it is still largely medieval in appearance. It includes a thirteenth century town hall, the *Denzelt*, originally a Court of Justice. The town was destroyed by fire in 1444 and by Dutch troops under the count of Brandembourg in 1552, but it was rebuilt each time. In WORLD WAR II, Echternach was caught between the American and German lines from October 1944 to March 1945, and a large part of the city was destroyed by bombardment. It was rebuilt after World War II with help from the Luxembourg state, largely through the efforts of the mayor, Robert Schaffner, who had spent a large part of the war in German concentration camps. (*See also* ABBEY OF ECHTERNACH, BASILICA OF ECHTERNACH, DANCING PROCESSION AT ECHTERNACH.)

EDUCATION. Luxembourg has a state-supported system of universal public education for pupils from four to nineteen years of age. KINDERGARTENS and PRIMARY SCHOOLS are supported by and under the supervision of local government. SECONDARY SCHOOLS are supported by the national government and come under the supervision of the Ministry of National Education. Luxembourg has no university, but post-secondary education is provided at the CENTRE UNIVERSITAIRE, the SCHOOL OF COMMERCE AND MANAGE-

MENT, and the TEACHER TRAINING COLLEGE. (*See* HIGHER EDUCATION)

In addition to the state schools, there are a number of Catholic secondary schools, which are partly supported by the government. The battle between church and state for control of public education was fought out in the years before WORLD WAR I; the liberals and socialists, who favored state control, won the battle.

Besides the state and Catholic schools, there are a few special schools in Luxembourg including the AMERICAN INTERNATIONAL SCHOOL OF LUXEMBOURG, the COLLEGE VAUBAN, and the EUROPEAN SCHOOL which exist mainly, but not entirely, for expatriates. (*See also* MUSIC CONSERVATORIES and VOCATIONAL SCHOOLS)

ELECTIONS OF 1994. Eleven parties filed lists of candidates for the elections held on 12 June 1994, but only five won seats in the CHAMBER OF DEPUTIES. The CHRISTIAN SOCIAL PEOPLE'S PARTY (CSV) and the LUXEMBOURG SOCIALIST WORKERS PARTY (LSAP) each lost a seat and the DEMOCRATIC PARTY (DP), the GREEN ALLIANCE and the ACTION COMMITTEE FOR DEMOCRACY AND SOCIAL REFORM (ADR) each won a seat. The COMMUNIST PARTY (KP), which had been represented in the Chamber of Deputies since WORLD WAR II, reaching a maximum of six seats in the election of 1968, lost its sole remaining seat.

A summary of the representation in the Chamber of Deputies shows the following allocation of seats:

Seats	
CSV	21
LSAP	17
DP	12
ADR	5
Green Alliance	5
Total	**60**

Grand Duke Jean asked the outgoing prime minister, JACQUES SANTER, to form a new government and the CSV and the LSAP agreed to renew the coalition that had governed the Grand Duchy for the past ten years. The membership of the government remained the same, although a few cabinet portfolios were redistributed. Six ministers from the CSV and five ministers from the LSAP formed the new government.

In the elections for the European Parliament, the CSV lost one seat, which was won by the Green Alliance. The Luxembourg delegation of six members includes two Christian Socialists, two Socialists, one Democrat, and one Green.

With a majority of thirty-eight seats out of sixty, the CSV-LSAP coalition has had no difficulty so far getting its legislation passed by the Chamber of Deputies. No major conflicts have risen between them to date. (*See also* POLITICAL PARTIES IN LUXEMBOURG)

Jacques Santer succeeded Jacques Delors as president of the EUROPEAN COMMISSION in January 1995 and his place as prime minister was taken by Jean-Claude Juncker.

ELIZABETH OF GOERLITZ. Niece of WENZEL II and SIGISMUND, both dukes of Luxembourg and Holy Roman Emperors. Wenzel, in need of money, pawned the Duchy of Luxembourg to Elizabeth in 1411. Sigismund challenged this transaction and appointed a governor for Luxembourg to act in his name. When Wenzel died in 1419, however, Sigismund lacked the funds to pay off the mortgage and was forced to leave Elizabeth in control. When Sigismund died in 1437, she was still in charge.

Elizabeth made various efforts to sell Luxembourg for the next four years. Through the archbishop of Trier, she made an arrangement by which William of Saxony, married to Anna, the eldest daughter of Emperor Sigismund, would pay off the mortgage and become duke of Luxembourg. The archbishop would advance the money to William, receiving Luxembourg and the county of Chiny as security. In 1441, however, Elizabeth changed her mind and sold Luxembourg to PHILIP THE GOOD, duke of Burgundy. The infuriated citizens then drove Elizabeth from the city and welcomed the troops of William of Saxony into the fortress.

Philip the Good led a Burgundian army into Luxembourg in 1442, and his troops captured the city in 1443 by a surprise night attack in which only one citizen was killed. The duke of Saxony's garrison took refuge in the castle and held out until December 1443, when lack of food forced them to surrender. Philip persuaded William to give up his claims to Luxembourg for a payment of 120,000 Hungarian florins. Philip ruled the Duchy thereafter, although he did not become the legitimate ruler until 1457, after the death of Ladislus the Posthumus, last legitimate claimant to the Duchy by virtue of descent from Sigismund.

Elizabeth was married twice, first in 1411 to Anthony of Burgundy, duke of Brabant, who died at the Battle of Agincourt in 1415, and second in 1419 to John of Bavaria, bishop-elect of Trier, who died in 1425. She died in Trier in 1451, not greatly mourned.

EMIGRATION. During the nineteenth century, the general increase in population in the Grand Duchy, combined with the shortage of arable land, led to a large emigration to other countries, especially the United States. Many of the emigrants settled in the midwestern states, particularly those west of the Mississippi. Where possible, the Luxembourg emigrants established villages of their own in the New World, where they could continue to speak their own language. Ties were kept up with families back home in Luxembourg and these ties continue to be maintained today.

In the emigration of a substantial part of its population to the United States during the nineteenth century, Luxembourg emulated the experience of other European countries. Europe's population quadrupled in the years from 1800 to 1900, rising from 100 to 400 million. As in the case of Ireland, there may be more people of Luxembourg descent living in the United States today than there are in the Grand Duchy itself.

Another type of emigration—the emigration of talent—has had a serious effect on Luxembourg during at least the past two hundred years. Artists and intellectuals have been drawn to the larger population centers of Europe, particularly Paris, where they have found wider scope for their talents. These include ROBERT SCHUMAN, a Luxembourger who became foreign minister of France and was among the most important promoters of the EUROPEAN COAL AND STEEL COMMUNITY, AUGUSTE TREMONT, the great sculptor and painter of animals, and PIERRE REDOUTE, the famous painter of flowers, particularly roses. The educational system has facilitated the emigration of talented and educated people to other countries. Graduates of Luxembourg lycées speak both German and French fluently and, because the Grand Duchy has no university of its own, must go abroad for their university studies. Many university graduates return to Luxembourg, but others remain in the countries where they have attended universities.

ENNERT DE STEILER (UNDER THE ARCADE). This building, on a corner opposite the FISHMARKET, dates from 1350. The owner, Jean Shalop, a member of the town watch, was the only Luxembourger killed during the Burgundian surprise attack in 1443. The building was reconstructed after 1569, and the pillars were added in 1691. Goethe is supposed to have lodged here in 1792, when he accompanied the duke of Brunswick to the "Cannonade of Valmy".

EPONA. A Gallo-Roman goddess, patroness of horses and horsemen. She is generally depicted riding a horse, either astride or sidesaddle, frequently carrying a cornucopia. Roadside shrines to Epona lined the roads in Roman times, and were as common as shrines to Christian saints and to the Virgin Mary in medieval times. Several of these shrines to Epona are on display in the NATIONAL MUSEUM.

ERMESINDE. Countess of Luxembourg, 1196–1247. One of the most remarkable women of the Middle Ages, she was the daughter of HENRY IV, count of Luxembourg from 1136 to 1196. When her father died, leaving no direct male heir, Ermesinde was only ten years old. Since female rights of succession were not recognized under Salic law, Ermesinde could not succeed her father as ruler of Luxembourg in her own right. As an imperial fief, the County of Luxembourg technically reverted to the Holy Roman Emperor, who might bestow it upon whomever he pleased.

Within a year after her father's death, Ermesinde married Thibault, count of Bar, who vigorously asserted his own and his young wife's rights to the Luxembourg lands and regained by purchase and negotiation not only Luxembourg but also the other possessions her father had lost during his lifetime. By the time Thibault died in 1214, Luxembourg had once more become an important principality.

When Thibault died, leaving Ermesinde a widow at the age of twenty-eight with only one daughter, her inheritance was once more in danger. Thibault's heir to the County of Bar, a son by an earlier marriage, could lay claim to Luxembourg as well as to his father's other possessions. To forestall this, Ermesinde married Duke Waleran of Limbourg, another powerful lord and strong ruler, only three months after Thibault's death. Together Waleran and Ermesinde ruled over lands far greater in extent than the Grand Duchy of today. The lesser lords within their domains became their vassals, paying them homage in return for their protection.

Waleran died in 1225, leaving Ermesinde a widow once again. Their son Henry became heir to their Luxembourg possessions, but he was only nine years old. Ermesinde, as countess of Luxembourg, had ruled jointly with Waleran during his lifetime and now became sole ruler of Luxembourg during her son's minority. She did not, in fact, give up her rule when her son came of age, but continued to reign as countess of Luxembourg until her death in 1247.

Ermesinde is remembered as a capable ruler who governed her lands intelligently and even managed to expand them. She is also remembered for the charters she granted to the towns in her realm, guaranteeing them civil liberties and limited rights of self-government in exchange for cash payments and various feudal dues, including military service. None of her towns was large—Luxembourg city itself had no more than five thousand inhabitants during Ermesinde's reign—but they were reasonably prosperous, and by granting them charters of liberty Ermesinde acquired for her government a source of income more reliable than the feudal dues of the lords who were her vassals.

ESCH-SUR-ALZETTE. The second largest city in Luxembourg, with a population of twenty-four thousand. It is located right on the French border, and is the principal town in the MINETTE, the steel-producing district. Esch is a more attractive town than its location might suggest. It has an excellent small theater and an active cultural life. Many of the productions that appear at the Municipal Theater in Luxembourg are booked into the theater at Esch as well.

Italians and Portuguese, attracted to the region before and after WORLD WAR II by jobs available in the steel industry, make up a substantial part of the population of Esch-Sur-Alzette. The mix of nationalities in Esch is different from that in the capital city, where the population is much more cosmopolitan and includes nationals of the various states of the EUROPEAN UNION as well as executives of the many foreign banks and other commercial enterprises.

ESCH-SUR-SURE. A medieval town on the banks of the SURE River, dominated by the remains of a feudal castle. Esch is close to the eastern end of an artificial lake created by a high dam on the Upper Sûre, built in 1963 to supply water and electrical power to the Grand Duchy. It is somewhat isolated by the hills around it, and when it became desirable to link it with the highway between ETTELBRUCK and WILTZ, a passage had to dynamited through solid rock. It is one of the most popular tourist sites in the Luxembourg ARDENNES.

ETTELBRUCK. A town near the center of the Grand Duchy where the ALZETTE River joins the SURE River, sometimes known as the "Gateway to the Ardennes." An agricultural college and a large mental hospital are located here as well as a statue to General PATTON. A remembrance day in honor of General Patton is held in Ettelbruck each July.

EUROPEAN CITY OF CULTURE. Each year, some European city is selected to serve as the European City of Culture. Luxembourg was the city chosen for 1995.

EUROPEAN COAL AND STEEL COMMUNITY. Also known as the Schuman Plan, after its founder and chief promoter, ROBERT SCHUMAN, a native Luxembourger who received his higher education in France and later became foreign minister in the French government. In July 1952, the foreign ministers of Belgium, France, Germany, Italy, Luxembourg, and the Netherlands agreed to establish a European Coal and Steel Community, with its headquarters in Luxembourg. The High Authority for this community was inaugurated in August 1952, at a ceremony in the Luxembourg city hall. Jean Monnet, a leading proponent of the plan, was elected president of the High Authority, and eight other members were chosen to represent the six member nations.

The purpose of the European Coal and Steel Community was to create and maintain a single market for coal and steel, eliminating customs barriers, quota restrictions, and other forms of discrimination. A secretariat was set up in Luxembourg to administer this market.

The European Coal and Steel Community went into operation in February 1953 when a German coal train passed the Luxembourg and French borders duty free. The common market in steel began in May 1953. The operations of the European Coal and Steel Community were later merged with the operations of the European Economic Community established by the Treaty of Rome in 1957, now known as the EUROPEAN UNION.

The European Coal and Steel Community has not been

completely successful. The world-wide overexpansion in steel-making capacity, along with a decline in the use of steel as a major structural material, has created major economic problems. Between 1983 and 1985 a major crisis hit the steel industry; production went down from 6.4 million tons to 4 million tons in Luxembourg alone within that two-year period. The work force was cut from 25,000 in 1974 to 11,842 in 1987 without solving the problem of overproduction. The current economic crisis threatens even further cuts in employment and markets.

The European Union has devoted large sums to alleviate the hardships involved in the reduction of steel production in member countries. Luxembourg, where ARBED, the fourth largest steel industry in Europe and sixth in the world has its headquarters, has taken the lead in trying to rationalize steel production. After a number of years when its operations lost money, ARBED finally showed a profit during 1994 and 1995.

EUROPEAN COMMISSION. Sometimes described as the executive branch of the EUROPEAN UNION, the European Commission has its headquarters in Brussels. It is composed of a number of commissioners appointed to five-year terms by the member states, headed by a president appointed by the heads of the member states whose appointment must be approved by the European Parliament.

Each commissioner heads one or more of the EU departments such as agriculture, communications, culture, external relations, fisheries, and so forth. They preside over a bureaucracy that now numbers over seventeen thousand employees. Many of these employees of the European Commission reside in Brussels, but others are located in other EU cities such as Luxembourg.

The commission is charged with implementing EU legislation as well as creating the necessary machinery for carrying it out. It can issue directives which have the force of law in member nations, so long as they fall within the power granted the commission.

The president of the European Commission holds a key position in Europe, since one of his functions is to provide leadership in the movement toward closer European integration. He is sometimes referred to as the president of the European Union, in recognition of the key role he plays. The most active and effective recent president was Jacques Delors of France. Upon his retirement in January 1995 he was replaced by JACQUES SANTER of Luxembourg.

EUROPEAN SATELLITE SOCIETY (SES). The SES was formed in 1985 with both public and private funding and seems likely to establish the Grand Duchy as a world leader in satellite broadcasting. Transmission began on 10 December 1988 using an Astra 1A medium-power satellite capable of transmitting sixteen stations rather than the usual five. Since then the SES has launched several other satellites in the Astra series and is now capable of transmitting on sixty-four channels. Its programs can be picked up in most European nations.

The offices and ground station of the SES are located on a former royal estate in Betzdorf several kilometers east of Luxembourg city. The government is planning to build an audiovisual park at Betzdorf to encourage the production of television programs which can be transmitted via the SES.

EUROPEAN SCHOOL (ECOLE EUROPEENNE). The EURO-PEAN UNION has established six schools in five European cities, including two in Brussels and one in Luxembourg. These European schools exist primarily for the children of EU employees, although other children are sometimes admitted on a space-available basis. The schools follow a common curriculum. One year of kindergarten is followed by five years of primary education and seven years of secondary education. Those who complete the program take the examination for the European Baccalaureate. If they pass this examination they are eligible for admission to universities in all EU member states, although this is conditional on their having mastered the language of instruction in the university they wish to enter.

The European schools are organized into language sections, a separate section for each major language spoken in the EU. Students are expected to have mastered two additional languages by the time they complete the program. Pupils in the different language streams do not mix much at the primary level; mixing occurs in the secondary school, where students in different sections begin studying certain subjects together in the same language.

The European School in Luxembourg is located on the KIRCHBERG with other EU institutions, although, because it is overcrowded at the moment (enrollment in 1995 reached 3500), some classes meet in the school's original building in LIMPERTSBERG. The need for additional classroom space has been evident for some time, but provision of the additional space has been postponed because of the possibility that large numbers of EU employees might be transferred to Brussels in the near future. With the adhesion of four more nations to the EU, however, the need for more space has become so pressing that plans are being made to enlarge the Luxembourg campus as quickly as possible.

The European School curriculum is very demanding and some pupils find it too difficult, especially if they enter at the secondary level and have not yet mastered a second language. Students who fail to pass major subjects must repeat a year, and if they fail the following year they are dropped.

Teachers for the European School are recruited in the EU member countries, although a few teachers may be recruited locally to fill temporary positions. Teacher salaries are high and teachers, as EU employees, enjoy a good many other perquisites, including a virtually tax-free status. Headmasters and deputy headmasters are from EU member states and are appointed for five-year terms on a rotating basis.

EUROPEAN UNION (EU). Established by the TREATY OF ROME in 1958 as the European Economic Community (EEC), the European Union adopted its present name in 1992. The EEC united six nations (Belgium, France, Germany, Italy, Luxembourg, and the Netherlands) into an economic alliance with the goals of setting up a common market with common external tariffs, establishing common social and economic policies, and permitting the free movement of capital, labor, and goods among member countries. This new economic organization was given three capitals—Strasbourg, where the European Parliament meets; Brussels, the headquarters of the European Commission and the bureaucracy which administers its directives; and Luxembourg, where the secretariat of the European Parliament is based. The latter creates something of a problem, because every time the parliament meets, the secretariat has to move *en masse*, personnel and records alike, from Luxembourg to Strasbourg for as long as the session lasts.

Other European institutions, such as the European Investment Bank, the Court of Auditors, the European Court of Justice, and various agencies of the European Commission also have their headquarters in Luxembourg. Luxembourg failed in its recent bid to have the proposed European Central Bank located in Luxembourg, however. (It went to Frankfurt instead.) There is, moreover, a strong movement afoot to concentrate all the major European institutions in a single city. Brussels is the preferred location, because it is far larger than either Luxembourg or Strasbourg and has more amenities. A move to Brussels might cost Luxembourg dearly, since it would involve the loss of over two thousand European families with their purchasing power (European civil servants are not underpaid) as well as causing a glut in the local housing market.

Between 1957 and 1992, six other countries joined the EEC (Denmark, Great Britain, Greece, Ireland, Portugal, and Spain), and on 1 January 1995 four other nations joined the newly rechristened European Union (Austria, Finland, Norway, and Sweden). The Czech Republic, Hungary, Poland, Slovakia, and the Baltic States, along with other nations in eastern Europe, hope to be admitted at an early date.

The actual free movement of goods and people between EU member states went into effect on 1 January 1993 without changing anything much. Action had already been taken to eliminate many of the barriers, and some member states imposed limitations upon the process.

The TREATY OF MAASTRICHT, signed in 1992, aimed to integrate EU member states into a closer monetary, social, and political union, but progress toward this goal since then has been slow. 1997 was selected as the year the member states would adopt a common currency, but the target date was later changed to 1999. As of January 1996, the only EU member which met the economic preconditions for a common currency set at Maastricht was Luxembourg. There has been a considerable loss of momentum toward European integration since Jacques Delors retired as EU president in January 1995.

EYSCHEN, PAUL. Minister of State (prime minister) of Luxembourg from 1888 to 1915 who presided over the transition between the reign of the Dutch sovereigns and the present Nassau-Weilburg dynasty. A conservative politician, he managed to keep the transition orderly and peaceful. During his administration, the Grand Duchy was also passing through its greatest period of industrial expansion, during which its iron and steel industry, supported by an extensive railroad network, became one of the largest in Europe.

FELIX. Prince of Bourbon-Parma. A descendent of LOUIS XIV, Prince Felix married GRAND DUCHESS CHARLOTTE on 6 November 1919.

During WORLD WAR II, Prince Felix went into exile with

the rest of the grand ducal family, and served with his son
PRINCE JEAN, heir to the throne, in the British army. He
returned to Luxembourg with American troops on 10 September 1944. Prince Felix died in 1970.

FINDEL. Luxembourg's international airport, about ten kilometers out of Luxembourg city. Although the passenger terminal
is small, the airport's runways can accommodate the largest
jets. Findel serves as air terminal to LUXAIR, the national
airline, ICELANDAIR, and about twelve other airlines, including Aeroflot. In a recent survey by a German travel magazine
of twenty-nine airports in Germany and neighboring countries,
the airport at Findel was rated first in user-friendliness and
service.

FIRST TREATY OF LONDON. When Belgium revolted against
King WILLIAM I of the Netherlands in 1830, a Great Power
conference was called in London, which drew up a treaty that
recognized Belgian independence but left the status of the
Grand Duchy of Luxembourg to be settled by negotiation
between the Dutch and the Belgians. William I refused to
accept this treaty until 1839, at which time the Grand Duchy
was divided, with the French-speaking part, more than half of
its total area, becoming part of Belgium as the province of
Luxembourg. The LETZEBUERGESCH-speaking part remained under the control of William I, as grand duke. (*See
also* JOINT RULE, 1830–1839, and THREE PARTITIONS
OF LUXEMBOURG)

FISHMARKET. The Fishmarket or Old Market is a small town
square not far from the BOCK. It was included in the original
grant of land to SIGEFROI by the ABBEY OF ST. MAXIMIN
IN TRIER in 963, and contained within the first city walls. In
earlier times a Roman watchtower stood on the spot and a
Roman road, still in use today, climbed the hill from the
Petrusse to this tower.

Excavations now in progress at the Fishmarket have unearthed the remains of what may be medieval fortifications,
including a round tower. A sixteenth-century building on the
west side of the square displays the famous *Gelle Klack*,
the Golden Clock, on its outer wall. The buildings of the
NATIONAL MUSEUM, form the north side of the present
square.

FLESCH, COLETTE. Mayor of the city of Luxembourg from 1970 to 1980, and vice-premier of the Grand Duchy from 1980 to 1984. A leading member of the DEMOCRATIC PARTY, Mrs. Flesch is currently a member of the European Parliament.

FONTAINE, EDMOND DE LA (1823–91). Playwright and songwriter, known as "Dicks". He owned a cloth factory in Remich, but later became a judge and lived in Vianden. He was the author of a patriotic poem, *D'Letzebuerger Land.*

FRANKS. A group of German tribes who had established themselves along the northern and eastern bank of the Rhine by the second century A.D. in an arc stretching from the North Sea to the Middle Rhine. During the troubled times of the third and fourth centuries, they made a number of raids into northern Gaul. Frankish prisoners taken in battle were sometimes enrolled in the Roman army, and some were permitted to settle with their families in empty lands in Gaul. Other Frankish tribes were enlisted as Roman allies, and a few Franks even rose to high rank in the Roman army during the fourth and fifth centuries. In 451 A.D. Franks, as well as Visigoths and Burgundians, fought under the command of the Roman general FLAVIUS AETIUS at the battle of the Catalaunian Fields (Châlons) which halted the invasion of Gaul by the HUNS under ATTILA. (*See also* RHINELAND FRANKS and SALIAN FRANKS)

GAULS. A group of Celtic-speaking tribes who inhabited northern Italy, Helvetia, Spain, and most of the area between the Rhine, the Atlantic, and the Pyrenees in the early years of the Roman republic. The Gauls who invaded and conquered northern Italy around 400 B.C. entered Italy from central Europe. In 397 B.C. they defeated a Roman army, captured Rome, burned a good part of the city, and forced the Romans to pay tribute. They settled in the Po River valley and established their capital at Mediolanum (Milan), from which they ruled most of northern Italy and continued to form a threat to Rome. The Romans conquered northern Italy in the third century B.C. and made it the Roman province of Cisalpine Gaul. That part of Gaul that lay to the north and west of the Alps they called Transalpine Gaul.

The Gauls who lived in Transalpine Gaul were a prosperous people who grew grain, raised horses and cattle, coined money, made gold and silver ornaments, and forged iron weapons.

They carried on an extensive trade with the Mediterranean lands, particularly through the port of Massilia (modern Marseilles) established by the Greeks around 600 B.C., and with the Baltic region, from which they imported amber. They built a number of towns, where merchants and tradesmen lived.

The Gauls were divided into a number of tribes who warred against each other and the Germans who lived east of them on the other side of the Rhine. This lack of unity led to their eventual subjugation by the Romans.

When JULIUS CAESAR came to power in 60 B.C., the Romans controlled not only Cisalpine Gaul but also a strip of territory along the Mediterranean coast, sometimes called for short the Province (whence modern Provence). Between 58 and 52 B.C., using Cisalpine Gaul and the Province as bases and recruiting grounds, Caesar conquered the rest of Gaul. It was not an easy conquest, despite the Gaul's lack of unity. Several times tribes Caesar had defeated rebelled while his legions were occupied elsewhere. In 52 B.C., a number of Gallic tribes finally joined together into a confederation under a leader named Vercingetorix and rose in rebellion. Caesar put down this final rebellion of the Gauls with difficulty, in a campaign that culminated with the successful siege of the Gallic town of Alesia and the surrender of Vercingetorix.

Among the tribes conquered by Caesar were the TREVERI who occupied a large area in northeastern Gaul between the Meuse and the MOSELLE Rivers, within which Luxembourg was eventually founded.

GENERAL STRIKE OF 1942. In August 1942, the Germans, having annexed the Grand Duchy to Hitler's Third Reich, began conscripting Luxembourgers into the German army. A general strike to oppose the annexation and conscription was announced. It began in the north, where seven hundred citizens of WILTZ were the first to go on strike, but quickly spread throughout the country. The strike was put down with great brutality. Twenty-one Luxembourgers were executed, including six citizens of Wiltz, four of whom were school teachers. Thousands of people, including the families of the men who had been executed, were deported to Germany, and the strike was broken. (*See also* WORLD WAR II)

GERMAN CONFEDERATION. Set up by the CONGRESS OF VIENNA (1814–1815) to replace the defunct HOLY ROMAN EMPIRE, dissolved by NAPOLEON I in 1806. It consisted of thirty-nine states, large and small, of whom the two most powerful were Austria and Prussia. The new Grand Duchy of Luxembourg was the thirty-ninth member of the German Confederation, under the personal rule of WILLIAM I, king of the Netherlands, in his capacity as grand duke of Luxembourg. Incorporating Luxembourg into the German Confederation was a compromise between giving the territory outright to Prussia or including it with Belgium in the newly established kingdom of the Netherlands. The other European powers feared too great an extension of Prussia's powers, but at the same time doubted the capacity of the Dutch to garrison the fortress-city adequately. (At this point, France was still considered the greatest threat to the peace of Europe, even with Napoleon I removed from power.) A Prussian garrison was introduced into the fortress, where it remained until Luxembourg was made a neutral state and demilitarized by the SECOND TREATY OF LONDON in 1867, up to which point the Grand Duchy remained a member of the German Confederation

GOLDEN BOOK (*CODEX AUREUS*) OF ECHTERNACH. The ABBEY OF ECHTERNACH was a center for the production of illuminated manuscripts from the eighth through the eleventh century. These manuscripts were written in the Irish Celtic style exemplified by the Book of Kells, now on display in the library at Trinity College, Dublin. The style was introduced by the Anglo-Saxon monks from northern England whom ST. WILLIBRORD established in the abbey. Their most famous work was an eleventh century copy of the Gospels bound in a leather and gold cover, studded with precious stones, the gift of OTTO III.

The Golden Book remained in the abbey at Echternach until the monastery was dissolved during the French occupation of Luxembourg following the French Revolution. It was smuggled out of Luxembourg into Germany by the monks, who sold it to the Duke of Saxe-Coburg-Gotha. It remained in the possession of his family until 1955, when it was placed on the market by his descendents for a sum equivalent to £100,000. Luxembourg was too poor at the time to purchase it, and it was sold to the museum in Nuremburg, where it now reposes.

Reproductions of some of the pages of the Golden Book are on display in the museum attached to the BASILICA OF ECHTERNACH, which also contains a display of the methods by which illuminated manuscripts were produced. (*See also* ABBEY OF ECHTERNACH and ST. WILLIBRORD)

GOLDEN BULL. The Golden Bull was issued by EMPEROR CHARLES IV in 1356 to regulate the order of succession to the imperial throne. The emperor was to be elected by seven electors—three ecclesiastical lords and four secular princes. The ecclesiastical electors were to be the archbishop of Mainz, primate of the church in Germany, the archbishop of Trier, and the archbishop of Cologne. The four secular electors were to be the king of Bohemia, the margrave of Brandenburg, the duke of Saxony and the count palatine of the Rhineland. The person chosen by these electors took the title KING OF THE ROMANS until his election was confirmed by the pope, whereupon he became Holy Roman Emperor. He was to be crowned at Aachen (Aix-la-Chapelle), CHARLEMAGNE's ancient capital, where OTTO THE GREAT and his successors had also been crowned.

Other electors were added in later years, including the rulers of Bavaria and Hanover, but the basic system of election remained in place until Francis II of Hapsburg dropped the title in 1806, having taken the title of emperor of Austria in 1804. (*See also* HOLY ROMAN EMPIRE)

GOLDEN LADY (GELLE FRA). A statue of Victory standing atop a tall pillar in the PLACE DE LA CONSTITUTION on the southern side of the old city of Luxembourg. The pillar and its base originally formed a monument to the Luxembourgers who fought and died in Allied armies fighting against the Germans during WORLD WAR I. The Germans destroyed the monument when they occupied the Grand Duchy during WORLD WAR II, but it was reerected after the war, and rededicated to the memory of the Luxembourgers who had died fighting on the Allied side during both world wars.

GOVERNMENT, NATIONAL. The executive powers of the national government are exercised by the GRAND DUKE and his responsible ministers. After a national election, the grand duke asks the leader of the political party that has won the largest number of seats in the CHAMBER OF DEPUTIES to form a government. Since no single party ever wins a majority of the seats, this involves putting together a coalition of two or more parties with enough seats among them to form a majority. If the leader of the largest party, after negotiating with the other parties, is unable to form a government within a reasonable period of time, he informs the grand duke, and the grand duke asks the leader of one of the other parties to form a government.

The government, properly speaking, consists of the prime minister and the heads of the various government departments such as foreign affairs and finance. The various ministers and the secretaries of state, meeting with the prime minister, form the COUNCIL OF GOVERNMENT. Since there are more government departments than there are ministers, a minister may preside over more than one department. (The present prime minister, for instance, is also minister of finance.) A secretary of state may be appointed to assist a minister who has more than one department to supervise.

The government is responsible to the Chamber of Deputies and members of the government attend all sessions of the chamber. They do not hold seats or vote, however. If a deputy is chosen to become a member of the government, he resigns his seat as deputy and the person who received the next highest number of votes in his electoral district becomes deputy in his place.

The Chamber of Deputies may bring about the resignation of the government by refusing to support it on a major issue such as the annual budget. This has not happened since WORLD WAR II. (*See also* COUNCIL OF STATE)

GRAND DUCAL PALACE (PALAIS GRAND-DUCAL). The Grand Ducal Palace is the official residence of the grand duke in the capital, where he has his offices, receives official guests, holds receptions, and performs other ceremonial duties. It dates from 1572, during the period of Spanish rule, when COUNT MANSFELD was governor, and the facade reflects both Burgundian and Spanish-Moorish influences. It served as the Luxembourg city hall and government house until the French takeover in 1795.

From 1795 until 1815, the building was the Prefecture of the DEPARTMENT OF FORESTS, the name given to Luxembourg by the French. From 1815 until 1841, it served as the seat of the Luxembourg government under the Dutch sovereigns, finally becoming the Grand Ducal Palace in 1841. Many prominent visitors, including Winston Churchill, General John J. Pershing, and General Dwight D. Eisenhower have been received at the Grand Ducal Palace.

On the last day of the OCTAVE the grand ducal family traditionally attends mass at the cathedral, then marches in procession through the streets to the palace, where they appear on the balcony to receive the plaudits of the crowds.

The palace is located only a block down the rue de la Reine from the PLACE GUILLAUME, where the statue of WILLIAM II faces it. The facade recently underwent a major restoration in preparation for 1995 when Luxembourg served as the EUROPEAN CITY OF CULTURE.

GRAND DUKE OF LUXEMBOURG. The title of grand duke or grand duchess of Luxembourg is hereditary in the Nassau family. According to the Nassau Family Compact of 1783 regulating the order of succession to the various lands of the Orange-Nassau family in Germany, inheritance was to be by primogeniture in the male line. If the head of one branch of the family died without leaving a male heir, the closest male relative in another branch would inherit his title and possessions. It was under the terms of this family compact that ADOLF OF NASSAU-WEILBURG inherited the throne of Luxembourg in 1890, when WILLIAM III, king of the Netherlands and grand duke of Luxembourg, died, leaving only a daughter but no son to succeed him. Since the rules governing the succession to the throne of the Netherlands differed from those in Luxembourg, William III's daughter Wilhelmina became queen of the Netherlands, but Adolf became grand duke of Luxembourg.

Adolf's son, Grand Duke WILLIAM IV, who had six daughters but no son, changed the order of succession in Luxembourg in 1907 by getting the CHAMBER OF DEPUTIES to ratify a law giving his daughters, in order of birth, the right to succeed him when he died. Under this law, MARIE-ADELAIDE became grand duchess in 1912 and William's second daughter, CHARLOTTE, became grand duchess when Marie-Adelaide abdicated in 1919. The order of succession still provides that the eldest surviving son of the reigning grand duke or duchess will succeed his parent when he or she abdicates or dies, but if the grand duke or duchess has no surviving sons, his or her daughters may succeed him or her in order of their birth.

The grand duke is chief of state as well as chief executive and represents Luxembourg in its relations with other countries. He plays an important part in the legislative process, because his signature is necessary on all new laws. He appoints the members of the COUNCIL OF STATE, which functions to some extent as the upper house of the legislature, and he may preside over their meeetings if he chooses to do so. He may also dissolve the Council of State if he sees fit.

The grand duke's person is inviolable, and he may not be held legally responsible for his actions as grand duke. He is presumed to act only upon the advice of his ministers, and it is they who are responsible to the CHAMBER OF DEPUTIES for any actions committed in his name. Laws signed by the grand duke are countersigned by one or more of his ministers, who thus assume responsibility for them. The government as a whole acts in his name and assumes responsibility for his acts, and thus shares in the exercise of executive powers, which consist primarily in seeing that laws, decrees, and judgments are faithfully executed. The government directs the public administration of the state including the armed forces, of whom the grand duke is supreme commander.

All judicial actions are taken in the grand duke's name, and he has the power to pardon offenders or to commute their sentences. He may himself, or through his representatives, sign treaties with other nations, but these must be submitted to the Chamber of Deputies for ratification. He presides over the opening and closing sessions of the Chamber of Deputies, and may convoke extraordinary sessions. He may also adjourn or dissolve the chamber, with the provision that new elections must be held within three months of the dissolution.

The grand duke must sign a law within three months of its passage or it becomes null and void. He may also reject a law, giving his reasons for doing so, and thus possesses an absolute veto over proposed laws. Given the various ways in which the grand duke may influence the legislative process, however, this has become purely a formal right and is never exercised, although the fact that it *could* be exercised is a powerful incentive for the government to meet the grand duke's objections to any proposed measure rather than force him to take the extreme step of vetoing it.

The grand duke is a constitutional monarch, and exercises only those powers granted him by the constitution and laws. His status is somewhat similar to that of the ruler of Great Britain, although he plays a more important part in the government of the Grand Duchy than the British sovereign plays in the British government.

The laws provide for a regent to be appointed if the grand duke or grand duchess is incapacitated or a minor. Adolf of Nassau-Weilburg acted as regent twice during the reign of WILLIAM III, before succeeding him as grand duke in 1890, and the Grand Duchess Marie-Anne, wife of WILLIAM IV, acted as regent from 1908 to 1912 during the last illness of her husband, and again for a few months in 1912 during the minority of her daughter MARIE-ADELAIDE.

The grand duke may also appoint a lieutenant to act as governor of the Grand Duchy. PRINCE HENRY of the Netherlands was appointed lieutenant by his elder brother William III and held that position from 1850 until his death in 1879. Grand Duke Adolf also appointed his eldest son William as lieutenant during his old age. William served as lieutenant from 1902 until the death of his father in 1905, when he succeeded him as Grand Duke William IV. William IV in turn appointed his wife, Grand Duchess Marie-Anne, lieutenant, and she held that position from March to November 1908, when she was named regent. Finally, the Grand Duchess Charlotte appointed her son JEAN, heir to the throne, lieutenant in 1961, and he served as such until his mother abdicated in his favor in 1964, when he became grand duke.

The heir to the throne is known as the grand duke héritier (the grand duke apparent or presumptive). This title is not assumed automatically by the heir apparent, but is granted him by the reigning grand duke or duchess, normally when he comes of age. Grand Duke Jean named his eldest son, Prince Henri, grand duke héritier in 1973.

GREEN ALLIANCE. The Green movement split into two political parties a few years ago, largely because of quarrels among the leadership. One faction took the name Green List Alternative Initiative (GLEI) and the other the Green Alternative Party (GAP). Each faction won two seats in the CHAMBER OF DEPUTIES elected in 1989. To fight the 1994 elections, the Greens reunited and presented a combined electoral list. This Green alliance won an additional seat, and now has five members in the CHAMBER OF DEPUTIES. They also succeeded in electing one of their members to the European Parliament, but he has since been read out of the party.

The Greens have a considerable number of supporters in the Grand Duchy, and have achieved some notable successes. A major indication of their success has been that the other political parties have added ecological planks to their platforms.

As might be expected, the Green Party candidates are younger, more idealistic, and more intellectual than the typical candidates nominated by the other parties. They also, unfortunately, have a remarkable talent for fighting among themselves. The Greens may never become one of the major parties in Luxembourg, but they will have succeeded if their goals for preserving the environment are taken up by one or more of the major political parties.

GREENPEACE LUXEMBOURG. Greenpeace International opened an office in Luxembourg in August 1984, and this office has recently celebrated its tenth anniversary. Roger Spautz has been leader of the movement in Luxembourg since its inception.

Until 1987, Greenpeace's Luxembourg office was staffed entirely by volunteers. It now has four full-time and two part-time workers and ten thousand members who pay an annual membership fee.

Besides conducting educational and research programs, Greenpeace carries on an active campaign against companies suspected of polluting the environment. One of its local victories has been over Du Pont de Nemours, whose Tyvek production line in Luxembourg had been releasing 28.8 kilograms (63 pounds) of chlorofluoro-carbons (CFCs) per hour into the air, and had released 6 tons and 1.7 tons of CFCs into the air in two major accidents in 1988 and 1990. Du Pont is now building a new plant in Luxembourg which will not use CFCs in its production process.

Another Greenpeace victory was over Eurosol/Eurofloor in WILTZ, which uses polyvinylchlorine (PVC) in its manufacture of flooring. Eurosol/Eurofloor is in the process, under Greenpeace pressure, of changing its production methods. Most recently, Greenpeace has successfully urged ARBED, the steel giant, to switch to the new electric-arc method of steel production.

Greenpeace has not succeeded in getting the French government to shut down the nuclear plant at CATTENOM just across the Luxembourg border, but has made everyone aware of the threat it represents. In July 1994, they occupied two newly erected high-tension power line pylons in protest against the proposed use by ARBED of electric power from the Belgian atomic energy power grid, which has a direct link to the French nuclear plant at Cattenom.

GROMPEREKICHELCHER. The name for potato in LETZE-BUERGESCH is *Grompere*, and a Gromperekichelcher is a small, spicy potato pancake, fried in deep fat, and often topped with applesauce. They are sold from special booths at the various fairs and KERMESSES held throughout the Grand Duchy, and the recipes for making them are closely guarded secrets. The Chalet au Gourmet, owned by Edmond Thill and Serge Staes, makes some of the best currently available.

GRUND. The original town in the valley of the ALZETTE that grew up under the protection of the castle built by SIGEFROI on the BOCK during the tenth century. The name may be translated as valley or foundation. Three small towns, the Grund, Clausen, and Pfaffental, developed along the banks of the Alzette where it winds around the sheer cliffs of the plateau upon which the upper town was built. As the walls of the upper town were extended to the west and north, it became a refuge for the residents of the lower town in time of war. Roads and gates were built which gave the inhabitants of the Grund and the other towns in the valley access to its fortifications.

As time went on, the lower town was protected by new fortifications built on the high ground to the east of the city, including the KIRCHBERG and the PLATEAU DU RHAM. The WALL OF WENCESLAS, built during the fourteenth century and still standing, is an example of such fortifications.

The Grund includes many attractive buildings, including the new buildings of the ABBEY OF ALTMUNSTER built during the eighteenth century. During the nineteenth and twentieth centuries, however, as the town of Luxembourg extended to the west, north, and south, the Grund was abandoned by the descendants of the original inhabitants and became increasingly the home of new immigrants to Luxembourg. Many of the buildings were neglected, and the area was in danger of developing into a slum. In recent years a project to renovate the Grund has been launched by a foundation called VIEUX LUXEMBOURG. Many of the old buildings have been repaired and restored, and the work is still in progress. The Abbey of Altmunster, which served as a prison from 1869 to 1984, is included in the work of restoration, and some of its buildings will become a museum. Among the leaders in the work of restoring the Grund is Georges M. Lentz, Jr., a prominent member of the AMERICAN LUXEMBOURG SOCIETY.

GUILLAUME-LUXEMBOURG RAILROAD. The first railroad built in Luxembourg, largely between the years 1859 and 1866. It was operated by the French Eastern Railroad Company (the

Compagnie Française des Chemins de Fer de l'Est) until 1871, after France's defeat in the Franco-Prussian War and its loss of Alsace-Lorraine, when operation of the railway was taken over by the new German Imperial Government. The Germans continued to operate the Guillaume-Luxembourg railroad until their defeat in WORLD WAR I. In 1919 the French again took over the operation of the Guillaume-Luxembourg railroad until WORLD WAR II, when it was again incorporated into the German railway system (10 May 1940 to 10 September 1944.) In 1946, all of Luxembourg's railway lines were merged into a single national company, the Societe Nationale des Chemins de fer Luxembourgeoise (CFL). (*See also* NARROW-GAUGE RAILROADS, PRINCE HENRI RAILROAD, and RAILROAD SYSTEM)

HAEBICHT. The major ecological issue in the Grand Duchy at the moment is the siting of a new industrial waste dump at Haebicht in Capellen, near Mamer. The measure to establish the dump passsed the CHAMBER OF DEPUTIES by a vote of 38 to 21 in July 1993, but the inhabitants of the neighborhood are still fighting the project. The CHRISTIAN SOCIAL PEOPLE'S PARTY (CSV) and the LUXEMBOURG SOCIALIST WORKERS PARTY (LSAP) supported the measure in the Chamber of Deputies. The Greens, needless to say, opposed it, as did the DEMOCRATIC PARTY (DP), which called for further study. The government has modified the original proposal, reducing the size of the dump and limiting the types of waste that may be disposed of there, but opposition to the planned dump is still vocal.

HAMMELSMARSCH. At the time of the KERMESS in each village and town, the local band parades through the streets collecting money for the band's expenses. The tune the band plays as it marches along is the "Hammelsmarsch" (the sheep march). Members of the band committee call at the door of each house, and when a contribution is made the band serenades the contributor with a fanfare.

The "Hammelsmarsch" is commemorated by a statue, built in 1982 on the site of the former RED WELL in Luxembourg city, showing a group of town musicians with a flock of sheep clustering around their feet. The tune they play was adopted by Brown University in Providence, Rhode Island, and is familiar to Brown football fans as "Rah, Rah! Brunonia!"

HENRI, Grand Duc Héretier (Grand Duke Presumptive). Eldest son of Grand Duke Jean and Grand Duchess Josephine Charlotte, Prince Henri is heir apparent to the throne of Luxembourg. His father has increasingly shared his responsibilities and duties with his eldest son in recent years, to prepare him for his ultimate succession to the throne. Prince Henri has accompanied government missions abroad to lend weight to their efforts to encourage foreign investment in Luxembourg, and he represents his father on certain ceremonial occasions. He also serves as a member of the COUNCIL OF STATE.

Prince Henri is married to Princess Maria Teresa, whom he met during his student days in Switzerland. The couple has several children, so the succession to the grand ducal throne seems assured for the foreseeable future.

HENRY, Prince Lieutenant of Luxembourg, 1850–79. Henry, the younger brother of WILLIAM III, governed the country in his brother's name until his own death in 1879. His conciliatory manner and his genuine devotion to their interests made him popular with the Luxembourgers and helped offset the unpopularity caused by some of his older brother's more reactionary measures. Prince Henry continued the policy established by his father, WILLIAM II, of appointing Luxembourgers to most of the important positions in the Grand Duchy and consulting them about important matters.

Prince Henry's wife, Princess Amalia of Saxe-Weimar, was equally popular with the people of Luxembourg, both because of her charities and her affable manner. After her death in 1872, money was raised by popular subscription to erect a statue of her, which still stands today in one of Luxembourg's public parks.

HENRY IV (Henry the Blind). Count of Luxembourg from 1136 to 1196. The male line of SIGEFROI, founder of Luxembourg, came to an end in 1136 with the death of his seventh successor, Conrad II. Henry of Namur, a descendent in the female line of Conrad I, was recognized as count of Luxembourg that year by the German emperor. Three years later, with the death of his father Godfrey, Henry became count of Namur as well. Since he had also inherited the counties of Laroche and Durbuy, Henry IV was one of the most powerful feudal lords in Lorraine.

As patron of the ABBEY OF ST. MAXIMIN IN TRIER, Henry quarreled with both Archbishop Alberon and his successor Archbishop Hillin. By an agreement reached in 1155, he gave up his rights as patron of St. Maximin's in return for the village of Grevenmacher on the MOSELLE.

A good part of Henry's reign was spent in fighting with his neighbors. He had some successes, capturing the castle of Bouillon in 1147 and ARLON in 1172, but his last years were spent in a bloody war with Baldwin the Fearless, count of Hainault, over the question of succession to Namur and Luxembourg, which ended in a complete victory for Baldwin. When Henry IV died at ECHTERNACH in 1196, leaving only a teenage daughter, ERMESINDE, both Namur and Luxembourg passed out of his family. Namur was ceded to Baldwin and Luxembourg itself reverted to the German emperor, Henry VI, who awarded it to his brother, Otto of Burgundy. The family fortunes were restored by Ermesinde through two fortunate marriages, the first to Thibault of Bar, who regained the counties of Luxembourg, Durbuy, and Laroche, as well as part of the county of Namur for his young bride; the second to Waleron of Limburg, who regained the marquisate of Arlon, and added it to the county of Luxembourg.

HENRY VII, Count of Luxembourg 1288–1310. Educated at the French court and the University of Paris, Henry VII maintained the friendship and alliance of the French kings during the early years of his reign. He was only fourteen when he succeeded his father, Henry VI, as count of Luxembourg, and his mother Beatrix assumed the regency for the first four years of his reign. He engaged in a feud with the archbishop of Trier in 1299 over river tolls on the MOSELLE but ended it three years later with a compromise by which Henry became a citizen of TRIER and was paid an annual income of three hundred pounds, in return for which he pledged to come to the defense of Trier with fifty knights if the city were to be attacked. He married Margaret of Brabant, who bore him one son and five daughters, all of whom made brilliant marriages.

Henry VII reformed the judicial system in Luxembourg, eliminating trial by ordeal and setting up a police force. He also straightened out Luxembourg's finances, paying off his father's debts and building up the treasury. He authorized the establishment of the Dominican Order in Luxembourg in 1292, the Carmelites in ARLON in 1293, and the Augustinians at THIONVILLE in 1307.

In 1308, Henry was unanimously elected KING OF THE

ROMANS by the German electors, with the strong support of two of the most powerful prelates, his brother BALDWIN, prince archbishop of Trier, and PETER OF ASPELT, archbishop of Mainz. Henry was a compromise candidate, the ruler of a weaker state elected because the temporal princes of Germany did not want to be ruled by a member of a powerful family, and because support for the other two candidates was divided. Henry's coronation took place at Aix-la-Chapelle (Aachen) in 1309.

One of Henry VII's early successes as emperor was to marry his only son John (JOHN THE BLIND) to Elizabeth, heiress to the Bohemian throne, a marriage by which John became king of Bohemia (the heartland of the present Czech Republic). Since there were other candidates, an army under Peter of Aspelt had to be sent to install John on the Bohemian throne.

The major event in Henry's reign as emperor was his invasion of Italy in 1310. The invasion was a quixotic attempt to revive the almost defunct claims of the Holy Roman Emperor to Italy, at that time in a state of near-anarchy, with the popes absent in Avignon. His invasion met with initial success, and was welcomed by many eminent Italians, including the poet Dante. Henry occupied Milan in 1311, receiving the IRON CROWN OF THE LOMBARDS.

Resistance stiffened against Henry as he marched south towards Rome. He had to lay siege to Brescia for four months before he captured it, Florence and Naples declared against him, and Robert of Naples occupied Rome. After a battle in which both sides suffered heavy losses, Henry succeeded in capturing part of Rome in 1312, and was crowned Holy Roman Emperor at St. John's Lateran by certain cardinal-delegates of the pope, who was still absent in Avignon.

Retiring from Rome, Henry laid siege to and captured Florence in 1313. While marching against Siena in August of the same year, however, he died of a fever and was buried in the cathedral at Pisa. His invasion of Italy marked the last attempt of the German emperors to restore the medieval empire, in which their claim to universal monarchy was based on their control of Rome and northern Italy.

Before leaving Germany on his invasion of Italy, Henry VII had installed his son John as count of Luxembourg. Henry was the first of four counts of Luxembourg to be elected Holy Roman Emperors. (*See also* CHARLES IV, SIGISMUND and WENZEL II)

HERSTAL. Town north of Liège, now one of its suburbs. Birthplace of PEPIN OF HERSTAL, grandfather of PEPIN THE SHORT who became king of the Franks in 751. Pepin the Short died in Herstal in 768. His son CHARLEMAGNE is also supposed to have been born here. Herstal was originally part of AUSTRASIA, the area between the Rhine, the Moselle, and the Meuse in which the RHINELAND FRANKS settled during the fourth and fifth centuries, and in which the County of Luxembourg later developed.

HIGHER EDUCATION. Luxembourg has no university and the graduates of its secondary schools must earn their degrees in other countries. There are two major reasons for this: (1) local opinion holds that students from as small a country as Luxembourg should not gain their entire education here, but should have the experience of studying in another country; and (2) most universities in Europe are state-supported (all costs, including the salaries of professors, are paid by the government) and the cost of supporting a first-class university would be very heavy for a country as small as Luxembourg.

By agreement with other governments, Luxembourg students who have passed their baccalaureate examinations may be admitted to universities in other European countries. Most attend universities in Belgium, France, Germany, and Switzerland, where they speak the languages fluently. Very few study at American universities because of the high cost, although a few go on to graduate study in the United States. Universities in the United Kingdom are ruled out also, since they charge foreign students excessive fees.

The cost of studying at most European universities is small, since qualified students need pay only a small annual registration fee. They must pay for their own food and lodging, but the Luxembourg government grants them bursaries that help cover these costs.

The system works well except that, as universities in other European countries get more crowded, Luxembourg students have begun finding it more difficult to gain admission to the universities and faculties of their choice. They may, while waiting, attend courses at the CENTRE UNIVERSITAIRE for a year.

One solution to the shortage of places for European students in existing universities would be for the EUROPEAN UNION to set up one or more European Universities, open to students from all member countries. Luxembourg would be an excellent site for one such university.

Institutions at which postsecondary education is offered in Luxembourg include, besides the Centre Universitaire, the TEACHER TRAINING COLLEGE and the SCHOOL OF COMMERCE AND MANAGEMENT.

HOLY ROMAN EMPIRE. The Holy Roman Empire was the name given to the medieval kingdom that, in theory, united Germany, northern Italy, and various other European countries into a single realm. It aspired to be a universal empire, but never succeeded in getting the kings of France and England, as well as other rulers, to accept its sovereignty.

The Holy Roman Empire was founded by OTTO THE GREAT, duke of Saxony, who was elected king of Germany by the other dukes in 936 and, in conscious imitation of CHARLEMAGNE, had himself crowned at Charlemagne's old capital at Aachen (Aix-la-Chapelle). In 962, he was crowned emperor in Rome by Pope John XII. It was Otto's goal to restore the empire of Charlemagne, but he never succeeded in gaining the adherence of the West Franks, who set up their own kingdom in France.

The Holy Roman Emperors were never able to unite the Germans into a single kingdom, largely because of their attempts to include Italy in their domains, which was one of the reasons for their conflicts with the popes.

Popes and emperors each claimed to be head of the Christian Church. In the early days of the empire, emperors demanded the right to be consulted in the choice of the pope, and sometimes deposed popes they objected to. Popes in turn asserted their sole right to crown emperors, and in fact rulers were not considered to be Holy Roman Emperors until they had actually been crowned by a pope or his representatives.

The Holy Roman Empire was distinguished from most other European kingdoms by being an elective rather than a hereditary monarchy. In the beginning, the other German dukes elected one of their number to become king. Later, certain prelates of the church were included among the electors. CHARLES IV issued the GOLDEN BULL of 1356 in order to regulate the future succession to the imperial throne. Three ecclesiastical and four lay electors were to assemble at Frankfurt within three months of the death of an emperor and elect his successor, who was to be crowned at Aachen and take the title KING OF THE ROMANS until his accession was recognized by the Pope and he was formally crowned Holy Roman Emperor. When they could, in imitation of Charlemagne, the emperors also took the IRON CROWN OF THE LOMBARDS as a symbol of their right to rule Italy.

The Holy Roman Emperors received their strongest support from the wealthy German church, which furnished them with knights to fight in their armies, money to fight their wars, and educated clerics to administer their lands. They had less success in getting the support of the powerful German dukes, who cherished their independence and regarded the emperor as only first among equals. In this, the dukes were aided by the popes. Time and again, when emperors invaded Italy, to assert their rights, the popes stirred up rebellions among their vassals in Germany.

Control of the German church was thus vital to the emperors, who named their own relatives and supporters as bishops, archbishops, and abbots. The pope contested this, claiming the right to choose the German prelates himself. This was the Investiture Controversy, which was settled eventually by a compromise in which the emperors chose the prelates and gave them their symbols of rule over the church lands as imperial fiefs, but the popes invested them with the symbols of spiritual authority.

SIGEFROI, whose lands in Lorraine formed part of the German realm, was a strong supporter of Otto the Great, accompanying him on his campaigns in Italy and receiving in return Otto's support in controlling his possessions in Lorraine. Sigefroi's successors continued his policy in this respect, and four of them became Holy Roman Emperors themselves. Luxembourg continued to be part of the Holy Roman Empire until the reign of CHARLES V, who gained the consent of the imperial diet to the separation of his possesssions in the Netherlands, including Luxembourg, from the Holy Roman Empire in 1548.

HOUSE OF ORANGE-NASSAU. The House of Orange-Nassau originated in the principality of Orange in southern France but came to own wide estates in Germany. The junior branch of the dynasty eventually became rulers of the Netherlands, as well as COUNTS OF VIANDEN in northeastern Luxembourg. In 1815, the CONGRESS OF VIENNA recognized WILLIAM I, prince of Orange-Nassau, as not only king of the Netherlands but also grand duke of Luxembourg. When WILLIAM III of Orange-Nassau died in 1890 without male heirs, rule over the Grand Duchy reverted to the elder branch of the House of Orange-Nassau, the German family of Nassau-Weilburg, and ADOLF OF NASSAU-WEILBURG, founder of the present dynasty, became grand duke of Luxembourg.

HUGO, VICTOR. French novelist, author of *Les Miserables, Toilers of the Sea*, and other works. Hugo made at least five visits to the Grand Duchy during his exile from France. The house in which he lived in Vianden in 1870–71 has been made into the Victor Hugo Museum.

Hugo was a painter as well as a novelist, and great value is attached to certain sketches and watercolors he made of various sites in Luxembourg, including a tower in Schengen on the MOSELLE and the CASTLE OF VIANDEN.

HUNS. Tribes of horsemen from the steppes of Asia who appeared in the Don River basin sometime during the fourth century A.D. Moving westward, they attacked the Ostrogoths who lived in an area known today as the Ukraine, north of the Black Sea, setting in motion a westward movement of the German tribes, first against the eastern Roman empire, then against the western empire. The Huns themselves moved further west and settled north of the Danube on the Hungarian plain, from which they made raids into both the eastern and western empires. Some of their tribes took service as auxiliary troops under various emperors, fighting against other claimants to the imperial throne or against the German tribes.

The Huns had various chieftains, but none of these ruled over all the Huns. A substantial number of the Hunnish tribes were united under the leadership of ATTILA toward the middle of the fifth century A.D. In 451 he launched a great raid into Gaul, during which his horsemen passed through what later became Luxembourg lands, looting and burning as they went. Attila is supposed to have crossed the SURE River at a place which later came to be named ETTELBRUCK, "Attila's bridge", destroying many Roman settlements including MERSCH, and sacking TRIER. The Hunnish raiders were stopped by the Roman general FLAVIUS AETIUS at the Battle of the Catalaunian Fields, near the site of present-day Châlons. Attila and his Huns retreated to their camps in Central Europe, only to reappear the following year (452) in northern Italy, where they threatened the city of Rome, which was saved, according to tradition, by the intercesssion of Pope Leo I.

ICELANDAIR. FINDEL Airport in Luxembourg is the principal European terminal for Icelandair, which provides daily service to and from New York, Baltimore, and Orlando, via Keflavik in Iceland, where the new Leif Eriksson Airport has opened during the last decade. Icelandair has provided service between Luxembourg and the United States since 1955 and was for years the lowest-cost way of crossing the Atlantic. Hundred of thousands of Americans have flown to Europe via Icelandair, but unfortunately too many of them went on to other European destinations with only a cursory glance at the Grand Duchy.

Icelandair flew propeller-driven aircraft in its early years, succeeded by turbo-props in the 1960s, but has operated only jet planes since 1970. In 1990, they purchased a fleet of new Boeing 757-200 aircraft.

IMMIGRATION. Luxembourg, like most European nations, has experienced recurrent waves of immigration. Not much is known about the pre-Celtic inhabitants of Gaul, except that they may have been related to the pre-Celtic inhabitants of the Iberian peninsula, Ireland, and Britain. After the CELTS came the Romans who, although not present in great numbers, had some effect upon the culture, language, and religion of the GAULS. Then came the FRANKS, who brought a language and customs of their own. CHARLEMAGNE settled a certain number of Saxons from east of the Rhine in Luxembourg, witnessed by place names such as Sassenheim.

The medieval mix of Gauls and Franks provided a reasonably stable population core, but during the Middle Ages and early modern times new elements were added, particularly French-speaking people from the areas now included in France and Belgium that once formed part of Luxembourg. Having killed off a substantial part of the population of Luxembourg city during the siege of 1683–84, LOUIS XIV imported many Frenchmen to help rebuild the city.

Immigration has continued during more modern times. Germans, drawn by employment in the rapidly-developing steel industry, formed a large part of the immigration in the late nineteenth and early twentieth century, when Luxembourg was part of the ZOLLVEREIN, the German customs union. After WORLD WAR I, there was a heavy immigration of Italian workers, also attracted to jobs in the steel mills. Since WORLD WAR II, the largest immigration has come from Portugal.

The Grand Duchy may be unique, at least in western Europe, in that native-born people make up less than 70 percent of its total population. As of 1 January 1993, the most recent date for which such a breakdown is available, 69.7 percent of the population were native-born or naturalized citizens, 12.9 percent were Portuguese, 6 percent were Italians, 4 percent were French, 3 percent were Belgians, and 2.7 percent were Germans. Many of the resident aliens are employees of the EUROPEAN UNION, and may be considered temporary residents, but others undoubtedly intend to stay. The birth rate among native Luxembourgers is stationary or even in slight decline (in 1994, there were 3335 deaths compared to 3255 live births among native Luxembourgers) and many fear that in time Luxembourgers may become a minority in their own country. A new political party, the NATIONAL MOVEMENT, was formed to fight the elections of 1994 with the aim of restricting the voting powers of non-native residents (under the terms of the TREATY OF MAASTRICHT, citizens of member states of the EUROPEAN UNION resident in other member states are supposed to be eligible to vote in local and European elections) but failed to attract much support.

In addition to aliens resident in Luxembourg, over fifty thousand foreigners, mainly French, Belgian, and German, cross the border every day to work in the Grand Duchy, where employment opportunities are greater and wages higher. The unemployment rate in Luxembourg reached 3.2 percent in 1995, the lowest in western Europe, so foreign labor is not a great concern at the moment, but a feeling of unease is beginning to develop. A point worth noting is that during the Great Depression of the 1930s the Grand Duchy was able to restrict immigration, but Luxembourg's membership in the European Union would prevent it doing this today, because citizens of member states have the right to relocate freely within the Union.

Despite the above considerations, Luxembourg has granted asylum to a higher number of refugees from the fighting in the former Yugoslavia in proportion to its population than any other European nation and is doing its best to find work and housing for them.

IRON AND STEEL MANUFACTURE. Iron-making in Luxembourg goes back to Celtic times, when the GAULS smelted iron and made iron tools and weapons, using techniques they had brought with them from their earlier home in the Danube Valley. Iron-making continued during Roman times and into the Middle Ages. Iron was forged on the TITELBERG during the five centuries of Roman occupation.

Supplies of iron ore were originally secured from alluvial deposits that had been washed down the rivers from the MINETTE, whose rich underground deposits were not discovered and mined until 1842. In medieval times, iron forges were located in the central part of Luxembourg, near rivers like the ALZETTE. The heat needed to smelt the iron was supplied by charcoal from the forests, and later by coal mined in the ARDENNES.

During the nineteenth century, the ore found in the red soil of the Minette was discovered and mined. There was one major drawback to the iron ore found in the Minette, however—it was rich in phosphorus, which made it difficult to turn it into steel in the early Bessemer converters. Salvation came in the form of a new process developed by Englishman SIDNEY GILCHRIST THOMAS, which made it possible to remove the phosphorus by using large quantities of lime in the furnaces. The resulting slag, rich in phosphorus and lime, made a valuable fertilizer.

The Thomas process was introduced into Luxembourg in 1884, after which steel manufacture became the country's major industry. Membership in the German customs union, the ZOLLVEREIN, gave the Grand Duchy a market for its iron and steel manufactures, and coke made from the high-quality coal of the Ruhr district was imported in large quantities to use in Luxembourg's furnaces. German workers and engineers came to Luxembourg to work in the steel mills and production steadily increased, making the tiny Grand Duchy one of the major steel producers in Europe.

The steel mills were originally individual enterprises but soon joined together into conglomerates such as ARBED. These conglomerates became international in their operations, exploiting iron ore deposits in Lorraine and Belgium and erecting steel mills outside the borders of the Grand Duchy as well.

Until quite recently, steel manufacture was the largest industry in Luxembourg and ARBED was the country's largest employer. The Grand Duchy became the capital of the EUROPEAN COAL AND STEEL COMMUNITY in 1951, and steel production continued to expand. A glut in the world market for steel products in recent years and increased international competition has forced the Luxembourg steel industry to streamline its operations and cut back its work force, however, and the Grand Duchy has diversified its industrial base by encouraging foreign investment in plants to manufacture new products of different materials. Luxembourg is still one of the largest steel producers in Europe, however, and ARBED, with its recent acquisition of Stahlwerke Bremen, has become the sixth largest steel conglomerate in the world.

The Grand Duchy's iron deposits have been almost entirely depleted, and the last iron mine in the Minette closed in 1981. Luxembourg now imports iron ore from Lorraine as well as coal from Germany to keep her steel mills going. Operations in the mills have been computerized, and electric-arc furnaces are being introduced. With these improvements in technology, Luxembourg hopes to stay ahead of her European and international competitors.

IRON CROWN OF THE LOMBARDS. Symbol of rule over Italy. CHARLEMAGNE assumed this crown in 773 after crushing the Lombards, thereafter calling himself the king of the Franks and Lombards. Later rulers assumed the crown as a preliminary step to being crowned as emperors. (*See also* HOLY ROMAN EMPIRE)

JEAN, Grand duke of Luxembourg (1964–present). The reigning grand duke of Luxembourg is Jean, eldest son of GRAND DUCHESS CHARLOTTE and PRINCE FELIX OF BOURBON-PARMA. Born in 1920, Jean was named grand duc héritier by his mother in 1938 when he reached the age of 18. During WORLD WAR II he went into exile with the other members of the grand ducal family when the German army invaded Luxembourg in 1940. With his father, Prince Felix, he served in the British army during the war. Jean became an officer in the Irish Guards, landed in Normandy with the Guards Armored Brigade on 12 June 1944, and took part in the liberation of Normandy and France. On 10 September 1944, when American troops liberated Luxembourg, Prince Jean was serving with his brigade, which had just captured Brussels. At his father's urgent request, he came to Luxembourg to join in the victory celebration, but soon returned to his brigade, in which he served until the war was over.

Jean was appointed prince lieutenant of Luxembourg by his mother, Charlotte, in 1961, and became grand duke when she abdicated in his favor in 1964. By his wise and prudent conduct as ruler he has enhanced the respect and prestige in which Luxembourg and the grand ducal family are held, at home and abroad.

In 1953, Prince Jean married Princess Josephine-Charlotte of the Belgian royal family, sister of the late King Baoudoin and of Albert II, the present king of the Belgians, They have five children, of whom the oldest son, PRINCE HENRI, is grand duc héritier. The couple's oldest daughter, Princess Marie-Astrid, is married to a member of Austria's former imperial family, the Hapsburgs.

In addition to his title as grand duke of Luxembourg, Jean also holds the titles of duke of Nassau and prince of Bourbon-Parma. He is honorary colonel-in-chief of the Irish Guards, the regiment in which he served during World War II. Not only he, but all the members of his family, enjoy the respect and esteem of the entire population of the Grand Duchy, which they have merited by their prudent conduct.

JESUITS. The Order of Jesus established itself in Luxembourg in1594. In 1603 they opened the Jesuit College, the first secondary school in Luxembourg, which provided a superior education to Luxembourg youth until 1773, when the order was suppressed by MARIA THERESA, and their college became a state school. In 1817, the former Jesuit college was renamed the ATHENEE GRAND-DUCAL. The buildings of the original Jesuit college, among the most beautiful in Luxembourg, now house the NATIONAL LIBRARY.

The Jesuit church, a masterpiece of baroque architecture, was built next door to the Jesuit College, between 1613 and 1621. In 1870, when Luxembourg became a diocese, the former Jesuit church became the new Luxembourg cathedral.

JOHN THE BLIND (JEAN L'AVEUGLE). Count of Luxembourg, 1310–1346. The son of HENRY VII, John was installed as count of Luxembourg in 1310, before his father's ill-fated invasion of Italy. His father also arranged his marriage to Elizabeth, daughter of Wenceslas III of Bohemia, which took place in Speyer in 1311 and gave John a claim to the throne of Bohemia. Since there were rival claimants to the throne, an army had to be sent to install John and Elizabeth in their kingdom. The army was successful, and John and Elizabeth were crowned in Prague in 1312, but John was never easy on the Bohemian throne, his rule being resisted by the turbulent Bohemian nobles.

During his minority, John had the benefit of the wise advice of PETER OF ASPELT, archbishop of Mainz, who had secured the election of Henry VII to the imperial throne, but disapproved of Henry's subsequent invasion of Italy. Peter died, unfortunately, in 1320 when John was only twenty.

John was too young to be seriously considered as a candidate for emperor upon his father's death in Italy in 1313. Peter of Aspelt succeeded in winning the election for Louis of Bavaria by a narrow majority, but the election was contested by Frederick the Handsome of Austria, the unsuccessful candidate. An eight-year war between the two candidates followed, during which John supported Louis of Bavaria, distinguishing himself in several battles. During this war, John lost control of Bohemia for a time.

John spent little time in his Bohemian kingdom during his reign, and even less time in Luxembourg, although he found time to fight three wars against Luxembourg's neighbors in the intervals between his other campaigns. He was a sort of medieval knight-errant, who took delight in battle and engaged in tournaments when no war was actually going on. He joined the Teutonic Knights in three campaigns against the Lithuanians, in the second of which he contracted a severe inflammation of his eyes. A French physician who treated his eyes in Breslau made his condition worse, whereupon John had him sewn up in a leather sack and thrown into the Oder. An Arabian oculist who treated him in Prague was even less successful, causing him to lose the vision of his right eye entirely.

After his first Lithuanian campaign, John invaded Italy, where he won some initial successes in 1330, but left in 1331 to return to Germany, leaving his army in charge of his teenage son Charles. By the time John returned to Italy in 1332, Charles and his army were in severe trouble. John kept on fighting, but met several defeats and was finally forced to leave Italy for good in 1333. Shortly thereafter he fought his second campaign in Lithuania, the one in which he lost his right eye.

In 1340 John paid a visit to Pope Clement VI at Avignon and then traveled to Montpellier to see if the medical facility there could help his eyesight. They conducted an operation in which he lost the sight of his other eye, leaving him totally blind, after which he was known as John the Blind.

In spite of his blindness, John returned to Bohemia, where he was greeted by declarations of war from seven of his neighbors. Rallying the Bohemian nobility about him, he fought and defeated all of his enemies. He was helped by Pope Clement VI, who excommunicated Louis the Bavarian, whom John had helped become emperor but who had now turned against him. The pope declared the imperial throne vacant, and

John, against all odds, succeeded in getting his eldest son Charles elected emperor in Louis's place.

An English invasion of France by Edward III of England resulted in a call for help from the French king, Philip VI. Despite his followers' attempts to dissuade him, John hastened to Philip's aid with five hundred knights and his son Charles, arriving in time to take part in the BATTLE OF CRECY in 1346. At Crécy, the English longbowmen mowed the French knights down and won the battle for Edward. John, interlacing the reins of his horse with those of the knights on either side of him so that he would not lose his way, led his knights into battle and rode to his death.

John's oldest son by his first wife, Elizabeth of Bohemia, survived the battle of Crécy, and was crowned king of Bohemia and Holy Roman Emperor as CHARLES IV. John left Luxembourg to a son by his second marriage to Beatrice of Bourbon, count WENZEL I, who took the title of duke when his brother Charles raised the status of Luxembourg to that of a duchy in 1353.

Despite his endless wars, John managed to leave the County of Luxembourg in reasonably good condition, although heavily in debt, upon his death. He enlarged its boundaries, curiously enough, by purchase rather than by war, using the income from his Bohemian estates to do so. He is best remembered for founding the SHEPHERDS' FAIR in 1340.

After Crécy, John was buried in the ABBEY OF ALTMUNSTER, but his bones were removed after a fire destroyed the abbey in 1543, and thereafter were almost constantly on the move, being buried in at least ten different places over the centuries. During the French Revolution, they were even hidden in a baker's oven for a time. They ended up in the Chapel of Castell in the Saar. After WORLD WAR II they were returned to Luxembourg and are now buried in the crypt of the cathedral.

JOINT RULE (1830–1839). For nine years after the Belgian Revolution of 1830, Luxembourg considered itself part of Belgium, and sent delegates to the Belgium Congress, but the Prussian garrison installed in the fortress by the CONGRESS OF VIENNA continued to hold the city of Luxembourg and its fortress subject to the Dutch king WILLIAM I. In 1839, when the FIRST TREATY OF LONDON went into effect, the Grand Duchy was split in two, with the western French-speaking section incorporated into the Kingdom of Belgium as the province of Luxembourg, and the smaller LETZEBUERG-ESCH-speaking eastern part continuing under the rule of William I as the Grand Duchy of Luxembourg. The Grand Duchy dates its independence from 1839. (*See also* THREE PARTITIONS OF LUXEMBOURG)

JOSEPH II, Holy Roman Emperor (1765–90). Although elected emperor and co-regent with his mother MARIA THERESA of the Austrian dominions in 1765, Joseph II exercised no real power until his mother's death in 1780. Like his mother, he was a "benevolent despot" but his own reforms, unlike his mother's, were unsuccessful, largely because he was too impatient to carry them through to be cautious, and paid little attention to the rights, traditions, and customs of the different people over whom he ruled. He visited Luxembourg only once, in 1781.

On 12 November 1781 Joseph issued an edict of toleration, granting non-Catholics in his realms the right to worship as they pleased, and admitting them to public employment. On the other hand, he engaged in a struggle with his Catholic clergy, attempting to establish state control over the Church. He suppressed many of the monastic orders, which led to the closing of the convents of the Holy Spirit in Luxembourg, St. Claire in ECHTERNACH, the Cistercians at Differdange, St. Augustin at Hosingen, and the Dominicans at MARIENTHAL. (Joseph confiscated the goods of the convents he closed, sold their lands, and deposited the receipts in something he called the Funds of Religion.) He also closed most of the seminaries and required aspirants to the priesthood to study at either the seminary at Louvain or the one at Luxembourg, both of which were put under state control.

Joseph also interfered in church administration, meddled with the liturgy, and criticized papal bulls and episcopal mandates. He limited the number of religious processions, and ordered all villages to hold their annual fairs the same day.

An attempted political reorganization of the Austrian Netherlands in 1787, replacing the historic provinces with nine districts equal in size and population, as well as a series of judicial reforms introduced without prior consultation, led to an uprising against Austrian rule called the BRABANTINE REVOLUTION in 1789, in which all the Belgian provinces except Luxembourg took part. In 1790, the provinces in revolt set up a republic they called the United Belgian States. Joseph II died early that same year, and was succeeded by his brother

Leopold II who spent the whole of his short reign (1790–92) trying to undo the mischief Joseph II had caused by his reforms and restoring Austrian authority in the Netherlands. When the Belgians refused to submit, Leopold sent an army under FIELD MARSHAL VON BENDER, governor of Luxembourg, against them, which crushed the revolt.

JOYOUS ENTRY (JOYEUSE ENTREE). Celebrated the wedding of WENZEL I to Jeanne, heiress to the Duchy of Brabant in 1354 and their entry into Brussels in 1356. By this marriage, Wenzel I became in time duke of Brabant and marquis of Antwerp.

The Joyous Entry was confirmed by a document that set forth the terms under which Wenzel was to administer Brabant and included provisions protecting the rights of the nobility, citizens, and clergy.

JULIUS CAESAR. Roman proconsul who commanded the legions that conquered Gaul during the years 58 to 52 B.C. At the time of the Roman conquest, Luxembourg was not a separate entity but part of northeastern Gaul. The principal Gallic tribe in the region were the TREVERI, after whom the city of TRIER in Germany is named. Caesar's legions defeated the Treveri in 54 B.C. and established Roman rule in the region.

For approximately five hundred years after its conquest by Caesar, Gaul remained part of the Roman empire and was occupied by the Romans.

KERMESS. Each of the villages and towns of Luxembourg holds an annual kermess or local fair. It usually features rides, including a merry-go-round, restaurants and sausage stands, booths where customers can win tawdry prizes by lottery or by throwing balls to knock over wooden bottles, and similar amusements. Beer, Thuringers and Mettwurst (spicy German sausages) and pork cutlets are featured at these and similar events in Luxembourg.

KINDERGARTEN EDUCATION. Two years of preschool education is available to four- and five-year-old children in the Grand Duchy. Until 1994, attendance was compulsory only for five-year-olds, but in September 1994 it became compulsory for four-year-olds as well. Most kindergartens are attached to the state primary schools.

There are a number of crêches (child-care centers) and play

schools available for younger children, some of them privately operated, but there are not enough to meet the demand.

KING OF THE ROMANS. Title given to the ruler chosen as their king by the German electors before his coronation by the pope as Holy Roman Emperor. In an attempt to set up a hereditary succession, some emperors took the precaution of having their sons elected king of the Romans during their own lifetimes. (*See also* HOLY ROMAN EMPIRE)

KIRCHBERG. A plateau to the east of Luxembourg city, reached by crossing the valley of the ALZETTE over the modern RED BRIDGE, the Pont du Grand-Duchesse Charlotte. The Kirchberg contains many of the buildings of the EUROPEAN UNION including the Hemicycle (the meeting or congress center), European Court of Justice, European Data Processing Centre, General Secretariat of the European Parliament, European Investment Bank, Statistics Office of the European Commission (housed in the Jean Monnet Building), Court of Auditors, Eurocontrol (the air-traffic control organization), and the EUROPEAN SCHOOL (Ecole Européene) for the children of employees of the European Union.

The Kirchberg is bisected by a highway leading to the airport at FINDEL, and houses the new Luxembourg exhibition center and several commercial enterprises such as Euromotor (the Ford agency), Le Foyer (the largest Luxembourg insurance company), Olympia A.G. (the German typewriter company), and the Hotel Pullman. A Swedish consortium was planning a large industrial complex on the Kirchberg, but this plan has been shelved, at least temporarily, because of the present unfavorable economic climate in Europe.

KLOPP, NICO (1894–1930). A native of REMICH who studied in Germany, Nico Klopp painted many views of the MOSELLE valley, especially of the bridge at Remich. He was a master of the use of color.

KLOPPELKRIEG. In 1798, during the French occupation (1795–1815), the peasants of the ARDENNES rose in revolt against the newly announced French policy of drafting Luxembourgers into the French army. The uprising, which began in 1798, had little chance of success, because the peasants were poorly armed, many of them with nothing but clubs and farm tools. The word *Klöppelkrieg* itself means *stick war*. The uprising was put down with great severity, and eventually fourteen thousand Luxembourgers were drafted into the French army, of whom nine thousand died in Napoleon's campaigns. Two notable sayings came out of the Kloppelkrieg; one is "Et get fir de glaf!" (Here goes for the faith!), the motto the peasants adopted when they rose, and the other a statement made by the leaders of the uprising who were captured and court-martialed at Luxembourg. When urged by the sympathetic president of the court to plead extenuating circumstances, such as that their muskets were not loaded or that they did not intend to start an uprising, they responded: "Wir können nicht lügen!" (We cannot lie.)

WILTZ was the town in which the Klöppelkrieg began; over one hundred years later it was also the town in which the uprising of 1942 against the German conscription laws began. (*See also* GENERAL STRIKE OF 1942 and WORLD WAR II)

KOENIG, LUCIEN (1888–1961). Luxembourg poet who wrote under the name of "Siggy vu Letzebuerg". Author of "Letze-buerg de Letzebuerger" (Luxembourg for the Luxembourg-ers), which was adopted as one of the national anthems in 1939.

"Siggy" played an important part in the movement to return the bones of JOHN THE BLIND to Luxembourg after WORLD WAR II.

KUTTER, JOSEPH (1894–1941). The most outstanding Luxem-bourg painter, known for his vivid use of color and his dark, brooding landscapes. He worked mostly in oils on large can-vases. One of his most famous paintings, a landscape of CLER-VAUX shown at the World Exhibition at Paris in 1937, mea-sured 4 by 3.2 meters (about 13 by 10.5 feet), the same size as his landscape of Luxembourg painted about the same time.

Kutter is also famous for his portraits, the best known of which are a series of clowns he painted during the 1930s. He painted abroad as well as in Luxembourg, and his oils were better known in other countries for a time than they were in his own country.

Kutter was born in Luxembourg city and died there. He studied in Munich from 1917 to 1924. Many of his paintings are on display in the NATIONAL MUSEUM.

LANGUAGES. Although LETZEBUERGESCH is the language spoken by native Luxembourgers, and although it was pro-claimed to be the national language in a law passed in 1984, it was not taught in the schools until the past few years. Luxembourg pupils begin learning German in the first grade and French in the second grade, and by the time they are in the sixth grade of primary school they are taught half their subjects in German and half in French; this pattern continues in secondary school. English is introduced in the last year of primary school and a majority of pupils go on to study it in secondary school, although other foreign languages are offered as well.

Luxembourg authors write in either French, German, or Letzebuergesch, but seldom in all three. There is a determined attempt by several authors, based upon Luxembourg's experiences under the German occupation during both world wars, to keep alive the tradition of writing in French. A majority of the population, however, watches German-language television, listens to German-language radio programs, and reads a German-language newspaper, since German is closer to their native language.

The influx of large numbers of people from southern Europe during the twentieth century, particularly from Italy and Portugal, has created some problems for the school system. Up to 50 percent of the pupils in some schools speak Portuguese as their native language. Since Portuguese and French have the same roots they find it relatively easy to learn French but much more difficult to learn German and Letzebuergesch. This tends to limit their educational opportunities, because entrance to the good secondary schools requires a mastery of both French and German.

Both French and German have been official languages in Luxembourg since 1830. Official documents have been written in French since at least the thirteenth century, and the position of French as an official language was firmly established with the absorption of Luxembourg into the domains of the dukes of Burgundy during the fifteenth century. Later French occupations (1684–1697 and 1795–1815) strengthened the position of French, and the CODE NAPOLEON, introduced into Luxembourg during the latter French occupation, became the basis of the Luxembourg legal system. The position of German was strengthened in the years following Luxembourg's adhesion in 1842 to the German customs union, the ZOLLVEREIN, when Luxembourg was drawn into the German economic sphere and German influence became particularly strong, but the German invasions of Luxembourg during both world wars caused a reaction against that language.

LENTZ, MICHEL (1820–1893). The national poet, author of the two best-known Luxembourg patriotic poems, "De Feierwon" ("The Fire-wagon") which celebrates the opening of the first railroad in Luxembourg in 1859, and "Ons Hémecht" ("Our Homeland") which, set to music by Johann Anton Zinnen, became the national hymn.

LENUS. A Gallic war god whose cult was assimilated to that of the Roman Mars. A funeral monument to a Roman officer, a priest of Lenus Mars, prefect of the second cohort of Spanish cavalry stationed at TRIER and tribune of the IXth Spanish legion, was located in the Roman cemetery in MERSCH, and is now on display at the NATIONAL MUSEUM.

LETZEBUERGESCH. The native language of the people of Luxembourg. In its origins, it is one of the Moselle-Franconian dialects, spoken by the RHINELAND FRANKS who settled in the lands between the Rhine, the Moselle, and the Meuse rivers in the fourth and fifth centuries A.D. The language survives in the Grand Duchy of Luxembourg and in the border regions in Germany, Belgium, and France, formerly parts of the Grand Duchy of Luxembourg, that adjoin it. It is related to Flemish (Dutch), the language spoken by the SALIAN FRANKS from the lower Rhine, who settled in what is now the southern Netherlands and northern Belgium during the same centuries.

Letzebuergesch is not descended from High German, a dialect originally spoken in southern parts of Germany, which became the German national language during the sixteenth century. It is related to the Plattdeutsch (Low German) dialects spoken in northern Germany. It is not, as sometimes decribed , a mixture of German and French. Some French words and phrases have been incorporated into Letzebuergesch but these have not greatly affected its vocabulary and structure, which remain Germanic.

During most of its existence, Letzebuergesch has been a spoken rather than written language, and even today it is not a major part of the school curriculum. Until recently there was no dictionary of Letzebuergesch, but a five-volume dictionary of the language was published between 1935 and 1977. Spelling and vocabulary were not standardized until recent years, and different dialects developed in the north and south.

A conscious effort was made during the nineteenth century to develop Letzebuergesch into a written language, and a respectable number of works were written and published by authors such as Antoine Meyer, Felix Thyes, "Dicks" (ED-MOND DE LA FONTAINE), MICHEL LENTZ, MICHEL RODANGE, and others. Even today, most works written by Letzebuergesch authors are written in French or German, but a few works are still written in Letzebuergesch and plays and films have been produced in that language.

Luxembourgers take an enormous pride in their language; it is one of the ties which have bound them together over the centuries. During the German occupation in WORLD WAR II, the German authorities conducted a survey in which they tried to make Luxembourgers declare themselves as either basically German speaking or French speaking. Ninety-seven percent of the population crossed out the German and French options and wrote in "Letzebuergesch".

In 1984 a law was passed declaring the national language of Luxembourg to be Letzebuergesch, although the language of legislation was to be French, and either French, German, or Letzebuergesch could be used in legal proceedings. Debates in the CHAMBER OF DEPUTIES may be conducted in French, German, or Letzebuergesch, and official notices are sent out in both French and German. The principal newspaper, *The Luxemburger Wort*, is written, for the most part, in German.

In recent years Letzebuergesch has been added to the primary school and early secondary school curriculum but German and French continue to be the major languages of instruction, largely because the authorities realize that to cope in the modern world Luxembourgers must be able to speak, read, and write at least one or two, and preferably more, of the major European languages. (*See also* LANGUAGES)

LIBERATION OF LUXEMBOURG, 1944. On 10 September 1944, American troops of the 5th Armored Division advancing up the route de Longwy from Petange, which they had captured on 9 September, liberated the capital city from German occupation. The Americans met little resistance, because the Germans had already retreated across the border into Germany. PRINCE FELIX OF BOURBON-PARMA, the husband of GRAND DUCHESS CHARLOTTE, accompanied the American troops and was received by the inhabitants amid scenes of great jubilation. The road upon which the Americans troops advanced, or at least that portion of it within Luxembourg city, was renamed the "avenue 10 September", a name it still bears.

The first liberation of Luxembourg had to be followed by a

second one after the German army reoccupied the northern part of the country three months later. In December 1944, FIELD MARSHAL GERD VON RUNDSTEDT launched a final offensive in the west in a desperate attempt to capture the port of Antwerp through which supplies were beginning to flow to the Allied armies. German troops swept across northern Luxembourg and Belgium, causing more destruction than this area had sustained in the entire war until then. (*See also* BATTLE OF THE BULGE; PATTON, GENERAL GEORGE S., JR.; and WORLD WAR II.)

LIMPERTSBERG. Limpertsberg is a northern suburb of Luxembourg city, originally outside the city walls. In earlier days, Limpertsberg was a famous rose-growing center and shipped plants all over the world, although that activity came to an end during the first world war. Now Limpertsberg is better known as the home of Villeroy and Boch, producers of fine pottery. Buses are run regularly from American military bases in Germany so that Americans can shop at the factory outlet on the rue de Rollingergrund.

Limpertsberg has also become one of the most important educational centers in Luxembourg. The Lycée Robert Schuman (formerly known as the Lycée des Jeune Filles), Lycée des Garcons, Lycée Technique des Arts et Metiers (the vocational school), Lycée Technique Michel Lucius, CENTRE UNIVERSITAIRE, AMERICAN INTERNATIONAL SCHOOL OF LUXEMBOURG, and COLLEGE VAUBAN are all located in Limpertsberg, as well as several primary schools.

LITTLE SWITZERLAND (PETITE SUISSE). A region in the eastern part of Luxembourg, between La Rochette and ECHTERNACH, also known as the Müllerthal, with picturesque scenery, swift-running streams, waterfalls, cliffs, forests, and caves. A number of beautiful small villages such as Berdorf, Consdorf, Altrier, Reuland, Christnach, Heffingen, Waldbillig, Altlinster, Nommern, Rippig, Bech, Lauterborn, and Junglinster are located in the area, and hiking trails wind through the forests. Bones of a woolly rhinoceros, wild oxen, cave bears, and mammoths have been found in the caves, as well as skeletons of prehistoric man and rock paintings. Traces of Neolithic and Bronze Age settlements have been discovered, as well as a Mesolithic skeleton, a four-sided monument depicting Apollo, Hercules, Minerva, and Juno, and the remains of a Roman villa.

The ruins of medieval castles are found at La Rochette, Beaufort, Heringen, Lauterborn, Bourglinster, and Steinborn, some of which have been restored. The castle at Bourglinster houses a youth hostel connected by trails to castles and youth hostels in other parts of the Grand Duchy.

At one time an iron foundry operated at Consdorf, and cannon were cast there during the eighteenth century for the use of the English army. Mills were located on several of the streams, although none of them are any longer in operation. A narrow-gauge railroad once connected Grundhof and Beaufort, but the line was abandoned after the second world war. The line was known familiarly as the "Charley", but American soldiers stationed in the Petite Suisse in the closing months of WORLD WAR II referred to it as the "Bubble and Squeak". The entire Petite Suisse region forms part of a German-Luxembourg nature park, established in 1965, which covers a total of 725 square kilometers. The district is a favorite holiday resort for Germans and visitors of other nationalities. There are several camping places and a number of hotels in the area and there is even a rock-climbing school at Berdorf.

LOTHAIR I. Eldest grandson of CHARLEMAGNE. Lothair was awarded an area stretching from northern Italy to the Netherlands by the TREATY OF VERDUN, signed in A.D. 843, and was also given the title of emperor. The rest of the Frankish empire was divided between Louis (Ludwig), who was given the eastern lands that eventually developed into Germany, and Charles the Bald, who was given the western section, which developed into the kingdom of France. Lothair established his capital at Aachen, Charlemagne's former capital.

The lands given to Lothair I never developed into a single state. When Lothair died in 855, at the Abbey of PRUM, he divided his lands among his three sons, and his kingdom disintegrated. Lothair II, the eldest of his three sons was named emperor, but the title soon died out among the descendants of Charlemagne. The last Carolingian emperor, Berengar, died in 924, but even before his death the imperial title had been awarded to Conrad of Franconia, in Germany.

Of the lands awarded to Lothair I, only Belgium, Luxembourg, the Netherlands, and Switzerland have emerged as independent states. The remaining parts of the lands he once ruled have been absorbed by France, Germany, and Italy.

LOTHARINGIA. The lands awarded at the TREATY OF VER-
DUN of 843 to LOTHAIR I included a stretch of territory
which extended from northern Italy to the Netherlands. These
lands never became a single kingdom. They were divided
among Lothair's three sons upon his death in 855, with the
northern part, the country between the Rhine and the Meuse,
going to his eldest son, Lothair II. These lands became known
as Lotharingia, a name later corrupted into Lorraine.

When Lothair II died without heirs in 870, Lotharingia was
divided from north to south between his uncles, Louis (Ludwig) the German, and Charles the Bald, rulers of Germany
and France respectively, at the TREATY OF MERSEN. The
eastern part, which included most of the present-day Grand
Duchy, fell to Germany, the western to France. In 959, OTTO
THE GREAT further divided Lotharingia into High and Low
Lotharingia, with the SURE River forming the dividing line.
High Lotharingia, south of the Sûre River, included the present
BON PAYS. Low Lotharingia included the ARDENNES and
the country north of the Ardennes as far as the Rhine.

Upper Lorraine was given as a royal fief to WIGERIC, count
of the Ardennes, as count palatine. In 963 Wigeric's youngest
son, SIGEFROI, acquired title to a small tract of land along
the ALZETTE River, which included a rocky promontory
called the BOCK, from Wicher, abbot of ST. MAXIMIN IN
TRIER. Sigefroi built a castle on the Bock, around which a
town grew up that formed the nucleus of the later city and
county of Luxembourg.

LOUIS XIV. King of France 1643–1715. One of his goals was to
expand France to its "natural boundaries", the Pyrenees in
the south and the Rhine in the north and east. his goals were
partly realized while he was still in his childhood when Cardinal
Mazarin succeeded in annexing the THIONVILLE area from
Luxembourg and Perpignan from Spain under the terms of the
TREATY OF THE PYRENEES (1659).

This did not put an end to the French annexations of Luxembourg, because Louis XIV interpreted the wording of the
Treaty of the Pyrénées to give France a claim to additional
Luxembourg territories. Between 1659 and 1683 he annexed
Rodemacher, Hesperange, Rollingen, Preisch, Outlingen, Orchimont, Virton, St. Mard, REMICH, and Grevenmacher, and
in 1683 his armies laid siege to the fortress of Luxembourg.

In 1684, following the siege, French troops captured the
fortress, after a bombardment that destroyed a substantial part

of the city. The French occupied Luxembourg from 1684 until
1697, when they were forced to give it up under the TREATY
OF RYSWICK. During the French occupation, the great
French military engineer VAUBAN redesigned the fortifications of Luxembourg, making it into the "Gibraltar of the
North." Louis XIV also distributed a certain amount of lar-
gesse to the town, to help repair the damage the French
artillery fire had caused. The baroque onion-shaped dome
on the CHURCH OF ST. MICHAEL (the oldest church in
Luxembourg) dates from the French occupation.

Louis XIV failed in his attempt to annex the Spanish Netherlands, largely because of alliances formed against him by other
European powers. The rise of France to the first rank among
European nations naturally alarmed other nations. The Austrian Hapsburgs came to the aid of the Spanish Hapsburgs as a
matter of course, bringing with them many of the other German
states that formed the HOLY ROMAN EMPIRE. The Dutch,
alarmed by Louis's early successes in the southern Netherlands, joined the alliance against him, fearing they would be his
next victims. (The Rhine flowed through the United Provinces
rather than through the Spanish Netherlands.) Great Britain
joined the alliance when the reigning stadholder of the Netherlands became king of England in 1689 as WILLIAM III.
William helped organize the League of Augsburg, and the
allies' successes in the war that followed, the WAR OF THE
LEAGUE OF AUGSBURG (1689–1697), forced Louis to give
up many of his gains, including Luxembourg.

Louis XIV's last attempt to conquer the Spanish Netherlands came during the WAR OF THE SPANISH SUCCES-
SION (1702–1713). The death in 1700 of Charles II, the last
Hapsburg king of Spain, leaving no heir, left the Spanish throne
open and Louis succeeded in having one of his grandsons
named king of Spain. His armies again invaded the Spanish
Netherlands. The usual coalition of other powers formed
against him, led by Great Britain and Austria. During the war,
the French reoccupied Luxembourg. Although French armies
won some victories, they were defeated in several decisive
battles by the allied armies led by the famous Duke of Marlborough and Prince Eugene of Savoy. By the TREATY OF
UTRECHT, Louis XIV's grandson, Philip V, was allowed to
keep the Spanish crown, but the Spanish Netherlands, including Luxembourg, were placed under the rule of the Austrian
Hapsburgs.

The Luxembourg territories were laid waste time and again

by the various invading armies during the wars of Louis XIV. Many of the castles on Luxembourg territory were destroyed or dismantled, mostly by French artillery under MARSHAL BOUFFLERS.

LUCILINBURHUC. A Celtic name meaning "little fortress on a hill", from which the name Luxembourg (Letzebuerg) is apparently derived. This may refer to a small fort built in Gallo-Roman times on or near the BOCK where SIGEFROI later built his castle. The hill continued to be fortified during Frankish times, although the remains of those early fortifications as well as Sigefroi's own castle have not survived. The castle itself was destroyed by fire in 1554 during the reign of CHARLES V. Excavations at the site just prior to the thousandth anniversary of the founding of Luxembourg in 963 uncovered some of the foundations of Sigefroi's castle.

LUXAIR. Luxembourg's own airline, partly owned by ICE-LANDAIR. Luxair operates regularly scheduled flights to Amsterdam, Athens, Brussels, Frankfurt, London, Munich, Paris, Rome, and Zurich, as well as charter flights to a number of destinations in Europe, North Africa, and the Near East. Connecting flights to other cities such as Frankfurt, London, Brussels, and Amsterdam enable travelers to reach major cities on all continents. (*See also* CARGOLUX and FINDEL)

LUXEMBOURG CHRISTIAN LABOR FEDERATION (LCGB). One of the two largest federations of labor unions in the Grand Duchy, closely affiliated with the CHRISTIAN SOCIAL PEOPLE'S PARTY (CSV).

LUXEMBOURG CITY HALL (HOTEL DE VILLE). The "new" city hall, built between 1830 and 1844 in neoclassical style, on the PLACE GUILLAUME and dedicated in 1844 by WILLIAM II. Bronze lions by AUGUSTE TREMONT were added in 1931, flanking the steps to the entrance.

LUXEMBOURG INDEPENDENT LABOR FEDERATION (OGB-L). The largest federation of labor unions in the Grand Duchy, affiliated with the LUXEMBOURG SOCIALIST WORKERS PARTY (LSAP).

LUXEMBOURG SOCIALIST WORKERS PARTY (LSAP). A social democratic political party which may be compared in its general aims and aspirations to the SPD (Social Democratic Party) in Germany. It was founded by Michel Welter in 1902. The LSAP normally garners the second-largest number of votes in national elections, and in order to share in government must form a coalition with at least one other party. From 1974 to 1979 it formed a coalition with the DEMOCRATIC PARTY, but since 1984 it has formed a coalition with the CHRISTIAN SOCIAL PEOPLE'S PARTY. This coalition governed the Grand Duchy from 1984 to 1994, and will govern it at least until the next national elections in 1999. (*See* ELECTIONS OF 1994).

The foreign minister and vice premier, Jacques Poos, a leading figure in the LSAP, stands a reasonable chance of becoming prime minister if the LSAP ever becomes the major partner in a coalition.

The LSAP is also supported by a large labor federation, the LUXEMBOURG INDEPENDENT LABOR FEDERATION (OGB-L).

The LSAP suffers the same handicap as the British Labour Party, in being widely seen as a party of industrial workers. In a country where the combined votes of farmers, committed Catholics, and members of the business community outweigh the labor vote, this makes it difficult for the LSAP to win an absolute majority. Its policies, moreover, are not seen as significantly different from those of the CSV, with whom it has formed a governing coalition for the past eleven years, so that voters have no great incentive to shift their votes from other parties to the LSAP.

MAGYARS. A nomadic tribe of horsemen, distantly related to the HUNS, who settled on the Hungarian plain during the ninth century after CHARLEMAGNE's defeat of the Avars. In 906, in alliance with the king of the East Franks, Arnulf of Carinthia, they conquered the Slavic kingdom of Moravia (today part of the Czech republic). From their base on the Danube, like the earlier Huns, the Magyars made raids into western Europe. In 911, 919, 926, and 950 they invaded the ARDENNES, destroying various Frankish towns including Malmédy.

In 954, OTTO I inflicted a major defeat on the Magyars at Lechfeld, ending the menace they posed to western Europe. They were converted to Christianity and settled down in their Hungarian territories, where their descendents live to this day.

The invasions of the Magyars from the east, like those of the

NORTHMEN from the north and west, gave great impetus to the growth of feudalism, a system by which strong local rulers like SIGEFROI provided the protection against invaders that more distant rulers were unable to provide.

MAISON DE CASSAL. Located on the CORNICHE, the Maison de Cassal was built during the seventeenth century, at approximately the same time as the GRAND DUCAL PALACE. It was a typical bourgeois dwelling of the time and passed through the hands of several prominent families, from the Cassals to the Reuters, over the centuries. Although it had been one of the finest residences in the city, it had fallen into poor condition by 1956 when the Luxembourg government purchased and restored it, largely at the initiative of Victor Bodson, minister of public works, during one of the administrations of JOSEPH BECH.

MAMER. A town to the west of Luxembourg city that lay on the original Roman road from ARLON to TRIER. Excavations at Mamer have uncovered a Roman bath and other artifacts from Roman times.

MANSFELD, COUNT PETER ERNEST VON. Count Mansfeld was governor of Luxembourg during the late Burgundian-early Spanish period of rule (1545–1604). In 1563 he built a magnificent palace in the lower town of which, unfortunately, few traces exist today. This palace was filled with relics of earlier times, including some dating from the Roman occupation of Gaul.

In 1572, Count Mansfeld built a town hall to replace the one that had been destroyed in the great fire and explosion of 1554. The building's facade displayed both Burgundian and Spanish-Moorish influences. It served as the town hall until 1795, as the seat of the Luxembourg government from 1815 to 1841, and as the Grand Ducal Palace from 1841 to the present. The facade was recently renovated and sandblasted in preparation for Luxembourg's year as EUROPEAN CITY OF CULTURE in 1995.

MARIA THERESA, Archduchess of Austria, queen of Bohemia and Hungary (1740–1780). One of the "benevolent despots" of the eighteenth century, Maria Theresa was duchess of Luxembourg as well as ruler of the rest of the Austrian Netherlands. Although her father CHARLES VI had tried to assure her peaceful succession to the lands he ruled by the Pragmatic Sanction of 1723, agreed to by all the major European rulers, he had no sooner died than Maria Theresa had to defend her possessions against attacks by most of her neighbors, including the kings of France, Spain, Poland, and Prussia, and the electors of Bavaria and Saxony, all anxious to seize some part of her inheritance. Maria Theresa, only twenty-three years old when her father died, had to fight the War of the Austrian Succession (1741–1748) against the armies of most of the European powers, in which she was supported only by her own subjects and by Great Britain. During this war, French armies under the famous Marshal Saxe (Maurice of Saxony) invaded the Austrian Netherlands, winning a great battle at Fontenoy in 1745. The Duchy of Luxembourg was, fortunately, spared invasion during this war.

Maria Theresa held on to most of her major possessions except for Silesia, which Frederick the Great of Prussia had seized at the outset of the war and successfully defended against all Austrian counterattacks. She spent most of the next eight years successfully organizing a coalition against Frederick, and in the Seven Years War that followed (1756–1763), he was attacked by Austrian, French and Russian armies. In this war, Prussia was aided by Great Britain, but even with British help it was nearly destroyed, being saved only by the timely death of Empress Elizabeth of Russia, one of Frederick's most formidable enemies. Prussia did succeed in holding on to the province of Silesia, whose return to Austrian rule had been one of Maria Theresa's major objectives. Luxembourg was again left free from invasion during the Seven Years War.

With this second war over, Maria Theresa was able to spend the rest of her reign carrying out reforms in her various dominions. She reformed the judicial system, abolishing many of the cruelest punishments left over from the Middle Ages, including death by strangulation, drawing and quartering, and cutting off hands. To reform the finances of her empire, she carried out a census of all property and wealth—including that held by religious communities, the Church, and lay persons—and used it to set up a fair system of taxation.

Maria Theresa reformed education by requiring every parish to set up a primary school and by establishing a system of teacher examinations. Secondary education in the Duchy of Luxembourg had largely been provided by the JESUITS, but Maria Theresa suppressed this order throughout her domains in 1773 and replaced their schools with state schools. She also built roads, including a great highway linking Luxembourg with Brussels and TRIER, and encouraged industry by taxing imports from France and England. She stimulated agriculture by reducing feudal dues, lowering taxes on the export of grain, and exempting farm workers from military service.

Maria Theresa also spent money on repairing and improving the fortifications of the city of Luxembourg. She had two deep wells dug to supply the defenders with water during a siege, including the famous RED WELL, and had new CASEMATES dug under the BOCK in 1744–45. She never visited Luxembourg during her reign, but the duchy benefitted greatly from her reforms.

As a woman, Maria Theresa could not become Holy Roman Emperor, but she succeeded in having her husband, Francis I, elected emperor in 1745 and her son JOSEPH II elected upon the death of her husband in 1765. She kept power over her various realms in her own hands until her death, however.

MARIE-ADELAIDE, Grand Duchess of Luxembourg, 1912–1919. Marie-Adelaide succeeded to the throne at the age of seventeen, and was the first ruler since WENZEL I to have been born in Luxembourg. Her reign began amid an outburst of popular enthusiasm, but she had the misfortune of ruling during WORLD WAR I when Luxembourg was occupied by the German army. Marie-Adelaide kept her German advisors, received the Kaiser on a state visit to Luxembourg, and continued to visit her family and friends in Germany during the war. Since the majority of her subjects favored the cause of the Allies, her apparent pro-German sympathies did not enhance her popularity.

Unlike her father and grandfather, Marie-Adelaide was a Catholic, and some of her unpopularity also came from her bitter opposition to a law passed by the CHAMBER OF DEPUTIES in 1912 to secularize religious education, which she delayed putting into effect. She favored conservative politicians and appointed a conservative government in 1915, even though it did not have a majority in the Chamber of Deputies. When this government was overthrown, she dissolved the Chamber of Deputies and called for new elections, which were won by the parties of the left, which opposed her policies.

When the war ended, Marie-Adelaide was forced to abdicate (*See* CRISIS OF 1919). She was succeeded by her younger sister CHARLOTTE. After her abdication, Marie-Adelaide entered a convent, where she died in 1924.

MARIENTHAL. Site of a convent founded by COUNTESS ERMESINDE in 1235, "for noble ladies". Most famous of its noble ladies was YOLANDE of Vianden. Because she objected to a marriage arranged for her by her parents, she was shut up in one of the towers of the CASTLE OF VIANDEN, from which she escaped by knotting bedclothes together and sliding down them. She fled to the convent at Marienthal in 1238 and spent the rest of her life there, eventually becoming abbess. She died in 1283.

The convent was suppressed during the reforms of JOSEPH II. In 1890, the Pères Blancs (White Fathers) built a monastery on the site. This order was founded in 1872 by Charles Lavigerie, archbishop of Algiers and primate of Africa, to do missionary work in Africa. To make their work easier among the Moslems the fathers adopted Arab dress, including a white robe and burnoose and a red fez. At one time the order had over one hundred houses in Europe and Africa. The White Fathers did some of their missionary work in North Africa but most of it in equatorial Africa, from Timbuktu to Uganda. They were the first missionary order to penetrate many parts of central Africa.

The monastery at Marienthal prepared missionaries for service in English-speaking countries. It was still in operation in 1956 when BERYL MILES visited it, but was closed by the order in 1974. Since then, the monastery buildings have been used for a variety of purposes, including lay retreats, meetings, and conferences. They are empty most of the year, and thus subject to neglect and vandalism. A fire destroyed part of the monastery several years ago.

MARSHALL PLAN. A project by which the United States poured hundred of millions of dollars into western Europe after WORLD WAR II to rebuild the economies of the various nations and keep them from falling to communism. The plan got its name from General George Caitlett Marshall, chief of staff of the American armed forces during World War II, and secretary of state under President Harry S Truman. Marshall announced the plan during his speech at the Harvard commencement in 1948. Luxembourg joined the Marshall Plan in 1948, as did most of the western European nations, but the Soviet Union prevented the eastern European states from joining. The Czechoslovak government, which initially had asked to join, was overthrown by a communist coup in 1948 and withdrew its request for membership.

By 1951, the level of productivity in western Europe had reached prewar levels, largely due to the huge influx of American aid brought about by the Marshall Plan.

MARY OF BURGUNDY. Only daughter of CHARLES THE BOLD, duke of Burgundy. At the age of twenty, she succeeded her father after his death on the battlefield of Nancy in 1477. Louis XI of France seized some of her father's possessions in France, but Mary held on to Franche-Comté and the Burgundian possessions in the Netherlands, including the Duchy of Luxembourg, through her marriage to MAXIMILIAN OF AUSTRIA that same year. Maximilian brought Mary the aid she needed to repel the French siege of Luxembourg in 1479 and to defeat the feudal lords in her territories who had rebelled against her in support of the French.

Mary and Maximilian were popular rulers in Luxembourg, restoring the privileges of the towns, monasteries, and corporations of which PHILIP THE GOOD had deprived them.

Mary died at the age of twenty-five from a hunting accident, when the couple's only son, PHILIP THE FAIR, was four years old. Maximilian assumed the regency and ruled in his son's name but had considerable difficulty in maintaining his rule after Mary's death. The French succeeded in annexing several of the Burgundian lands, although Maximilian's victories over the French in several battles forced them to restore the territories they had seized. Maximilian became Holy Roman Emperor in 1493, and died in 1519.

Mary's marriage to Maximilian of Austria, began the process by which Luxembourg fell into the hands of the Hapsburgs of Austria and Spain.

MASONIC LODGE. Located in the old city, near the FISHMARKET. The building dates from 1655, and served from 1655 to 1795 as the seat of the merchants' guild. The Masons have met there ever since 1818.

MAXIMILIAN OF AUSTRIA. Maximilian became sole ruler of the Burgundian possessions in 1482 upon the death of his wife, MARY OF BURGUNDY, daughter of CHARLES THE BOLD. In 1493, when he was elected Holy Roman Emperor, he appointed his son, PHILIP THE FAIR, his regent in the

Netherlands and the other Burgundian possessions. When Philip died in 1506, his son Charles, grandson of Maximilian and Mary, became ruler of the Burgundian territories, including Luxembourg, at the age of six. Charles was a native of the Netherlands, born in Ghent in 1500. During his childhood, the Burgundian possessions in the Low Countries were ruled by Charles's aunt, Margaret of Austria, acting as regent. (*See also* CHARLES V)

MELUSINA. The heroine of the best-known Luxembourg folktale. According to the legend, SIGEFROI, the founder of Luxembourg, saw a beautiful girl while hunting near a ruined castle on the BOCK, but she instantly vanished when he appeared. Sigefroi persisted in wooing her and eventually won her consent to marry him. The only condition to the marriage was that she be given a room of her own to which she could retire every Saturday night, and to which Sigefroi would never attempt to gain access. Overcome by curiosity, however, Sigefroi entered her room one Saturday night and discovered that his wife was a mermaid. Melusina disappeared into the solid rock of the castle, from which she emerges every seven years with a golden key in her mouth, hoping that someone will rescue her. Since no one has rescued her yet, she spends her time sewing a shirt of fine linen, adding a stitch every seven years. If she finishes it before she is rescued, the castle and the town will vanish in a clap of thunder.

The legend resembles similar stories that pervade European folklore, and it is unlikely to have originated in Luxembourg. More likely, it has been adapted by storytellers to local circumstances.

MEROVINGIANS. A dynasty of Frankish kings descended from CLOVIS, who became king of the SALIAN FRANKS in 481. The Merovingians derived their name from an ancestor of Clovis, perhaps his grandfather Merovech, about whom little is known. Clovis extended Merovingian rule over most of Gaul as well as the Frankish lands in West Germany and AUSTRASIA, but followed the Frankish custom of dividing his kingdom among his sons, so that within a short time the Frankish lands were once more divided into separate kingdoms.

The later Merovingians declined rapidly in power, becoming mere puppets of their hereditary mayors of the palace who, in the end, deposed them and took over their thrones as well as their power.

MERSCH. A small town about twenty kilometers north of Luxembourg city, where the ALZETTE, MAMER, and Eisch Rivers join. It has been inhabited since pre-Roman times, and Stone-Age tools and weapons have been discovered there.

A Roman graveyard and the remains of a large Roman villa on a ridge called Mersch-Mies have been excavated. The Romans called the area "Marisca", refering to the marshes which surround the town when the rivers overflow.

Mersch is a small market town, with a large abattoir and meat-packing plant as well as grain silos. It is on the railroad line from Luxembourg to Liège as well as on the highway from Luxembourg to ETTELBRUCK and the north.

A medieval castle and an eighteenth century bell-tower, the tower of St. Michael (called locally the "Hexenturm" or witches tower), all that is left of a church that was destroyed by lightning in 1851, are among the attractions of Mersch, and there are many footpaths in the surrounding hills. Mersch is the eastern terminus of the VALLEY OF THE SEVEN CASTLES.

Mersch has been overrun and destroyed by a number of invaders over the centuries, beginning with the HUNS, and continuing with the Burgundians, Swedes, and French. MARSHAL BOUFFLERS battered the often-restored castle with his cannon in 1683. It was purchased and restored by Count Jean-Frederick d'Autel, governor of Luxembourg, in 1700, but fell into ruins later. In 1975, the national government purchased the castle and began the work of restoring it again.

On a hill above Mersch stands a column erected in 1939 to celebrate the hundredth anniversary of the Grand Duchy's independence. The Germans destroyed it during their occupation of Luxembourg during WORLD WAR II, but it was rebuilt after the war. A poem by NIKOLAUS WELTER, a native of Mersch, is engraved on the base of the monument.

MERTERT. Luxembourg's port on the MOSELLE, opened in 1966. The port handles goods shipped from and delivered to the Grand Duchy along the network of rivers and canals that link northern and southern Europe. The port has its own docks and warehouse facilities on a site totaling 60 hectares (about 132 acres) owned by the Luxembourg state, but it is operated by a mixed company, the Society of the River Port of Mertert, in which the government owns 50 percent of the shares; the other 50 percent is owned by companies and banks. ARBED is the largest private stockholder, with 36.2 percent of the shares. The site is served by 16.5 kilometers of railway and 5 kilometers of road, which connect it to the national and international rail and road networks.

About a quarter of the freight landed at Mertert is trans-shipped to other countries, including the frontier regions of Belgium, France, and Germany. Approximately one million tons of goods are handled by the port annually. Its principal customer is the Luxembourg steel industry, but coal, cement, sand, oil, construction materials and agricultural products are also handled. An industrial estate for companies wishing access to the waterways has recently been opened on the site.

MESTA, PEARL. Appointed ambassador to Luxembourg by President Harry S Truman, Pearl Mesta was undoubtedly the most popular American ambassador ever to serve in the Grand Duchy. Her winning personality, warm hospitality, and the famous picnics she sponsored every year on the Fourth of July won the hearts of the Luxembourg people. She is the thinly disguised heroine, played by Ethel Merman, of Irving Berlin's musical *Call Me Madam*.

MIAMI UNIVERSITY EUROPEAN CENTER. The Miami University European Center, which celebrated its twenty-fifth anniversary in 1993, offers a junior year abroad to selected students from Miami University in Oxford, Ohio. Students live with Luxembourgish families and attend classes in European history, international relations, French, German and other subjects at the center on avenue Monterey. Approximately eighty to one hundred students from the United States participate in this program every year.

Attached to the center is the Miami University Library, whose collection was begun with the donation of a number of books by the United States Information Service. Anyone in Luxembourg may apply for a library card and use the library's facilities.

The center participates in a program which awards five scholarships to Luxembourg students each year to study at Miami University's Ohio campus and another program in which a certain number of Luxembourg students are selected to study and travel in the United States each summer.

The center was renamed the John E. Dolibois European

Center in 1986 in honor of the former American ambassador to Luxembourg, JOHN E. DOLIBOIS. The present director of the center (1996) is Ekkehard Stiller.

MIDDLE STONE AGE (MESOLITHIC AGE). In western Europe, the dates of the Mesolithic Age fall roughly between 9000 and 5300 B.C., and seem to have been distinguished by a marked rise in average temperatures and the spread of forests. Deer and elk replaced the woolly mammoths, rhinoceri, and aurochs of earlier times, and man hunted with bows and arrows and domesticated dogs. Although weapons and tools had been made of wood and bone as well as stone in Paleolithic times, the use of wood and bone increased during Mesolithic times.

Mesolithic man buried his dead, and a Mesolithic tomb has been discovered in the Müllerthal (*See* LITTLE SWITZERLAND). At Oetrange, animal bones and tools from both late Paleolithic and Mesolithic times have been found. (*See also* OLD STONE AGE and NEW STONE AGE)

MILES, BERYL. British travel writer who spent several months in Luxembourg in 1955 and wrote a book called *Attic in Luxembourg*, which gave an interesting portrait of the Grand Duchy as it was then.

MINETTE. A region in southern Luxembourg next to the French border, once rich in iron ore. This part of the country is also known as the "Terre Rouge" because of the red color imparted to the soil by the iron oxides that permeate it. The iron ore is rich in phosphorus, which makes it difficult to smelt. The introduction of a new steel-making process by an Englishman during the nineteenth century made Luxembourg a major steel-producing country, and thus a valuable prize during both world wars, when it was occupied by the Germans. The last iron mine in the Minette was closed in 1981, and Luxembourg now imports iron ore for her steel mills from Lorraine. (*See also* ARBED, IRON AND STEEL MANUFACTURE, and THOMAS, SIDNEY GILCHRIST)

MODEL OF THE FORTRESS (MAQUETTE DE LA FORTERESSE). Reached by a side entrance to the CERCLE MUNICIPAL, a model of the fortress of Luxembourg is on display daily. A Sound and Light show traces the history of the fortress from its beginnings to its final development during the first part of the nineteenth century. Tapes in English, French,

German, and Dutch are played at fixed hours during the day, and special showings for groups can be arranged.

The original model of the fortress, of which this is a copy, is located in the Musée des Invalides in Paris and is part of a collection of models of fortified cities begun by LOUIS XIV. Another copy is located in the NATIONAL MUSEUM.

MONDORF-LES-BAINS. A town on the French border, the only spa in Luxembourg. Medicinal springs with water rich in sulfur were discovered here during the twentieth century. Twenty years ago it was a typical turn-of-the-century watering place, with a modest thermal establishment, an old casino, and a number of old hotels and restaurants, as well as a beautiful park and garden where band concerts were performed on Sunday afternoons. In recent years, government and private money has been invested in building a modern clinic and thermal establishment, with a heated pool, badminton courts and other athletic facilities. An expensive new casino has been built, which attracts a prosperous clientele from France and Germany as well as from Luxembourg. Mondorf has lost much of its old charm, although it still has its gardens, some elegant buildings (of which the Orangerie in the park is the most attractive), and a fairly pleasant atmosphere.

The old casino, which still stands, was used as a place of confinement for some of the top Nazi leaders, including Hermann Goering, for a time after WORLD WAR II, before they were tried at Nuremburg.

MOSELLE. A major European river that rises in the Vosges in eastern France, flows north past Nancy, Metz, and THION-VILLE, then turns and flows in a northeasterly direction until it joins the Rhine at Coblenz. During a small part of its course, the Moselle forms the border between Luxembourg and the Saarland in Germany.

The Moselle was canalized between 1956 and 1964 and is navigable for a good part of its length. Barge traffic can pass down the Rhine and Moselle, then be carried by canal to the Rhone, down which it can travel to the Mediterranean. The Moselle is thus an important link in the river transportation system of Europe. Early counts of Luxembourg, including HENRY VII, set up stations on the Moselle in an attempt to collect tolls on the river traffic, which brought them into conflict with their neighbors in TRIER.

The Moselle is the wine district of Luxembourg. (*See also* WINE MAKING)

MUSIC CONSERVATORIES (CONSERVATOIRES). Luxembourg and several other cities in the Grand Duchy have conservatories that offer instruction in vocal and instrumental music. Secondary students attend classes at the conservatories Tuesday and Thursday afternoons, when they are free from classes at their other schools. The cost of instruction is minimal, and the conservatories are open to students attending foreign schools in Luxembourg as well as to students attending Luxembourg schools.

All entering students must take and pass a course in *solfegge*. This course is advertised as being conducted in French, but instruction may be conducted in LETZEBUERGESCH since both instructors and students are more at home in that language. The instructors generally make every effort to help foreign students who don't speak Letzebuergesch, so this is not much of a problem. Individual instruction in voice and in the various musical instruments is of very high quality.

The Conservatoire in Luxembourg was formerly located in a set of historic buildings in the Old City, once the Refuge House of the ABBEY OF ORVAL, but is now located in a modern building in the western suburb of Merl, close to the ATHENEE GRAND-DUCAL, with a splendid auditorium and fine practice rooms.

NAPOLEON I. Napoleon Bonaparte seized control of France by a *coup d' état* in 1799, becoming first consul, and was crowned emperor of the French in 1804. When Napoleon came to power, Luxembourg was already a part of France, having been conquered in 1795 by the armies of the French Revolution.

Napoleon was not as unpopular in Luxembourg as his predecessors, the agents of the French Republic, had been. To begin with, he put an end to religious persecution and concluded a concordat with the pope in 1801 which reestablished the free exercise of the Catholic religion and restored the legal status of the church. Since Luxembourg was devoutly Catholic, these measures were popular there, as was his coronation as emperor by Pope Pius VII in 1804.

In 1804, after his coronation, Napoleon paid a state visit to Luxembourg, at which he was given the keys to the city. Told that one of the keys was normally suspended from the right hand of a statue of the Virgin Mary, he restored it at once, declaring that it was in good hands. During his visit, Napoleon stayed at the former city hall, then the seat of the French prefecture, now the GRAND DUCAL PALACE. He made a gift to the city of the former church and convent of the Franciscans along with their gardens. The gardens were shortly afterwards made into a public square named the Place Napoléon. Today it is called the PLACE GUILLAUME.

Over fourteen thousand Luxembourgers served in Napoleon's armies, of whom nine thousand never returned. In addition, the costs of Napoleon's wars and the Continental System he established bore heavily upon Luxembourg as well as the rest of the French territories. Nevertheless, after Napoleon's defeat at the Battle of Leipzig in 1813 and the crossing of the Rhine by the Allies' armies in 1814, Luxembourg and its French garrison held out against two attempts by Hessian troops to capture it, before the French commander decided to surrender.

Napoleon's greatest contribution to Luxembourg was the CODE NAPOLEON, the law code which forms the basis of Luxembourg's present legal system. He remains popular today. The story goes that the statue of WILLIAM II which adorns the Place Guillaume was intended to bear a plaque commemorating him as one of the victors of the Battle of Waterloo, but that this plaque was deliberately left off, because Luxembourgers had fought in Napoleon's defeated army.

NAPOLEON III. Nephew of NAPOLEON I and son of Napoleon's brother Louis Bonaparte, whom Napoleon I had made king of Holland. Louis Napoleon, as he was known in his early years, was elected president of the Second French Republic after the Revolution of 1848, and declared himself emperor of the French as Napoleon III in 1851.

Napoleon III attempted to purchase the Grand Duchy of Luxembourg from WILLIAM III in 1866. (*See* CRISIS OF 1866–67) William III agreed to the sale and a price of five million Dutch florins was agreed upon (and probably paid). At this point Otto von Bismarck, the Prussian chancellor, came out publicly against the purchase, although he had privately agreed to it earlier.

War between France and Prussia seemed likely, but a compromise was reached by the Great Powers at a conference in London by which the Grand Duchy would remain under the rule of William III, but the Prussian garrison of the fortress of

Luxembourg would be withdrawn and the fortfications dismantled. (*See also* SECOND TREATY OF LONDON, 1867)

NARROW-GAUGE RAILROADS. In additon to its two standard-
gauge railroads, Luxembourg built a system of narrow-gauge
lines to serve areas not reached by the other two railroads.
By 1940, this narrow-gauge rail network, operated by the
Luxembourg state, comprised 139 kilometers of track. The
narrow-gauge lines were gradually eliminated after WORLD
WAR II, although one of them was still operating in 1954.
One narrow-gauge line still runs old-fashioned steam trains in
Rodange on Sundays and holidays. (*See also* RAILROAD
SYSTEM)

NATIONAL LIBRARY (BIBLIOTHEQUE NATIONALE). The
National Library is the inheritor of the first public library in
Luxembourg, founded by the French authorities in 1798, when
Luxembourg was the DEPARTMENT OF FORESTS. It was
given the name Bibliotheque Nationale in 1899. Since 1973 it
has been located in the buildings of the former ATHENEE
GRAND-DUCAL next to the CATHEDRAL OF NOTRE
DAME.

The National Library has a collection of more than eight
hundred thousand volumes in its main buildings and in its
annexes on the KIRCHBERG and the boulevard Prince Henri.
Its rare book collection contains 140 early printed books, 3500
maps and plans dating before 1950, 200 atlases, including 50
very old ones, and 250 historic and artistic book bindings. Its
archives of works of art contain 800 early drawings and portraits, a collection of 15,000 postcards of the Grand Duchy,
and 20,000 posters. It also contains more than 800 manuscripts
dating from the ninth to the twentieth centuries, including some
of the illuminated manuscripts of the ABBEY OF ECHTER-
NACH and the ABBEY OF ORVAL, as well as the works of
many of the best-known Luxembourg writers.

The present librarian is Jul Christophory, former professor
at the Lyceé Michel Rodange, and author of a well-known
textbook for teaching LETZEBUERGESCH.

NATIONAL MOVEMENT (NATIONAL BEWEGONG). A small
antiforeign political party which entered candidates in a national election for the first time on 12 June 1994. The National
Movement wanted to halt immigration (impossible under present treaties as far as citizens of other countries belonging to

the EUROPEAN UNION are concerned); set up customs and gendarmerie posts at every border crossing (removed from the borders of all European Union countries except Great Britain on 1 January 1993); expand the teaching of LETZEBUERG-ESCH in the schools; provide more housing at affordable prices for native Luxembourgers (they blame the current high rents and purchase prices on the presence of foreigners); force companies in Luxembourg to hire more Luxembourgers; put an end to the large number of workers from France, Belgium, and Germany who cross the borders every day to work in the Grand Duchy; and prevent foreigners from voting in local elections (made posssible in 1993 under the terms of the TREATY OF MAASTRICHT, although restricted to citizens of other countries in the European Union).

Since most of what the National Movement wants cannot be achieved without repealing parts of the various treaties governing the European Union, the National Movement's foreign policy calls for a looser European Union rather than a closer federation. In that respect they resemble the Euroskeptics in the Conservative Party in Great Britain.

The National Movement cannot be compared to the extreme right-wing movements in France (the National Front under Le Pen), the neo-Nazi Republican Party in Germany, or the neo-Fascist party in Italy. They are not racist and they do not advocate or practice violence. They fly in the face of most political sentiment in Luxembourg, moreover, because the Grand Duchy has been one of the strongest supporters of a closer European Union and is committed to the free movement of people and goods throughout Europe. In the ELECTIONS OF 1994, the National Movement gained only about 3 percent of the total vote in the Grand Duchy, and did not win a single seat in the CHAMBER OF DEPUTIES. The movement was disbanded in December 1995.

NATIONAL MUSEUM (Musée de l'Etat.) The National Museum is located on the north side of the FISHMARKET in the older part of the city. It contains an excellent collection of Roman, Frankish, and medieval artifacts found on Luxembourg soil, Gallic and Roman coins, and even the tomb of a Frankish warrior. It also has paintings, drawings and sculptures by Luxembourgish and foreign artists, and collections of antique furniture, clocks, firearms, and other weapons. The natural history section has stuffed specimens of animals and birds found in the Grand Duchy and other parts of the world.

The archaeological section of the museum has carried out digs all over the country and has made many important discoveries. The museum publishes books about these finds, about the museum's collections, and about some aspects of Luxembourg history.

NATO. The North Atlantic Treaty Organization, formed in 1949 to combat the perceived menace to western Europe posed by the Soviet Union after WORLD WAR II. The United States was the principal power behind the organization of NATO and provided most of its military strength.

The Grand Duchy of Luxembourg was proclaimed a permanently neutral state by the terms of the SECOND TREATY OF LONDON, signed in 1867, and guaranteed by the major European powers including Germany. German violations of Luxembourg's neutrality during WORLD WAR I and WORLD WAR II convinced Luxembourg of the uselessness of neutrality as a foreign policy, and so it joined NATO in 1949 and contributed a battalion to its armed forces. This battalion serves with the Belgian army but is called back to the Grand Duchy to take part in various ceremonial occasions.

Luxembourg also serves as the headquarters of the NATO MAINTENANCE AND SUPPLY AGENCY. It has sent volunteers to participate in NATO and United Nations operations in Bosnia-Herzegovina as well.

The principal headquarters of NATO forces is at Mons, Belgium.

NATO MAINTENANCE AND SUPPLY AGENCY (NAMSA). Located in Capellen, NAMSA is the center for planning the logistics and supply of NATO forces in Europe. Representatives of all the NATO countries, including the United States, are employed at NAMSA, most of them seconded for duty by their own governments.

Besides NAMSA, the United States army has two depots in southern Luxembourg for the storage and supply of weapons and other items that might be needed by American forces in Europe.

NEUSTRIA. The "new lands" conquered by CLOVIS and his Frankish successors during the sixth century as opposed to the "old lands" the FRANKS had occupied during the second through fifth centuries. The principal distinction between Neustria and the lands that the Franks had settled earlier was that

Neustria had a large Gallo-Roman population which spoke vulgar Latin, the tongue which eventially developed into modern French. In the old lands, the Franks had settled in large enough numbers so that their Germanic language prevailed.

Neustria became a separate kingdom for a time, comprising most of what is today modern France and southern Belgium (Wallonia) where the language spoken is French, but eventually it was united with AUSTRASIA into a single Frankish kingdom. (*See also* RHINELAND FRANKS and SALIAN FRANKS)

NEW STONE AGE (NEOLITHIC AGE). The New Stone Age is distinguished from the OLD and MIDDLE STONE AGES largely by the development of agriculture and the domestication of animals, which began around 8000 B.C. in the Middle East on the Iranian uplands and spread in all directions from that center. Neolithic culture seems to have spread to western Europe from the Danube valley by approximately 5300 B.C. Wheat, barley, millet, and rye were grown as well as other crops. The potter's wheel and pottery were introduced, and more settled communities developed. Flax was cultivated, and cloth and leather replaced animal skins as garments, although animal skins continued to be worn in colder climates. Sheep, goats, cattle, and pigs were domesticated.

Many Neolithic sites have been found in Luxembourg, including a Neolithic camp with an encircling wall at Beaufort and a Neolithic tomb in the Vichten-Grosbous area. Neolithic sites are often overlaid by later BRONZE AGE settlements.

NOPENNY, MARCEL (1877–1966). Luxembourg author who spent more than ten years in German prisons and camps during WORLD WAR I and WORLD WAR II. He wrote in French, and it was his aim to fight the Germanization of Luxembourg by demonstrating that Luxembourg was also a bastion of French culture.

Marcel Nopenny lived in the Chateau Bofferdange, which was taken over by the Germans during World War II. They destroyed or took almost everything in the house, including his books, pictures, manuscripts, and photographs. They threw almost all his possessions into a huge bonfire on the lawn, which burned for three days. They also drank, within a few days, the entire contents of his four-thousand-bottle wine cellar.

NORTH GERMAN CONFEDERATION. In 1867, Chancellor Otto von Bismarck, following Prussia's victory over Austria in the Seven Weeks War, established the North German Confederation, from which Austria and four states in south Germany were excluded. Luxembourg, although a member of the GERMAN CONFEDERATION formed in 1815, did not join the North German Confederation, which, with the addition of the four South German states, transformed itself into the Second German Empire in 1871 after the Franco-Prussian War. The king of Prussia became emperor of Germany. (*See also* CRISIS OF 1866–67 and SECOND TREATY OF LONDON)

NORTHMEN. The Northmen who ravaged the coasts of England, Scotland, Ireland, and France during the ninth and tenth centuries, making permanent settlements in each country (such as the Danelaw in England and Normandy in France), made raids deep into France and Lorraine as well. From a camp they established on the Meuse, they made incursions into what later became Luxembourg, pillaging and burning the abbeys at PRUM, St. Hubert, ECHTERNACH and, on Easter Day in 882, the ABBEY OF ST. MAXIMIN IN TRIER. They were met at REMICH by an army hastily assembled by the bishops of Trier and Metz, Count Abelard of Lorraine, and the lay abbot of Echternach. The Normans defeated this army, killing Bishop Walo of Metz, and sacked Remich, but the losses they suffered were heavy enough to prevent them from carrying out their planned attack on Metz. They retired to their camp on the Meuse, where they were defeated the following year by an army led by Arnulf of Carinthia, king of the East Franks, a descendent of CHARLEMAGNE who claimed the overlordship of Lorraine by virtue of the TREATY OF MERSEN, which divided LOTHARINGIA between the West Franks and the East Franks in 870.

OCTAVE. An annual spring fair in honor of the Holy Virgin, protectress of Luxembourg. It originally was held over an eight-day period, but has proved somewhat flexible, having now expanded to at least two weeks. It is held on the PLACE GUILLAUME in front of the LUXEMBOURG CITY HALL, within sight of both the CATHEDRAL OF NOTRE DAME and the GRAND DUCAL PALACE. It consists largely, like most similar events in Luxembourg, of booths devoted to eating and drinking.

Each of the cantons in Luxembourg has a day allotted to it

The Grand Ducal Palace in Luxembourg City (sixteenth-century Spanish town hall).

The Cathedral of Notre Dame in Luxembourg. Next to it stands the seventeenth-century Jesuit college, now the home of the National Library.

Statue of William II, King of the Netherlands and Grand Duke of Luxembourg (1840–1849).

The Pont Adolf, spanning the gorge of the Petrusse at Luxembourg.

The "Gëlle Fra" (Golden Lady) atop the Victory Monument in Luxembourg City. The statue honors the Luxembourgers who died fighting on the Allied side in the First and Second World Wars.

One of the Trémont lions, which guard the entrance to the nineteenth-century
town hall on the Place Guillaume in Luxembourg.

The "Denzelt" at Echternach, which served as both a grain market and a hall of
justice.

The eleventh-century feudal castle at Vianden.

Ruins of the feudal castle at Useldange.

The Orangerie at Echternach, which served during the eighteenth century as the home of the abbotts of the Benedictine monastery founded by Saint Willibrord in 698.

at the Octave. Residents of the cantons walk through the night to Luxembourg, attend early mass at the cathedral, and then have breakfast on the Place Guillaume. On the last day of the Octave, the GRAND DUKE and his family attend mass, and then walk to the palace, where they appear on the balcony to be cheered by their loyal subjects.

The number of people who actually walk through the night to reach the cathedral gets smaller every year, but large numbers of people, including many foreigners, still attend the Octave at least once during the fortnight.

OLD STONE AGE (PALEOLITHIC AGE). Stone tools and weapons from both the Mousterian Period (c. 500,000–150,000 B.C.) and the Aurignacian Period (c. 150,000–35,000 B.C.) have been found in Luxembourg, as well as the bones of animals such as the aurochs, rhinoceros, and woolly mammoth. Paleolithic sites have been discovered in the valleys of the SURE and MOSELLE Rivers, as well as in the MINETTE and at Burglinster. The Mousterian period is the era of Neanderthal Man who roamed western Europe during the period when Mousterian culture flourished. The Aurignacian culture is thought to have been introduced into Europe by later immigrants such as the Cro-Magnons. Cave paintings, which may date from Aurignacian times, have been discovered at Asbach and Loschbour.

During the Old Stone Age, man lived by hunting, fishing, and gathering and populations tended to be sparse. Paleolithic man followed the migrations of game animals, and his dwellings, in caves or in the open, were temporary, although certain sites were constantly revisited. (*See also* MIDDLE STONE AGE and NEW STONE AGE)

OTTO I (OTTO THE GREAT). Son of Henry the Fowler, duke of Saxony who was elected king of Germany in 918. Otto succeeded his father in 936, and was crowned king in Aachen, CHARLEMAGNE's ancient capital. Otto was determined to restore the empire of Charlemagne, and succeeded insofar as Germany and central Europe were concerned, although he was never able to add France to his dominions.

As elected king of the Germans, Otto was considered by the other German dukes not as a reigning monarch, but only as first among equals. The other dukes resisted Otto's attempts to establish his rule over them, so Otto turned to the church for support, forming a close alliance with the wealthy Benedictine abbeys and the bishops and archbishops who controlled the extensive lands of the church in Germany. The church supplied Otto not only with knights to serve in his armies but also educated clerks to administer his domains. To assure himself of their cooperation, Otto had his own relations and close supporters elected bishops and abbots whenever an episcopal see or abbacy fell vacant.

Otto invaded Italy in 951, ostensibly to rescue Adelaide of Burgundy, a young widow who was being held prisoner by Berengar II. Otto not only rescued her but married her, and assumed the title King of the Lombards held by Charlemagne and his successors. (*See* IRON CROWN OF THE LOMBARDS)

Returning to Germany, Otto successfully put down several uprisings against him and then, in 955, defeated the MAGYARS at the battle of Lechfeld, after which he was referred to as Otto the Great. In 961, Otto returned to Italy, where he was crowned Roman emperor in 962 by Pope John XII, who took an oath of fealty to Otto at the same time. Otto later deposed John XII for violating this oath and forced the Romans to elect his own nominee, Leo VIII, in his place.

Otto returned to Germany in 965, but when the Romans rebelled against him and his appointed pope, he returned and sacked the city in 966. Otto died in 973, having established his rule over both Germany and Italy.

SIGEFROI, the founder of Luxembourg, took care to maintain good relations with Otto and his successors who were the overlords of Lorraine. In 950, he received ECHTERNACH from Otto I as a royal fief. In 963, when Sigefroi acquired the land along the ALZETTE where he built his castle from the ABBEY OF ST. MAXIMIN IN TRIER, one of the witnesses to the title was Otto's brother Bruno, archbishop of Cologne. Sigefroi accompanied Otto I on his invasion of Italy in 966, and helped suppress an uprising against Otto by the Greeks (the adherents of the Eastern Roman Emperor). He also accompanied his son, OTTO II on his invasion of Italy in 981.

OTTO II (955–983). Son of OTTO I, Otto II was elected king of Germany in 961 and crowned joint emperor by Pope John XIII in 967. In 972 he married Theophano, daughter of the eastern Roman emperor. Having been crowned during his father's lifetime, he was able to succeed him directly upon his death in 973 as both king and emperor. During his reign he had to put down uprisings against his rule in Germany and resist an invasion of Lorraine by King Lothair II of France. In 981 he returned to Rome where he restored Benedict VII to the papal throne. In 982 he launched an attack against Apulia where the Saracens had gained a foothold on the Italian mainland, but he was defeated and forced to retreat to Rome. In 983, after holding an imperial diet at Verona to plan a fresh attack on the Saracens, he returned to Rome, where he secured the election of one of his supporters, Peter of Pavia, to the vacant papal throne as John XIV. He died in Rome the same year.

SIGEFROI of Luxembourg accompanied Otto II on his Italian expedition and was with him when he died. He was asked by Otto to intervene with the French king to maintain the alliance between the royal houses of Germany and France, but failed in his mission when Lothair II saw in the emperor's death a new opportunity to seize Lorraine. Sigefroi and his nephew, Godfrey of Verdun, saved Verdun from capture, but both he and his nephew were taken prisoner shortly afterward and held captive until 985, when they were released by the intercession of Hugh Capet, count of Paris, who became king of France two years later.

OTTO III (980–1002). At the age of three, Otto III succeeded his father OTTO II as king of the Germans. He was crowned in Aix-la-Chapelle (Aachen), CHARLEMAGNE's capital, in 983, but was seized by Henry the Quarrelsome of Bavaria, who claimed the right to act as regent, in 984. Opposition from the other dukes forced Henry to release Otto to the custody of his mother, Theophano, who governed Germany as regent until her death in 991, after which a council took over Otto's guardianship until he was declared of age in 995. Otto III took part in wars against the Bohemians and the Wends even before he came of age, and in 996 he invaded Italy by invitation of Pope John XV. At Pavia, Otto received the IRON CROWN OF THE LOMBARDS, the crown held by Charlemagne and by OTTO I.

By the time Otto III reached Rome, John XV had died, so Otto raised his cousin, Bruno of Carinthia, to the papal throne as Gregory V, and was, in turn, crowned emperor by Gregory.

Having been crowned emperor, Otto III returned to Germany. After his departure, Gregory V was deposed and driven from Rome by the Romans, who elected a new pope, John XVI. Otto returned to Italy in 998, restored Gregory V to the papal throne, and put the leader of the uprising to death. Upon the death of Gregory V in 999, Otto appointed his former tutor, Gerbert, pope as Sylvester II. Sylvester II reigned for only four years (999–1003), but did a great deal to restore the prestige of the papacy. The greatest scholar of his time, he collected old manuscripts, introduced the use of arabic numerals, and built clocks and astronomical instruments.

Otto III served as patron of the ABBEY OF ECHTER-NACH and presented the abbey with a splendid leather book cover, ornamented in gold and studded with precious stones, produced in TRIER. The cover was used to bind the famous GOLDEN BOOK OF ECHTERNACH, an edition of the Gospels produced in the scriptorium of the Abbey of Echternach during the eleventh century.

OUR LADY, CONSOLATRICE OF THE AFFLICTED. In 1666, the city council of Luxembourg, faced with the ravages of the bubonic plague and the threat to the city posed by a French army encamped on the frontiers, chose the Virgin Mary, Consolatrice of the Afflicted, as patroness of the city. A great procession in her honor was held on 10 October 1666 and annually thereafter. Later, the procession was transferred to the fifth Sunday after Easter. (*See also* OCTAVE)

PARMA (ALEXANDER FARNESE, DUKE OF PARMA). A nephew of PHILIP II who was sent to the Netherlands in 1578 to put down opposition to the king. By a policy of alternate conciliation and military victory, he succeeded in restoring most of the southern Netherlands to Spanish rule. By 1585 he had captured Antwerp and was preparing to conquer the seven northern provinces that were still in rebellion. His plan to complete the reconquest of the Netherlands had to be postponed, when, after the execution of Mary, Queen of Scots, Philip II decided that priority must be given to the conquest of England. The failure of the Spanish Armada in 1588 put an end to any possibility that Spain would be able to reconquer the northern Netherlands.

The southern Netherlands, which had been reconquered by the dukes of ALVA and Parma, remained under the control of Spain as the Spanish Netherlands until 1713. The Duchy of Luxembourg was included in the Spanish Netherlands.

PARTITIONS. (*See* THREE PARTITIONS OF LUXEMBOURG)

PATTON, GENERAL GEORGE S., JR. Patton is a national hero in Luxembourg. When the Germans under FIELD MARSHAL GERD VON RUNDSTEDT launched their winter offensive across northern Luxembourg and Belgium in 1944, the head-quarters of Patton's Third Army was in Metz, some forty miles south of the Luxembourg border. He immediately swung a substantial part of his army north, racing across Luxembourg and western Belgium in time to relieve the 101st Airborne Division at Bastogne and pinch off the German salient. His prompt action drove the Germans back across the German border and liberated the Grand Duchy a second time.

A statue of General Patton has been erected in ETTEL-BRUCK next to a memorial to the American liberators and an American tank. His fieldglasses in his hand, Patton faces east, the direction of the enemy, in death as he did in life.

Although Patton died after the war in an automobile accident in Germany, he was buried according to his own wishes in the AMERICAN MILITARY CEMETERY IN HAMM among the troops he had commanded during the liberation of Luxembourg.

A parade is held in Ettelbruck on the second Sunday of July every year in honor of the liberation of the city by American troops. In addition, the film *Patton,* starring George C. Scott, was shown annually at the Victory Theatre in Luxembourg until the theatre was pulled down a few years ago to make way for a bank. It is still shown from time to time at the CINEMATEQUE MUNICIPALE.

PEPIN I (PEPIN THE SHORT). Founder of the Carolingian dynasty, Pepin succeeded his father CHARLES MARTEL as mayor of the palace in NEUSTRIA in 741. His older brother Carloman became mayor of the palace in AUSTRASIA at the same time, but in 747 Carloman retired to a monastery and Pepin became the sole ruler of the FRANKS, as mayor of the palace to Childeric III, last of the Merovingian kings. In 751, Pope Zacharias, menaced by the Lombards of northern Italy, recognized Pepin as king of the Franks. Pepin deposed Childeric III, who retired to a monastery. Pepin then had himself elected king by the Frankish nobles and crowned at Soissons in 752. In 754, Pope Stephen III, successor to Pope Zacharias, traveled to Châlons in France and offically crowned Pepin as king of the Franks, recognized his dynasty as the sole ruling family of the Franks, and gave him the title of Roman patrician.

In turn Pepin invaded Italy in 755 with a Franklish army, defeated the Lombards, and confirmed the pope's rule over a large section of central Italy, the famous Donation of Pepin, which created what later came to be called the States of the Church. By this donation of land, the pope became a temporal as well as a spiritual ruler.

Pepin spent the rest of his reign subduing his enemies in different parts of the Frankish kingdom. Upon his death, he ruled all the lands from the English Channel to the Mediterranean and from the Rhine to the Pyrenees, with the single exception of Brittany.

PEPIN OF HERSTAL. Mayor of the palace to the Merovingian kings of AUSTRASIA. After a series of wars against his rivals, the mayors of the palace of NEUSTRIA, he became sole mayor of the palace of the entire Frankish realm in 687. His illegitmate son, CHARLES MARTEL, succeeded him.

PESCATORE, JEAN-PIERRE (1793–1855). A nineteenth century merchant who played a leading part in the industrial and political development of the Grand Duchy. Among his benefactions was the Foundation Pescatore, built at a cost of 400,000 francs to serve as a retirement home for the elderly. The former family mansion in Luxembourg was left to the city as an art museum, the Musée Pescatore. During the renovations of the GRAND DUCAL PALACE in 1993–94, the Musée Pescatore served temporarily as the palace.

PETER OF ASPELT. A Luxembourger born in Aspelt, Peter joined the church at an early age, and was educated in TRIER, Bologna, Padua, and Paris, where he studied theology and medicine. He became chaplain to Emperor Rudolph of Hapsburg, and a canon in the cathedral at Mainz. He next entered the service of Wenceslas III of Bohemia, whom he served for seven years, rising to the rank of chancellor. He was called in to treat the pope for an ailment of which his physicians had failed to find the cause, and was lucky enough to cure him, after which further ecclesiastical preference followed. He became bishop of Basel, then archbishop of Mainz, the highest position in the German church.

Peter was instrumental in securing the election of HENRY VII of Luxembourg as king and emperor, and also helped to arrange the marriage of Henry's son John to Elizabeth of Bohemia, making John the first count of Luxembourg to become king of Bohemia. After Henry VII's death in Italy, Peter secured the election of Louis of Bavaria as king and emperor. Peter died in 1320. (*See also* HOLY ROMAN EMPIRE and JOHN THE BLIND)

PETIT TRAIN. The "little train" which takes passengers on a guided tour of the GRUND and the PLATEAU DU RHAM under the cliffs of the city. Earphones are provided for passengers, who may listen to a condensed history of the city in English, Dutch, French, or German. The petit train leaves from the PLACE DE LA CONSTITUTION.

Similar little trains now serve the cities of ECHTERNACH and REMICH.

PETRUSSE. A small river that, over the millennia, cut a deep gorge through the soft sandstone on which the city of Luxembourg was later built. It joins the ALZETTE which cut an equally deep gorge on the eastern side of the city. The two rivers together helped make the site of Luxembourg a natural fortress.

The Petrusse is narrow enough to be stepped across, but the gorge it cut is very deep. It has been spanned in modern times by two bridges, the VIADUCT and the PONT ADOLF.

PHILIP THE FAIR. The only son of MARY OF BURGUNDY and MAXIMILIAN OF AUSTRIA, Philip succeeded his mother at the age of four, after her tragic death in a hunting accident at the age of twenty-five. Maximilian assumed the regency and ruled in his son's name until 1494, when Philip reached the age of sixteen. Two years later Philip married Joanna, the Infanta of Spain, heiress of Ferdinand and Isabella, who became known in history as Joanna the Mad.

In 1506, Philip died of a fever during a visit to Spain, where he had been recognized as king of Castile following the death of Queen Isabella. He left his possessions in the Netherlands and France to his six-year-old son, Charles of Ghent. (*See* CHARLES V)

PHILIP THE GOOD (PHILIP LE BON). A descendent of a younger branch of the French royal house, Philip became duke of Burgundy in 1419 and ruled until 1467. Along with the Duchy of Burgundy, he inherited Charolais, Franche-Comté (the old imperial Burgundy), Nevers, and the County of Artois in France from his father, as well as Flanders in the Netherlands. He was granted other provinces in France, including Auxerre, Brie, and Champagne in 1423–24 in exchange for supporting the French against the English during the Hundred Years War. He purchased the County of Namur in 1428 and Brabant and Limbourg in 1430 with their dependencies in Antwerp and Mechlin.

Although born in Dijon in Burgundy, Philip moved his capital to Brussels, where he built up a brilliant court. Between his inherited possessions and those he acquired in his lifetime, he was easily the most powerful prince in western Europe, and the principal rival of Louis XI of France. In 1441 he rounded out his possessions by purchasing the Duchy of Luxembourg from ELIZABETH OF GOERLITZ. Since Elizabeth had already made arrangements to sell the Duchy to William of Saxony, who had placed a garrison in the city of Luxembourg, Philip was unable to take immediate possession of his new purchase, but he captured the city in 1443 by a surprise night attack, shutting the Saxon garrison up in the castle, which they surrendered a few months later.

Philip was not immediately recognized as the legitimate ruler of Luxembourg, since there were other claimants he had either to buy or frighten off, but he was recognized as their lawful ruler by the Luxembourg Estates in 1461.

Beyond allowing his troops to pillage the city after its capture in 1443, Philip proved a good ruler to his new province. He confirmed the county in its traditional customs and privileges and made few changes in its traditional form of government. He was strong enough to protect Luxembourg against its enemies, so that the county enjoyed two decades of peace.

Philip aspired to raise his possessions to the status of a kingdom, with himself as king, but never quite managed it. He died in Ghent in 1467, after having turned over his powers to his son CHARLES THE BOLD and confirmed him as his successor in 1465. His twenty-one bastards were also provided for, one of them becoming bishop of Utrecht.

Philip's acquisition of Luxembourg in 1443 put an end to almost four hundred years of Luxembourg independence. The country remained under foreign rule for the next four centuries, although retaining its identity and language.

PHILIP II, king of Spain (1556–1598). When CHARLES V became king of Spain in 1516, he agreed to have his son and heir, Philip, brought up in Spain, and Philip became a complete Spaniard. (Charles also had to agree to learn to speak Spanish himself.)

Philip II inherited Spain, the Spanish possessions in Italy, his father's Burgundian possessions in France and the Netherlands (including the Duchy of Luxembourg) and the Spanish empire overseas, which included the gold and silver mines of Mexico and Peru. In 1580, he invaded Portugal, laying claim to its crown, and made it part of the Spanish dominions, which gave him control of Portugal's fleet as well as of her overseas empire in Brazil, Africa, India, and East Asia.

Philip II was the most powerful ruler in the Europe of his day and brooked little opposition to his views in either religion or politics. Complaints by the nobility in the Netherlands about the policies of his government were little heeded. When the iconoclasts in the Netherlands broke into and desecrated a number of Catholic churches in 1566, Philip sent the duke of ALVA with a Spanish army to put down resistance. (The Spanish army did not have to be sent by sea, but could travel overland to the Netherlands from northern Italy by the Spanish Road through territory either held by or allied to Spain.) Alva had a two-fold mission: to stamp out resistance to Spanish rule and to eliminate Protestantism in the Netherlands, which at the time enjoyed greater support in the south (present-day Belgium) than in the more conservative north, which clung to the traditional Catholic faith longer than most of the southern provinces.

Alva did not find a rebellion in progress in the Netherlands but created one. One of his first acts was to establish a "Blood Council" that condemned eight thousand people to death, including the patriot leaders, the counts of Egmont and Horn. This marked the beginning of an eighty-year rebellion against Spain, led in the beginning by WILLIAM THE SILENT (William, prince of Orange), stadholder (governor) of Holland, Utrecht, and Zealand until his assassination in 1584. The northern provinces began the rebellion in 1572, fighting the Spanish largely on the sea.

After the Spanish army sacked the loyal city of Antwerp in 1576, all seventeen provinces of the Low Countries, Catholic and Protestant alike, joined in the rebellion. Luxembourg played little or no part, being more securely occupied by Spanish troops than the other provinces, and more inclined to maintain its traditional liberties by submission than by rebellion.

The temporary union of the seventeen provinces soon fell apart. In 1581, the seven northern provinces declared their independence from Spain. They continued to harass the Spanish by sea and defend themselves by land, but were unable to prevent the Spanish reconquest of the ten southern provinces. After the death of Alva, Philip II appointed DON JUAN OF AUSTRIA, victor of the battle of Lepanto, governor of the Netherlands. Don Juan tried to pacify the rebellious provinces by peaceful means, but failed. In 1577, Alexander Farnese, duke of PARMA, nephew of Don Juan, joined his uncle in Brussels. When Don Juan died, Philip appointed Parma to succeed him as governor.

Parma was one of the ablest generals of his day, and although frequently hampered by shortages of men, supplies, and money, he systematically reconquered the southern Netherlands, beginning with the Walloon provinces in the south (largely loyal anyway) and ending with the Flemish (Dutch-speaking) provinces in the north. Antwerp, a vital center of opposition, fell to the Spanish army in 1585. The line reached by the Spanish armies under the duke of Parma marks, in fact, the boundary between the modern kingdoms of Belgium and the Netherlands.

The reconquest of the seven northern provinces was prevented largely by English intervention. Elizabeth I of England was alarmed enough by the prospect of complete Spanish control of the Low Countries to begin reluctantly to send money and troops to help the Dutch maintain their independence, although she remained nominally at peace with Spain. Elizabeth's execution in 1587 of Mary, queen of Scots, Catholic heiress to the throne of England, triggered an attempted invasion of England by Philip II. His plan called for a Spanish fleet to enter the English Channel and ferry Parma's army across it to conquer England.

The plan was a futile one to begin with. There was no deep-water harbor in Flanders which the Spanish Armada could enter to embark Parma's army, the English fleet both outnumbered and outgunned the Spanish fleet, and the shallow offshore waters were controlled by the Dutch fleet under Justin of Nassau. The Spanish fleet, ably commanded by the duke of Medina-Sidonia, who has never received full credit for his able seamanship, sailed up the English Channel pursued by the English fleet and anchored off Calais. English fire-ships launched into the center of the Spanish fleet helped scatter it, and the English navy and storms completed the rout of the "Invincible Armada," which finally returned to Spain by sailing north around Scotland and Ireland, losing a third of its ships along the way. Parma, lacking the necessary shipping, made no attempt at all to join the Spanish fleet, but held his army along the channel coast instead.

One of the greatest effects of Philip's attempt to conquer England was that it prevented his complete reconquest of the Netherlands. In September 1587, Parma had for the first time enough soldiers, supplies, and money to enable him to reconquer the seven northern provinces. After waiting a year along the channel coast for the Spanish fleet, his army had been wasted by disease and attrition to a third its size, his supplies had largely run out, and he never again had enough men, money, and munitions to finish the job. The Dutch fought on until 1640, when the Spanish king Philip IV finally recognized their independence. The ten southern provinces, including Luxembourg, remained under Spanish rule until 1714, during which time they were known as the SPANISH NETHERLANDS. During this time they were subject to many attacks from the French who, as Spain's power declined, made a determined effort to rid themselves of the Spanish cordon that surrounded France.

PLACE D'ARMES. A square in the heart of the city of Luxembourg. The Place d'Armes is so named because the town watch, stationed in medieval times in the town hall on the east side of the square, used it as a drill field and parade ground. The old town hall was destroyed in the great fire of 1544 and replaced by a new one built in 1572, which now serves as the GRAND DUCAL PALACE.

A bandstand, recently rebuilt and enlarged, stands at one end of the Place d'Armes, and concerts are given by various organizations during the spring and summer. The Place d'Armes is lined by trees. Restaurants and cafés set out tables on both sides during warm weather, but a space is left clear in the middle. Several of the older and better-known restaurants have closed their doors in recent years; they have, unfortunately, been replaced by fast-food restaurants such as McDonald's, Quick and Chi Chi's. The fast-food restaurants are popular with both Luxembourgers and tourists, but detract from the old-fashioned charm of the square.

A flea market is held on the Place d'Armes on Saturday mornings, and the annual Christmas market is held there in December. In former times the Place was a favorite rendezvous for Luxembourgers, especially after Sunday mass. By tradition, groups of girls would walk around the square one way and boys the other, while their parents sat at tables eating sausage and drinking a glass or two of beer or wine.

At one end of the Place d'Armes stands the CERCLE

MUNICIPAL and at the other a house dating from 1673, built by a prosperous ironmaster, which served as the seat of the intendent during the French occupation under LOUIS XIV (1684–1697) and as the official residence of the commander of the fortress during the Prussian occupation (1815–1867). At this time it was known to Luxembourgers as the *Kommandatur*. Next to this house is a column erected in 1903 in honor of MICHEL LENZ, author of the national hymn, and EDMOND DE LA FONTAINE, a well-known Luxembourg author and composer, commonly referred to as "Dicks" (the fat one).

PLACE DE LA CONSTITUTION. Located above the gorge of the PETRUSSE, the Place de la Constitution is the site of a memorial to the Luxembourgers who lost their lives during both world wars fighting on the Allied side. The monument is crowned by the famous GOLDEN LADY.

One of the entrances to the CASEMATES is located on the Place de la Constitution. The PETIT TRAIN, which takes passengers on a guided tour of the GRUND and the PLATEAU DU RHAM, leaves from the Place de la Constitution.

PLACE GUILLAUME. One of the two principal town squares in Luxembourg. The present LUXEMBOURG CITY HALL, built between 1830 and 1844 in the neoclassic style, stands on the southern side of the square. The steps are guarded by two bronze lions, created in 1931 by AUGUSTE TREMONT, the famous sculptor and painter of animals. A statue of Renert the Fox, in honor of MICHEL RODANGE, also stands on the south side of the square. On the east side, facing the GRAND DUCAL PALACE stands an equestrian statue of WILLIAM II, dedicated in 1884 by WILLIAM III in honor of his father.

A Franciscan priory stood on the present site of the Place Guillaume from 1250 to 1795, and the Place Guillaume is still called the Knuedeler in LETZEBUERGESCH, in reference to the knotted cord Franciscan friars wore around their waists.

A market is held on the Place Guillaume on Wednesday and Saturday mornings, and a fair is held there annually during the OCTAVE. A flight of stairs leads down to the cathedral from the southern side of the Place Guillaume, and two passageways connect it with the PLACE D'ARMES.

PLATEAU DU RHAM. Located to the east of the city, across the valley of the ALZETTE, the Plateau du Rham contains traces of habitation dating from Gallo-Roman times. During the fourteenth century, the plateau was incorporated into the city's defenses when the WALL OF WENCESLAS was built. During the French occupation of 1684–1697, MARSHAL VAUBAN, the great military engineer, strengthened the city's defenses by building several forts on the Plateau du Rham. Some of the barracks he built there for the French troops are still standing, although the forts were dismantled after 1867, in compliance with the terms of the SECOND TREATY OF LONDON. The Wall of Wenceslas was partially dismantled in 1875, but four towers, each 12 meters high, were left standing, as well as the Porte de Trèves which guarded the old road from Luxembourg to Trèves (TRIER).

POLITICAL PARTIES. There are three major political parties in Luxembourg, and several smaller ones, some focused around a single issue.

The largest party is the CHRISTIAN SOCIAL PEOPLE'S PARTY (CSV), a center-right party with a strong Catholic orientation. The second largest is the LUXEMBOURG SOCIALIST WORKERS PARTY (LSAP), a social democratic party that might be described as center-left. Although once strongly anticlerical, it can no longer be so described, having achieved one of its principal aims, the secularization of education, prior to WORLD WAR I. The DEMOCRATIC PARTY (DP), the third largest, may be described as a center party, closely resembling the present British Liberal Democrats. Like the British Liberals, the DP achieved its principal aims— political democracy, social insurance, and free public education—in the first two decades of the twentieth century with the cooperation of the socialists. Since then the DP has had difficulty finding new goals to distinguish it from the two other major parties.

None of the three major parties has been able to win an absolute majority in the CHAMBER OF DEPUTIES for decades, and so no party has been able to govern the nation alone, but has had to form a coalition with at least one other party. The country was governed from 1974 to 1979 by an LSAP-DP coalition, from 1979 to 1984 by a CSV-DP coalition, and has been governed from 1984 to the present day by a CSV-LSAP coalition.

PONT ADOLF. A single-span stone bridge, 46 meters (149 feet) high and 84 meters (185 feet) long, which spans the valley of the PETRUSSE, connecting the old city with the newer district on the other side of the valley. It is one of the longest single-span stone bridges in the world.

The Pont Adolf was constructed between 1899 and 1903 during the reign of GRAND DUKE ADOLF and was dedicated by Adolf himself.

PRIMARY SCHOOLS. The primary schools in Luxembourg are supported by local government and offer a six-year program of instruction. Pupils begin to learn German in the first year and French in the second. By the time pupils reach their sixth year, they are taking half their subjects in French and half in German. Instruction in English begins in the sixth year.

Not much formal instruction in LETZEBUERGESCH is given, although it is used to give explanations in the classroom and spoken on the playground. Pupils are trilingual when they finish their primary education, and have the beginnings of a fourth language. Secondary-school entrance examinations are given in French and German.

Primary school teachers are trained at the TEACHER TRAINING COLLEGE. Primary schools have no principals, but school inspectors are responsible for a group of schools in a given area.

The biggest problem faced by the primary schools today is the need to educate a large influx of children, the majority of them Portuguese, who speak no Letzebuergesch and who find French much easier to learn than German. In some districts, they outnumber the children who speak Letzebuergesch. Special classes and, in some cases, special schools have been set up for these children. (*See also* EDUCATION and SECONDARY SCHOOLS.)

PRINCE HENRI RAILROAD. After the Franco-Prussian War, when the Germans had taken over management of the GUILLAUME-LUXEMBOURG RAILROAD, Luxembourg built a second rail system, the Prince Henri Railroad, to provide Luxembourg with a direct line to Paris through French rather than German territory, and to link together various other towns in the Grand Duchy. Capital to build the new railroad was raised privately, much of it from Belgian investors.

The Prince Henri Railroad, like the other Luxembourg railroads, was taken over by the Germans during both world wars. In 1946, it was merged with the other railroads into the Société Nationale des Chemins des Fer Luxembourgeoise (CFL). (*See also* NARROW-GAUGE RAILROADS and RAILROAD SYSTEM)

PRUM. A town now in German territory, famous for its abbey, that once belonged to the Grand Duchy but was annexed to Prussia in 1815. (*See* THREE PARTITIONS OF LUXEMBOURG)

RADIO-TELEVISION LUXEMBOURG (RTL). Radio-Television Luxembourg, with its studios in the Villa Louvigny in Luxembourg and its powerful transmitters in Junglinster, broadcasts programs in French, German, Dutch, and English over most of western Europe. A few programs in LETZEBUERGESCH are broadcast for local reception. Radio Luxembourg was Europe's leading popular music station during the post–WORLD WAR II years, when its music programs, with British disc-jockeys, were especially popular in Great Britain at a time when the BBC broadcast only a limited selection of popular music. Millions of young Britons tuned in to Radio Luxembourg regularly, even though many of its listeners had no idea where Luxembourg was.

Radio-Television Luxembourg now broadcasts regularly on at least five channels (it keeps adding more) providing a steady diet of news, drama, films, music, and special programs on various subjects. It maintains a symphony orchestra, the RTL Symphony, which not only broadcasts over the airwaves but also provides a regular series of classical music programs at the municipal theater in Luxembourg, the conservatory and other locations. Its programs of classical music for young people are especially popular.

RTL has recently become part of an international consortium and is no longer independent. It has also signed an agreement with the government to give up its present headquarters in the Villa Louvigny and build new studios in Junglinster. The RTL Symphony will become an independent organization supported by the national government.

RAILROAD SYSTEM. Since shortly after WORLD WAR II, the Grand Duchy has had a single, unified national railroad system under the control of the Société Nationale des Chemins de Fer Luxembourgeoise (CFL), in which the government holds a major share. This system was formed by joining together the two standard-gauge railroad systems that had existed before World War II, the GUILLAUME-LUXEMBOURG RAIL-

ROAD and the PRINCE HENRI RAILROAD, and a number of NARROW-GAUGE RAILROADS that operated in different parts of the country.

The first Luxembourg railroad, the Luxembourg-Guillaume Railroad, was built between 1859 and 1866. All but one section of this railroad was operated by the French railway company of the east, largely because the cost of building the railroad had left the Luxembourg government with insufficient funds to operate it. After the Franco-Prussian War of 1870 and the German annexation of Lorraine, the German government took over the operation of the Guillaume-Luxembourg Railroad and incorporated it into the German railroad network, of which it formed a part until the end of WORLD WAR I.

Between 1880 and 1902, a second railroad was built in the Grand Duchy, the Prince Henri Railroad, which connected Luxembourg directly to Paris. This railroad was built largely with private capital, most of it raised in Belgium. The Luxembourg government also built and operated a number of narrow-gauge railroads

By the terms of the Treaty of Versailles, the French recovered Lorraine and with it the right to operate the Guillaume-Luxembourg Railroad. Between 1919 and 1940, there were three railroad lines operating in Luxembourg, the Guillaume-Luxembourg line operated by the French National Railways, the Prince Henri line operated by a private company, and 139 kilometers of narrow-gauge lines operated by the Luxembourg government. All three were integrated into the German railroad network during World War II. After the war, all of these lines were incorporated into a single railroad system, the Luxembourg National Railways.

Almost the entire railroad system has now been electrified except for the line between Luxembourg and TRIER, which still uses diesel locomotives. In 1994 the Luxembourg government signed an agreement with the French government to connect Luxembourg with Metz by an extension of the high-speed TGV (Trains de Grand Vitesse) line. Luxembourg will thus be connected with the new European high-speed rail system. The Grand Duchy will pay most of the cost of the new Luxembourg-Metz line. (*See also* TRANSPORTATION, PUBLIC AND PRIVATE)

RAVANGER, ABBOT OF ECHTERNACH. In 973, SIGEFROI replaced the lay canons of the ABBEY OF ECHTERNACH with forty Benedictine monks from the ABBEY OF ST. MAX-

IMIN IN TRIER led by Ravanger, whom the monks elected as their abbot. This was part of a movement within the church for reforming the monasteries, in which Sigefroi's brother Adalbert, bishop of Metz, played a leading part.

RED BRIDGE (PONT GRAND-DUCHESSE CHARLOTTE). A modern single-span cantilever bridge, completed in 1966, which spans the valley of the ALZETTE, linking the city of Luxembourg with the KIRCHBERG, home of the institutions of the EUROPEAN UNION. The highway which crosses the bridge joins the Boulevard John F. Kennedy on the other side, which continues on past the European institutions to the Luxembourg international airport at FINDEL.

The Red Bridge was the favorite spot for suicides in the Grand Duchy until 1994, when it was fitted with plexiglass barriers to prevent people jumping. Prospective suicides now tend to use the PONT ADOLF.

REDEMPTORISTS. Established in Luxembourg in 1851, the Redemporists were the first new Roman Catholic order to settle in the Grand Duchy following the French Revolution. The Redemptorists built a church and a cloister in the capital city. The original buildings were completed in 1856 and consecrated by Monsignor Nicholas Adames, the apostolic vicar in Luxembourg, who became the country's first bishop in 1870.

The church, known as the Cloister Church of St. Alphonse, is located on the rue des Capucins, not far from the PLACE D'ARMES. It suffered some damage during WORLD WAR II but was restored after the war.

REDOUTE, PIERRE JOSEPH (1759–1840). Perhaps the world's most famous painter of flowers, Redouté was born in St. Hubert in the ARDENNES, then part of the Duchy of Luxembourg but now part of Belgium. His first teacher was Brother Abraham at the ABBEY OF ORVAL, a well-known painter during his own time.

At the age of eighteen, Redouté went to Luxembourg city, where he painted portraits of some of the notable figures of his day, including MARSHAL BENDER, governor of the fortress. He also painted portraits of wealthy ladies, one of whom sent him to Paris with money and letters of introduction. In Paris he met a noted flower painter, Van Spaendonck, who hired him to do some flower paintings for the collection of Louis XVI.

In 1783, Redouté was appointed court flower painter and

drawing master to Queen Marie-Antoinette. He survived the French Revolution, and continued to paint for Josephine Bonaparte, wife of NAPOLEON I, who became empress when her husband became emperor, and for Napoleon's second wife, Marie-Louise. After Napoleon's downfall and the restoration of the Bourbons, Redouté was sponsored by the duchesse du Berry, and after the Revolution of 1830 he became court flower painter to King Louis-Philippe. He died in Paris in 1840 and is buried in the cemetery of Père-Lachaise.

Between 1817 and 1824 Redouté published a three-volume book about roses, illustrated with 164 of his paintings, which made him famous. He subsequently published volumes illustrated with paintings of other flowers, including lilacs, tulips, and irises, but he is best known for his roses.

Redouté's paintings, especially his roses, are known worldwide. The NATIONAL MUSEUM in Luxembourg has a number of reproductions of his work, including several albums of his paintings.

RED WELL (PUITS ROUGE). A well two hundred feet deep dug by the Austrians in 1740 to supply water to the city. It continued in use until 1857. Over the spot where it once came to the surface, there now stands a statue of a group of musicians with a flock of sheep, symbolizing the HAMMELSMARSCH.

REMICH. An important town on the MOSELLE, one of the centers of the Luxembourg wine industry. A bridge crosses the Moselle at Remich linking it to the Saarland. A battle was fought here in A.D. 882 in which the NORTHMEN defeated the combined armies of the bishops of TRIER and Metz and the abbot of ECHTERNACH. Although the Northmen won the battle, they suffered heavy losses and retreated to their camp on the Meuse, abandoning their original plans to sack Metz.

Excursion boats such as the *Princess Marie Astrid* dock at Remich, and trips can be taken to other towns and cities along the Moselle.

REUTER, EMILE. Prime minister who headed the Luxembourg government from 1918 to 1925. He failed to secure an economic agreement with France in 1918 to replace the favorable ties with Germany that the Grand Duchy had enjoyed under the old ZOLLVEREIN but steered Luxembourg safely through the troubles that followed—an attempt to set up a left-wing republic, the abdication of GRAND DUCHESS MARIE-ADELAIDE, and an attempt by the Belgians to annex the Grand Duchy.

A patriotic demonstration took place on 27 April 1919, in which the people of Luxembourg affirmed their desire for their country's independence, and a delegation headed by Emile Reuter managed to convince the peace conference at Paris to delay action until a referendum could be held on the question of Luxembourg's future destiny. The referendum, held in September 1919, showed an overwhelming majority in favor of continuing Luxembourg's independence under its current dynasty, represented by the GRAND DUCHESS CHARLOTTE.

In 1919, the Reuter government pushed through a law guaranteeing universal suffrage and extending the right to vote to all men and women twenty-one years of age and older. In addition, having failed to secure an economic treaty with France, the Reuter government negotiated a treaty creating a CUSTOMS AND MONETARY UNION with Belgium in 1921. This treaty was not popular in the Grand Duchy and the CHAMBER OF DEPUTIES delayed ratifying it until the following year.

The unpopular treaty with Belgium, postwar inflation, and a plan to place the Luxembourg railroad system under the administration of a company controlled by the Belgian government led to the downfall of the Reuter government in 1925, and it was replaced by a coalition government headed by Joseph Bech.

RHINELAND FRANKS. Often called Ripuarian Franks, a term indicating that their original home was along the banks of the Rhine between Düsseldorf and Coblenz. Beginning in the second century A.D., the Rhineland Franks made raids into Roman Gaul, into the area between the Rhine, MOSELLE, and Meuse rivers that later became known as AUSTRASIA. Many of the Franks were enlisted in the Roman armies, either voluntarily or after being captured in battle, and some tribes became Roman allies. Franks, along with Visigoths and Burgundians, formed an important part of the army under the Roman general FLAVIUS AETIUS which defeated the HUNS under ATTILA at the Battle of the Catalaunian Fields in A.D. 451.

Most of the Frankish penetration of Austrasia was peaceful. The Romans settled some Frankish soldiers and their families in colonies among the GAULS. Others flocked across the borders into lands left vacant by the death of a large part of the population in the plagues that followed the great Plague of Antoninus, which struck the western parts of the Roman empire in A.D. 170, during the reign of the Emperor Marcus Aurelius Antoninus.

LETZEBUERGESCH, the language spoken by Luxembourgers, is derived from the Moselle-Franconian dialect spoken by the Rhineland Franks.

RODANGE, MICHEL (1827–1876). Author of *Renert*, a long epic poem in LETZEBUERGESCH satirizing nineteenth century politicians, political parties, elections, newspapers, the courts, the church, business leaders, the army, the police, and every other aspect of Luxembourgish life, from high to low. His protagonist is Reynard the Fox, hero of many animal tales in European folklore. A statue of a fox with an inscription to Michel Rodange stands on one side of the PLACE GUILLAUME next to the city hall.

Michel Rodange was born in Waldbillig and spent most of his working life as a primary school teacher. *Renert* was published in 1872.

ROMAN ROADS. Two major roads crossed what is now the Grand Duchy of Luxembourg in Gallo-Roman times. The first followed a route from Reims through ARLON, MAMER, and Niederanven to TRIER, and on to Cologne, the major Roman base on the Rhine. The second road came north from Lyons and Metz, crossed the MOSELLE at Stadtbredimus, and went on through Dalheim and Roodt, joining the other Roman road near the Widdenberg, a large hill where many Roman artifacts have been found. The remnants of the Roman bridge that crossed the Moselle between Stadtbredimus and Palzem have also been located.

Secondary roads linked various Roman settlements in the area, including one road that crossed the valley of the PETRUSSE and climbed the hill to the Roman watchtower that stood on the site of the present square called the FISHMARKET. This road, now paved with cobblestones, is still in use. It enters the square under an arched gateway erected in later days.

A third Roman road linking Reims directly to Cologne crossed the northwest corner of the present-day Grand Duchy.

ROMAN RULE (c. 50 B.C.–A.D. 450). Gaul enjoyed a considerable degree of peace and prosperity while it was part of the Roman empire, especially during the two hundred years of the *Pax Augustorum* which followed the accession of Augustus to the imperial throne in 44 B.C. Commerce flourished; roads, bridges and aqueducts were built, and towns and cities sprang up everywhere. Internal warfare between the tribes ceased, and wars were fought only along or beyond the Rhine frontier.

The country occupied by the TREVERI shared in the general prosperity. Although there were no major Roman towns in what is now the Grand Duchy of Luxembourg, the nearby town of TRIER was a major Roman center, housing part of a Roman legion. Later emperors made it the capital of the entire diocese of Gaul.

The Romans left many traces of their occupation in Luxembourg, despite having built no major city there. The TITELBERG and DALHEIM in particular have yielded a treasure trove of Roman ruins and artifacts, but archaeologists have found Roman remains everywhere. Milestones and shrines to Roman and Celtic deities such as EPONA lined the roads, and Roman cemeteries, tools, coins, and the ruins of ROMAN VILLAS have been found throughout the land. An excellent collection of Roman artifacts can be found in the NATIONAL MUSEUM as well as in the museums in TRIER and ARLON. In 1995, a Roman mosaic depicting Homer and the nine muses was discovered in Vichten.

During the later centuries of Roman rule, Gaul was neither so peaceful nor so prosperous as it had been during the Age of Augustus. Incursions of German tribes from the other side of the Rhine began during the second century, but did not become really serious until the fifth century. Struggles between rival claimants for the imperial throne and plagues that caused a serious decline in population weakened the empire and left it less able to defend itself against the barbarians. The fifth century German invasions finally put an end to the Roman empire in the West. The RHINELAND FRANKS settled in the lands of the TREVERI, intermarried with the local population, and established their rule in the lands between the Rhine, the MOSELLE, and the Meuse. (*See also* AUSTRASIA)

ROMAN VILLAS. The most magnificent Roman villa discovered in the present-day Grand Duchy was located in ECHTERNACH. It had central heating, ornamental pools, and imposing buildings, and has sometimes been described as a palace. This villa was the center of extensive agricultural domains, whose surplus production helped support the population of the Roman city of TRIER.

Another large Roman villa was located on a ridge called Mersch-Mies overlooking the Roman settlement at MERSCH. This villa boasted central heating, columned porticos, mosaics, and a large ornamental pool. Destroyed when the HUNS passed through Mersch in A.D. 451, it was excavated during the late nineteenth century. Most of the ruins were covered up again and houses were built on the site, but the Roman hypocaust has been preserved as well as the outlines of the ornamental pool.

RUNDSTEDT, FIELD MARSHAL GERD VON. German commander on the western front during the closing years of WORLD WAR II. Marshal von Rundstedt was actually in command of the German army in the west during the Allied invasion of Normandy in June 1944. Removed from his post when the Allied invasion succeeded, Rundstedt was restored to command just prior to the Battle of Arnhem. He succeeded in halting the German retreat and reestablishing a line of defense.

In December 1944, Rundstedt launched the last German offensive in the west, the famous BATTLE OF THE BULGE, sometimes known as the Rundstedt Offensive. This offensive, although it caught the allied armies off guard and caused considerable damage, failed in the end.

Rundstedt is famous for his reply to German headquarters, which asked him what to do after the Allied breakout from Normandy. "Make peace, you fools," was his reply. (*See also* PATTON, GENERAL GEORGE S., JR.)

RUNDSTEDT OFFENSIVE. (*See* BATTLE OF THE BULGE)

SALIAN FRANKS. Frankish tribes who lived along the lower reaches of the Rhine. They crossed the Rhine and settled in large numbers in what is now the southern Netherlands and northern Belgium during the fourth and fifth centuries. Their language, a Plattdeutsch dialect, developed into modern Dutch, the language still spoken in the Netherlands and northern Belgium (where it is known as Flemish). Under their greatest leader, CLOVIS, the Salian Franks moved south from their capital at Tournai in present-day Belgium to conquer most of the rest of Gaul, which they called NEUSTRIA, the "new lands". Since they were greatly outnumbered by the people they conquered in western Gaul, the vulgar Latin spoken by the conquered Gallo-Romans, which developed into French, prevailed over the language of their Frankish conquerors, which persisted only in Flanders and the Netherlands. (*See also* RHINELAND FRANKS)

SANDWEILER. A town to the east of Luxembourg city, location of the principal inspection station for automobiles, trucks, and motorcycles. New vehicles need not be inspected for the first three years, but after that must be inspected annually. In addition, every time a motor vehicle changes ownership it must be inspected, even if it is less than three years old.

The inspection is very thorough, and the lines have become so long that taking a car for inspection can use up the best part of a morning or afternoon. In an attempt to speed up the process, new inspection stations have been opened up at Wilverwoltz in the north and ESCH-SUR-ALZETTE in the south.

SANTER, JACQUES. Successor to PIERRE WERNER as head of the CHRISTIAN SOCIAL PEOPLE'S PARTY (CSV). Santer served as prime minister of Luxembourg from 1984 to 1994, leading the CSV to victory in the elections of 1984, 1989, and 1994. His governments were a coalition between the CSV and the LUXEMBOURG SOCIALIST WORKERS PARTY (LSAP). The number of seats controlled by the coalition in the CHAMBER OF DEPUTIES gave them such a strong majority that their policies went virtually unchallenged. The DEMO-CRATIC PARTY (DP) was in such a hopeless minority that it could offer only token opposition to any measures favored by the coalition.

Jacques Santer is a skillful politician whose strength lies in uniting the disparate elements in the governing coalition. He took no bold, decisive initiatives, but worked hard to create a consensus, which guaranteed a period of calm government, relatively free of strife. Even the recession which hit western Europe in 1992 did little to diminish the government's popularity, although the CSV and LSAP each lost a seat in the ELECTIONS OF 1994. Santer's own share of the vote ran behind that of his finance minister, JEAN-CLAUDE JUN-CKER, and the Democratic mayor of Luxembourg, LYDIE WURTH-POLFER, however.

On 16 July 1994 the European heads of state selected Santer to succeed Jacques Delors as president of the EUROPEAN COMMISSION, to take office for a five-year term in January

1995. Santer is a committed European, in favor of the closer integration and expansion of the EUROPEAN UNION and a single European currency. He was one of the principal architects of the TREATY OF MAASTRICHT, but he is seen as a compromiser rather than an activist and was expected to bring a period of calm to the European Union, in contrast to the turmoil which distinguished the administration of his predecessor, Jacques Delors. Unfortunately for Santer, the situation in Bosnia, rising unemployment in the member states, and the general slowdown of the European economy seem likely to make his presidency a troubled one.

SCHÖNFELS. A village between MERSCH and Kopstal, site of a feudal castle dating back to the thirteenth or fourteenth century. The castle at Schönfels is considered to be one of the seven castles in the VALLEY OF THE SEVEN CASTLES, although strictly speaking it is located in the valley of the Mamer River rather than of the Eisch River.

A few years ago, the current owner of the castle tore down one of the historic buildings to provide more parking space for his cars. This caused a tremendous public outcry, although no action could be taken against the owner. There was a law prohibiting the alteration or destruction of historic buildings without specific permission from the government, but the law provided no penalties for those who violated it. Fortunately, the square tower of the old chateau is still standing.

Legend has it that Schönfels was once inhabited by a race of cave-dwelling dwarfs.

SCHOOL OF COMMERCE AND MANAGEMENT. Formerly the Ecole du Commerce et de Gestion, the school has been renamed the Lycée Technique du Commerce et de Gestion. It is located in Merl, close to the ATHENEE GRAND-DUCAL and the Conservatoire.

The school offers one- and two-year programs in business subjects and languages, and most of its graduates are employed by banks, insurance companies, and similar enterprises. With the great increase in the number of banks and insurance companies in recent years, the school's graduates are in great demand, and its enrollment has increased dramatically.

Normally, students have completed a course at another secondary school (generally a lycée technique) and worked for a year or two before applying for entrance to the School of Commerce and Management. Their greater maturity makes them more attentive to their studies than the typical secondary student. The study of the languages used in business (French, German, and especially English) is stressed, since most international enterprises, including banks, need employees who can speak several languages. (*See also* HIGHER EDUCATION)

SCHUMAN, ROBERT. French statesman, born at Clausen in Luxembourg in 1886. He attended the ATHENEE GRAND-DUCAL, from which he received his baccalaureate in 1902, then attended university in France. Adopting French nationality, he entered French politics, rising to the position of foreign minister, which he held in several French governments. At one point, he even served as premier.

Schuman was one of the architects of the EUROPEAN COAL AND STEEL COMMUNITY, founded in 1952, whose capital he helped establish in his native Luxembourg, and of the TREATY OF ROME of 1957, which established the European Economic Community (since renamed the EUROPEAN UNION).

SECOND TREATY OF LONDON, 1867. The Second Treaty of London provided for the permanent neutrality of Luxembourg, its continued separate existence under the Dutch crown, and the demolition of its fortifications. The Prussian garrison was to be withdrawn. The Great Powers, including Prussia and France, agreed to respect the Grand Duchy's neutrality.

In some respects, the Second Treaty of London went further toward establishing Luxembourg independence than the FIRST TREATY OF LONDON that went into effect in 1839, because it ended foreign occupation, kept Luxembourg out of the NORTH GERMAN CONFEDERATION and the Second German Empire, and left it free to continue its separate national development under the loose rule of the Dutch king/ grand duke. Complete independence was achieved twenty-three years later when Luxembourg was separated from the Dutch crown and given its own monarch.

The neutrality guaranteed by the Great Powers turned out to be a myth when Luxembourg was occupied by German troops in both world wars of the twentieth century. (*See also* CRISIS OF 1866–67 and NAPOLEON III)

SECONDARY SCHOOLS. Luxembourg has a system of state secondary schools of several types. The highest-rated are the athenées and lycées, which offer seven-year programs leading to the examinations for the baccalaureate, which is needed for entrance to higher education. (The original distinction between athenées and lycées was that the athenées offered both Latin and Greek as classical languages and the lycées offered only Latin, but this distinction has disappeared.) Because there are more lycées than athenées, the superior secondary schools will be referred to as lycées hereafter.

Each lycée sets its own entrance examinations, with tests in certain subjects given in French and in other subjects in German. The various secondary schools do not all hold their examinations on the same day, so pupils may take the entrance examinations for more than one secondary school.

The course of study at a lycée is rigorous. Secondary students who fail to pass the annual examination in a single major subject may be required to repeat an entire school year. Students who fail two years are dropped and must complete their secondary education in another type of secondary school. Students must study a third foreign language in lycées, and most elect to study English, although other languages are offered.

There are lycées in most major towns and cities, but some towns, particularly in the north, do not have one and students in these towns must travel to one that does. Since the most prestigious secondary schools are located in the capital city, large numbers of secondary students travel daily to Luxembourg by train or bus.

Students who do not take or do not pass the examinations for entrance to lycées normally attend schools that were known as middle schools (écoles moyennes) until a few years ago, but are now called technical high schools (lycées techniques) in an attempt to upgrade their status. Students in a technical high school follow four- to six-year courses of instruction, followed in some cases by two-year apprenticeships during which they attend classes on a part-time basis.

In addition to the state schools, there are a few Catholic secondary schools in the Grand Duchy. Provided they follow the normal Luxembourg curriculum in most subjects, they receive state aid, with the government paying 80 percent of the teachers' salaries.

There are other special types of secondary schools in Luxembourg, such as the VOCATIONAL SCHOOLS, the MUSIC CONSERVATORIES, and the SCHOOL OF COMMERCE AND MANAGEMENT.

Most teachers in Luxembourg secondary schools, especially

in the lycées, are graduates of foreign universities. They must serve a three-year temporary appointment as apprentices (stagiaires), after which they may receive permanent appointments.

Secondary schools in Luxembourg are supported by the national government and fall under the jurisdiction of the Ministry of National Education, although the school buildings are under the jurisdiction of the Bureau of Public Buildings, which is itself a division of the Ministry of Public Works. (*See also* ATHENEE GRAND-DUCAL, EDUCATION, HIGHER EDUCATION, and PRIMARY SCHOOLS)

SEPTFONTAINES. A village in the western part of Luxembourg, in the valley of the Eisch river (VALLEY OF THE SEVEN CASTLES). The ruins of a medieval castle crown one of the hilltops nearby. The name is also given to an eighteenth century chateau in LIMPERTSBERG on the rue de Rollingergrund. This latter chateau is owned and maintained by VILLEROY AND BOCH, a well-known firm that manufactures fine pottery in its factories on the same road. In LETZEBUERGESCH, Septfontaines becomes "Sieweburen," and a popular restaurant nearby carries that name.

SERVAIS, EMMANUEL. A nineteenth century Luxembourg statesman. In 1844–49, with two other deputies from the Grand Duchy, he attended the meeting of the Vorparlement in Frankfurt, which was charged with drawing up a new, liberal constitution for Germany. The three Luxembourg deputies, along with the majority of other deputies, cast their votes in favor of offering the crown of Germany to the king of Prussia as German emperor, but the king refused this "crown from the gutter."

Servais opposed the proposed constitution of 1856 granting increased powers to the Dutch monarch and was dismissed from the government. In 1867 he and the baron de Tornaco represented the Grand Duchy at the meeting of the Great Powers in London that produced the SECOND TREATY OF LONDON guaranteeing Luxembourg's independence and neutrality. Servais became prime minister in 1867, and presided over the government until 1874. During these years he had to contend with Germany's attempt to take over the administration of the Luxembourg post and telegraph system and the GUILLAUME-LUXEMBOURG RAILROAD, the continued willingness of WILLIAM III to sell the Grand Duchy to the highest bidder, and a move to restore the Prussian garrison and link Luxembourg more closely with the new German empire. The opposing ambitions of the larger nations tended to cancel each other out, however, leaving Luxembourg free, independent, and neutral, although still ruled by the Dutch king/grand duke.

SHEPHERDS' FAIR (SCHUEBERFOUER). Founded by JOHN THE BLIND in 1340 and still held annually in Luxembourg in late August and early September. It normally lasts for eighteen days, but every fifth year it lasts for 25 days. Although originally a livestock fair, the Schueberfouer today consists largely of amusements, rides, a huge Ferris wheel, and food stalls. The only sheep evident are a small flock trotted around the fairgrounds during the first day of the fair by a shepherd dressed in a medieval smock. The fair is held on the "glacis", originally a field of fire for the fortress of Luxembourg, but now a large parking lot on the outskirts of the city.

SIGEFROI. The founder of Luxembourg, Sigefroi was the youngest son of WIGERIC, count of the Ardennes and count-palatine of Upper Lorraine, who held his lands and governed them in the name of OTTO I, elected king of the East Franks (Germany) in 933 and crowned Holy Roman Emperor in 962.

Sigefroi inherited various lands from his father in the Saar, MOSELLE, and ALZETTE valleys, in the ARDENNES, and around BITBURG in the Eifel. He held ECHTERNACH as a fief from Otto I, and was solicitor or advocate of the ABBEY OF SAINT MAXIMIN IN TRIER, whose lands he administered. Needing a place to serve as the center for his scattered domains, Sigefroi made an attempt to acquire Stavelot in the Ardennes. Failing in that, he made an agreement in 963 with Wicher, the abbot of St. Maximin, by which he gave up title to some lands at Feulen near ETTELBRUCK in exchange for a small tract of land on the Alzette River, and a rocky outcropping overlooking it called the BOCK, upon which he proceeded to build a castle.

The castle Sigefroi built on the Bock and the town which grew up around it became the nucleus of a feudal state ruled over by Sigefroi and his descendents, who eventually became known as the counts of Luxembourg. (The name Luxembourg derives from the Celtic name "Lucilinburhuc" meaning "little fortress on a hill".) Besides the valley of the Alzette below the castle, in which the original town grew up, Sigefroi owned part of the plateau adjoining the Bock, which he enclosed within a defensive wall. Included within the wall were the first town square, which later became the FISHMARKET, and the CHURCH OF ST. MICHAEL, construction of which began in 987. As the upper town grew, a second and third wall were built to enclose it.

Sigefroi maintained close relations with the Abbey of St. Maximin in Trier. In 973, he replaced the lay canons of Echternach, which he held as an imperial fief, with Benedictines from St. Maximin, under RAVANGER, who became their abbot. When Sigefroi died in 998, he was buried in the Abbey of St. Maximin.

Sigefroi also maintained close relations with the Saxon emperors of Germany, who were his feudal overlords. He accompanied OTTO I on his expedition to Italy in 966 and fought against his enemies there. Sigefroi and his son also accompanied OTTO II during his invasion of Italy in 981, in which Otto died fighting the Saracens.

Sigefroi had some problems with the French. When the bishop of Verdun invaded Luxembourg in 982, Sigefroi took him prisoner, but he was forced to release him under pressure from the church. In 983, after the death of Otto II in Italy, Lothair I of France attacked Verdun, held at that time by Sigefroi's nephew Godfrey, to whose aid Sigefroi came. Both he and his nephew were taken captive and were not released until 985, through the intercession of Hugh Capet, count of Paris, who became king of France in 987. Thereafter, although they remained vassals of the German emperors, the counts of Luxembourg normally remained on friendly terms with the kings of France.

Sigefroi is sometimes referred to as count of the Ardennes, one of his father's titles, but he was the youngest son, and one of his older brothers inherited that title. Historians have also questioned whether a Sigefroi II succeeded his father in 987. The existence of this second Sigefroi is surmised from land grants made to him by his father, but not much is known about him, and he probably predeceased his father. In any case, Sigefroi was succeeded by another son, Henry I, in 998.

The spelling of Sigefroi's name has also been disputed. In German, he is referred to as Siegfried, and at least one Luxembourg historian insists that his name should be spelled Sigefroid. Other possible spellings exist. Sigefroi is the spelling commonly used in Luxembourg.

SIGISMUND. Fourth ruler of Luxembourg to serve as Holy Roman Emperor, and younger brother of WENZEL II. (Wenzel, as emperor, was known as Wenceslas, the Latinized version of his name.) Sigismund became king of Hungary in 1387 upon the death of the reigning king, whose only daughter he had married. He spent a good part of his reign fighting against the Turks, who invaded Hungary several times while he was king. Even during the lifetime of Wenceslas, Sigismund contested the empire with him, being elected king of the Romans by the dissatisfied German princes in 1410 and crowned at Aachen in 1414. He became duke of Luxembourg in 1419 upon his brother's death, and king of Bohemia in 1420. During Wenceslas's lifetime, Sigismund allowed him to keep his title, although Sigismund actually ruled from 1410.

Sigismund was not particularly successful as a ruler. His own Hungarian subjects imprisoned him twice, and he was forced to pawn the margravate of Brandenburg to Josse of Moravia for ready cash, and later to sell it to Frederick of Hohenzollern in 1415. Being short of money again when he inherited Luxembourg in 1419, he was unable to pay off the money owed to ELIZABETH OF GOERLITZ, to whom Wenceslas had transferred the Duchy in 1411, and so was forced to leave Elizabeth in control. Sigismund took no further interest in Luxembourg, and died in 1437 without ever having visited the country.

STEICHEN, EDWARD. Born in Bevange in Luxembourg, Edward Steichen became one of the most influential and important photographers of the twentieth century.

Steichen is best known for having assembled the collection of photographs known as the "Family of Man," which was first exhibited at the Museum of Modern Art in New York on 24 January 1955. The collection, selected from over two million photographs, includes 503 photographs taken by 273 photographers from 68 countries. The collection, oddly enough, does not contain many photographs by Steichen himself.

The Family of Man traveled around the world and was seen by over nine million people. In 1962, the American government gave Luxembourg the traveling version of the collection. By Steichen's wish, this collection was to be housed at the castle at CLERVAUX.

Only part of the collection was put on display—nearly half the photographs were found gathering dust in the attic of a nearby school in 1989—and the photographs in the display suffered from thirty years of neglect. Within the past few years, however, the collection has been restored and has since been shown in Toulouse, Tokyo, and Hiroshima.

The entire collection is now housed in a new museum in the castle of Clervaux built by the Service of Sites and National Monuments and is on display to visitors from 1 March to 31 December each year.

SURE. A river that rises in the Belgian ARDENNES and flows east across the center of the Grand Duchy, before turning south to flow into the MOSELLE at Wasserbillig. It has been dammed above ETTELBRUCK, forming a large reservoir that provides both electricity and a major part of Luxembourg's water supply. The reservoir is also a recreation area and sailing is permitted. The water is very cold.

Below the dam, the Sûre continues east to Ettelbruck, where it is joined by the ALZETTE, then further east until it makes a deep turn to the south, shortly before it is joined by the waters of the Our, a river that rises in the Ardennes north of VIANDEN. On its southward course the Sûre forms the eastern border between Luxembourg and Germany.

Along the eastern border, the Sûre is more often referred to as the Sauer, a German name that seems similar but has a different origin and meaning.

From Ettelbruck to Wasserbillig, kayaking and canoeing are possible on the Sûre, and a bicycle path parallels the stream. Another artificial lake, where sailing is also permitted, has been created just north of ECHTERNACH.

Most of the Luxembourg rivers drain into the Sûre, which in turn drains into the Moselle.

TEACHER TRAINING COLLEGE (ECOLE NORMALE). Located in Walferdange, not far north of Luxembourg city, the Ecôle Normale trains teachers for the Luxembourg primary school. Until recently, the program took two years to complete, but it now takes three years.

Candidates must have passed their baccalaureate examinations and be accepted by the school. Since the need for primary teachers in the Grand Duchy can be easily predicted, the Ecôle Normale is careful to enroll only enough students to fill the positions that might become available. The number of new students admitted each year is small and it is said to be more difficult to gain entrance to the Ecôle Normale than to a foreign university.

Although primary teachers in the Grand Duchy are paid on

a lower scale than the secondary teachers, they have what amounts to a guaranteed lifetime job at a reasonable salary, so entrance to the Ecôle Normale is eagerly sought.

There is talk of moving the Ecôle Normale to the campus of the CENTRE UNIVERSITAIRE, which has recently been enlarged. (*See also* HIGHER EDUCATION)

THIONVILLE. A town in France south of Luxembourg on the autoroute to Metz. This town and the area around it once belonged to the Duchy of Luxemburg, but it was annexed by the French in 1659 by the terms of the TREATY OF THE PYRENEES engineered by Cardinal Mazarin.

Thionville had earlier served as one of the capitals of CHARLEMAGNE, to which he moved his court during the winter. Some of the people in the Thionville area still speak LETZEBUERGESCH.

THIRTY YEARS WAR (1618–1648). This war started as a quarrel between the Protestant princes of northern Germany and the Catholic princes of southern Germany led by Ferdinand II, the Holy Roman Emperor, but ended up by dragging in most of the major states of Europe. First the Danish king Christian IV, then the Swedish king Gustavus Adolphus, intervened on the Protestant side, with the victories of Gustavus Adolphus tilting the balance in the Protestants' favor. The death of Gustavus Adolphus at the Battle of Lützen in 1632 put an end to the Protestant hopes of victory, and thereafter they were hard put to defend themselves against the imperial armies led by General Wallenstein. Wallenstein's subsequent fall from power and his murder in 1634 deprived the imperial forces of their greatest general.

In 1635, Cardinal Richelieu involved France in the Thirty Years War in opposition to the Hapsburg powers of Austria and Spain. As a result of Richelieu's negotiations, the elector of TRIER placed his possessions under the protection of the king of France and admitted a French garrison to that city. The presence of a powerful French garrrison so close to the Luxembourg border seemed to threaten the fortress, and the governor of Luxembourg, the count of Emden, attacked Trier and captured the elector, sending him as prisoner first to Luxembourg then to Brussels. Philip IV of Spain then delivered the elector into the hands of Emperor Ferdinand II as a felon, whereupon Richelieu declared war on the king of Spain and entered into an alliance with Sweden, the Protestant princes of Germany, and the Dutch. This turned the Spanish Netherlands into a theater of war, and it was invaded in turn by the French and Imperial armies. The towns of Wasserbillig, Grevenmacher, Wormeldange, Canach, and REMICH in Luxembourg territory were sacked and burned by an imperial army in 1636, despite the fact that Luxembourg was a Spanish possession. Croats and Poles from the imperial army were quartered on Luxembourg territory from 1636 to 1639 and committed some frightful atrocities. About two-thirds of the Luxembourg population died either of famine or plague during this occupation by "friendly forces."

The imperial army left Luxembourg in 1639 but was succeeded by a French army, which overran the southern districts, holding them for the rest of the war. The Treaty of Westphalia ended the Thirty Years War in 1648, but France and Spain were unable to come to terms and the war in the Low Countries continued for another eleven years, during which the French armies continued to ravage the Duchy of Luxembourg. The war between Spain and France was finally brought to an end by the TREATY OF THE PYRENEES in 1659.

THOMAS, SIDNEY GILCHRIST. English inventor who developed a process by which phosphorus could be removed from iron in Bessemer converters. The process was especially useful in Luxembourg, where the iron ore deposits contained large quantities of phosphorus. Introduced in 1884, it made Luxembourg one of the largest steel producers in Europe.

A by-product of the steel-making process introduced by Thomas was a valuable fertilizer known as "Thomas Scoria," which contained large amounts of phosphorus and lime. This fertilizer was especially valuable in the mineral-poor soils of the ARDENNES, making farming possible in areas where it had previously been impossible. Thomas came to consider this the most valuable product of his steel-making process.

Thomas died of tuberculosis in Paris in 1885, at the age of thirty-four.

THORN, GASTON. Foreign minister of Luxembourg from 1969 to 1979 and prime minister from 1974 to 1979. He later served a term as president of the European Commission (1980–1984).

Thorn is a leading member of the DEMOCRATIC PARTY and is chairman of the board of directors of the Banque Internationale à Luxembourg.

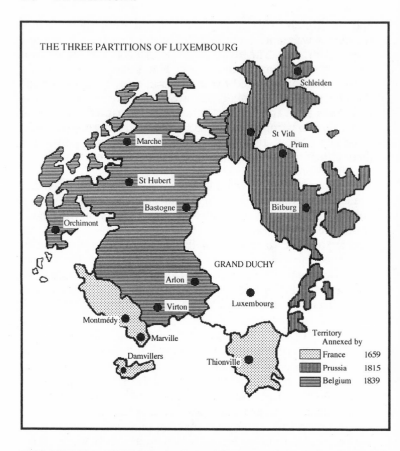

THE THREE PARTITIONS OF LUXEMBOURG

Schleiden

St Vith
Prüm

Marche

St Hubert

Bastogne

Bitburg

Orchimont

GRAND DUCHY

Arlon

Virton

Luxembourg

Montmédy

Marville

Damvillers

Thionville

Territory
Annexed by

France   1659
Prussia   1815
Belgium   1839

THE THREE ACORNS (LES TROIS GLANDS). When most of Fort Thungen, built during the eighteenth century by the Austrians on the KIRCHBERG, was demolished according to the terms of tthe SECOND TREATY OF LONDON of 1867, three towers crowned with acorn-shaped knobs were left standing. These towers are known in Luxembourg as the Three Acorns.

THREE PARTITIONS OF LUXEMBOURG. The First Partition of the Duchy took place in 1659, when LOUIS XIV of France, following a successful war against the Spanish, annexed a substantial part of Luxembourg's French-speaking territories (the areas around Montmédy, Carignon, Damvillers, Chauvency, and Marville) and the LETZEBUERGESCH-speaking area around THIONVILLE under the terms of the TREATY OF THE PYRENEES.

The Second Partition took place in 1815, when the CONGRESS OF VIENNA assigned the lands east of the MOSELLE, SURE, and Our Rivers, including Mandersfeld, St. Vith, PRUM, and BITBURG to Prussia. These lands were primarily Letzebuergesch-speaking and some of the people in this district still speak the language. In compensation, the new Grand Duchy acquired parts of the old principalities of Bouillon and Liège, which were French-speaking.

The Third Partition occurred in 1839, when the French-speaking part of the Grand Duchy, by far the larger part, was given to Belgium by the Great Powers under the terms of the FIRST TREATY OF LONDON. The section given to Belgium was renamed the province of Luxembourg. This partition had its roots in the successful Belgian revolution of 1830 against Dutch rule. The Grand Duchy as a whole sympathized with the Belgian revolution and sent delegates to the Belgian congress between 1831 and 1839. The whole of the Grand Duchy might have become part of the new kingdom of Belgium at that time if the fortress and capital city had not been held by a Prussian garrison. In the end, the First Treaty of London confirmed both Dutch rule over the truncated Grand Duchy and its continued membership in the GERMAN CONFEDERATION. The Grand Duchy was thus reduced to a Letzebuergesch-speaking core 1560 square kilometers (998 square miles) in size.

There is no irredentist movement in Luxembourg—no desire to reacquire its lost lands, which have been effectively integrated into Belgium, France, and Germany. Luxembourg, in fact, celebrates 1839 as its year of independence, the year in which its existence as a separate nation was confirmed, although it continued to be ruled by Dutch kings until 1890 and Prussian troops garrisoned the fortress until 1867.

TITELBERG. A large hill in the extreme southwest of the Grand Duchy, site of a pre-Roman Celtic oppidum and a Roman town, where the largest collection of artifacts from Gallo-Roman times in Luxembourg has been found. Ceramics, jewelry, Gallic and Roman coins, and altars to household gods have been discovered there, as well as objects from as far away as the Mediterranean. A mint and a glass factory were located on the Titelberg in Gallo-Roman times, as well as iron forges, houses, and other buildings. A major discovery on the Titelberg was a large bronze statue of a wild boar, now on display in the

Louvre. Other finds are on display in the NATIONAL MUSEUM.

TRANSPORTATION, PUBLIC AND PRIVATE. Since WORLD WAR II, Luxembourg has become one of the most prosperous nations in Europe. This has meant, among other things, a tremendous increase in the ownership of automobiles. Luxembourg is now second only to the United States in the number of private motor cars in circulation per capita. The great increase in the number of automobiles on the roads has brought the usual problems, including air pollution and traffic congestion. In recent years, Luxembourg has registered the second-highest number of deaths in road accidents per capita in Europe, second only to Portugal.

The Grand Duchy has a good network of secondary roads and is building autoroutes (expressways) as rapidly as it can. The first autoroutes were built in the southern part of the country and it is now possible to drive most of the way to Luxembourg city from the southern towns and cities by autoroute. The southern autoroute has been linked to the French and Belgian autoroute networks, and cars and heavy trucks may now travel directly from Metz and other French cities to Brussels and the Netherlands, bypassing Luxembourg city and other towns and cities in the Grand Duchy.

A new autoroute crosses the eastern frontier by a large bridge over the SURE River and joins the German autobahn network at TRIER. Work is under way on a ring road, to be completed in 1996, to enable traffic from the south to bypass the city of Luxembourg and join the autoroute to Trier. A northern autoroute is also under construction and some sections have been completed, although there is still controversy over the route it should follow from Luxembourg city to ETTELBRUCK. The government has proposed a route by which it would pass through the Grünewald, a large, picturesque forest, and nature-lovers are fighting this proposal.

The new autoroutes have the advantage of taking most of the heavy international truck traffic off the regular Luxembourg roads, but have had the negative effect of injuring the owners of small businesses along the former main highways between principal towns. They also allow foreigners to pass through parts of the Grand Duchy without seeing anything but a few kilometers of motorway. There have been some major accidents involving several cars on the autoroutes on foggy or rainy days, too, although nothing quite so bad as the pile-ups, involving hundreds of cars, that sometimes take place on the German autobahns.

Traffic congestion in Luxembourg city has become a major problem in recent years as private ownership of motor vehicles has increased. With more and more people driving to work in the city each day, a severe shortage of parking spaces developed, which the government met by building underground parking garages. This, unfortunately, has only increased traffic congestion on the city streets, because the larger number of parking spaces available has tempted more people to drive to work. Some of the larger enterprises have begun to move their headquarters out of the city. ARBED, for instance, opened a new, modern headquarters in ESCH-SUR-ALZETTE in 1994.

Increased use of private automobiles has resulted in fewer passengers using the railroads, which now run at a loss and must be subsidized by the government. There has been a steady decrease in the number of workers employed on the railroads, and some trains have been eliminated. Cutting train service, however, only leads to more patrons switching to the automobile.

The Grand Duchy has an extensive bus system, which includes municipal buses; buses operated by the CFL, the Luxembourg National Railways; and buses operated by private companies that serve localities not served by the municipal and CFL buses and also provide transportation for schoolchildren in some parts of the country.

The government could both save money and reduce traffic congestion by providing more school cafeterias and changing school schedules. Because most schoolchildren now go home for lunch, they now make two round trips a day between their homes and schools on Mondays, Wednesdays, and Fridays, and one round trip on Tuesdays, Thursdays, and Saturdays, which are half-holidays. The government has considered switching to a five-day school week and having pupils eat lunch at school, but this proposed change is opposed by the teachers, who like having two afternoons off a week, even if it means they have to teach Saturday mornings. Because the teachers have a strong union and both the union and the bus companies carry a good deal of political weight, it is not likely that the school schedule will change in the near future.

Forty years ago, Luxembourg city was still served by an extensive tram system, but the trams have now all been replaced by buses. Many European cities kept their tram systems and modernized them, and it has recently been proposed that

Luxembourg construct a new high-speed tram system to reduce traffic congestion and air pollution.

TREATY OF MAASTRICHT. The meeting of European heads of state in Maastricht in the Netherlands in 1991 led to momentous changes. Agreements were reached about measures leading to the development of common financial, foreign, and social policies among member states, and about the adoption of a common currrency.

The European Community's name was changed to EUROPEAN UNION, and it was agreed that nationals from member states living in other nations in the European Union would have the right to vote in local and European elections.

The powers of the European Parliament were strengthened and it was given a greater voice in the selection of the president of the EUROPEAN COMMISSION and in other important matters. (Ironically enough, JACQUES SANTER of Luxembourg, who had worked hard at Maastricht to increase the powers of the European Parliament, was almost the first to suffer from these increased powers. In July 1994, the Parliament approved his appointment as president of the European Commision by only a narrow majority, not from any objection towards Santer, but because the European heads of state had not consulted the Parliament in advance about his appointment.)

The only sour note at the Maastricht meeting was struck by John Major, prime minister of Great Britain, who insisted that Great Britain be allowed to opt out of the "social compact" that guaranteed common minimum working conditions and social benefits for workers in member countries.

TREATY OF MERSEN (870). When LOTHAIR II died without issue, his lands between the Rhine, the Meuse, and the MOSELLE were divided between his two uncles, Charles the Bald of France and Louis (Ludwig) the German at the Treaty of Mersen. The French received the western part, the Germans the eastern part. The County of Luxembourg was established in the part ceded to the Germans, although it later expanded to include lands to the west as well. (*See also* CHARLEMAGNE, LOTHAIR I, and LOTHARINGIA)

TREATY OF THE PYRENEES (1659). By the Treaty of the Pyrenees, which ended the eleven years of fighting between France and Spain following the THIRTY YEARS WAR,

France annexed the districts of THIONVILLE, Montmèdy, Ivoix-Carignon, Damvillers, Chauveney, and Marville, all of which were at that time parts of the Duchy of Luxembourg and among its most fertile and populous lands. (*See also* THREE PARTITIONS OF LUXEMBOURG).

This did not put an end to French encroachments on Luxembourg territory. LOUIS XIV interpreted some of the wording of the Treaty of the Pyrenees to justify further annexations. Between 1659 and 1683, the French annexed the counties of Chiny and Roussy, Rodemacher, Hesperange, Rollingen, Preisch, Puttingen, Orchimont, Virton, St. Mard, REMICH, and Grevenmacher, and in 1683 they laid siege to the fortress of Luxembourg itself, which they captured in 1684 and held until 1697. Only Louis XIV's defeat in the WAR OF THE LEAGUE OF AUGSBURG (1689–1697) forced him to give up these later annexations.

TREATY OF RYSWICK (1697). Ended the WAR OF THE LEAGUE OF AUGSBURG between LOUIS XIV and the alliance that had been formed against him by WILLIAM III of England. Louis was forced to evacuate the Duchy of Luxembourg and the other lands he had occupied in the Spanish Netherlands, although France retained the territories it had acquired in 1659 by the TREATY OF THE PYRENEES.

TREATY OF UTRECHT (1713). The Treaty of Utrecht put an end to the WAR OF THE SPANISH SUCCESSION. Philip V, the grandson of LOUIS XIV, was recognized as lawful heir to the Spanish kingdom, but many of Spain's possessions, including Naples, Milan, Sardinia, Mantua, and the Spanish Netherlands, were awarded to CHARLES VI, archduke of Austria and Holy Roman Emperor. The danger of French seizure of the Netherlands was ended, but France, now joined in a family alliance with Spain, remained the most powerful nation in Europe. Luxembourg gained eighty years of peace under Austrian rule.

TREATY OF VERDUN (A.D. 843). After the death of CHARLEMAGNE in 814, the empire he established fell apart. His son, Louis the Pious, was unable to assert the authority of his famous father, and in 843 Charlemagne's three grandsons divided his empire among them. The western part, allocated to Charles the Bald, developed eventually into the kingdom of France; the eastern part, given to Louis the German, developed into Germany. The oldest grandson, LOTHAIR I, was recognized as emperor and given a strip of territory that included northern Italy, Switzerland, Burgundy, Alsace, Lorraine, and the Netherlands, as far north as Frankish authority reached. It proved impossible to hold this strip of territory together as a single kingdom, although various attempts to do so were made over the centuries, with the Burgundians and the Spanish coming closest. What tended to happen instead was what happened in France and Germany at the same time: the feudal system became established, and local magnates assumed power in their own provinces, establishing independent or semi-independent feudal states. The kingdom of Lothair I was divided among his sons, with the northern part, which came to be called LOTHARINGIA, going to his son LOTHAIR II.

The process of disintegration and the growth of feudalism was speeded by the invasions of the NORTHMEN and MAGYARS from the north, west, and east, which the descendants of Charlemagne lacked the power to stem. Their inability to protect their kingdoms from invasions led to their eventual deposition and their replacement by local rulers who could provide the protection they could not. Hugh Capet, count of Paris, after fighting off a Viking attack on Paris, was recognized as king of France in place of the inept descendant of Charlemagne who claimed that office, although Hugh's authority barely extended beyond the Ile de France, the region around Paris.

Luxembourg was one of the feudal states that grew up in Lotharingia. (*See also* SIGEFROI, TREATY OF MERSEN, and WIGERIC)

TREMONT, AUGUSTE (1893–1980). Celebrated Luxembourg painter and sculptor of animals. Born in Luxembourg, he moved to Paris where he did most of his great work. Two of his bronze lions flank the steps of the LUXEMBOURG CITY HALL on the PLACE GUILLAUME and two guard the tomb of JOHN THE BLIND in the CATHEDRAL OF NOTRE DAME in Luxembourg.

The NATIONAL MUSEUM has several of Trémont's paintings and sculptures on display, including a magnificent sculpture of a black panther.

TREVERI. A Gallic tribe living in the area between the Meuse and MOSELLE Rivers in northeast Gaul, conquered by JULIUS CAESAR in 54 B.C. What eventually came to be Luxembourg grew up in the lands once inhabited by the Treveri, who must be numbered among the ancestors of the people of Luxembourg.

During the reign of the emperor Augustus, the Romans built a town on the Moselle that they named "Civitas Augusta Treverorum" (the city of Augusta among the Treveri) where they stationed part of a legion. The name was later shortened to "Trêves" in French, and "TRIER" in German. This town was the principal Roman center in the area.

Many of the Treveri served in the Roman army, and some of them even served in the Praetorian Guard.

TRIER. Founded by the Romans during the reign of the emperor Augustus, Trier (Civitas Augusta Treverorum) was an important Roman town on the MOSELLE. Because Trier was located on the Roman road to Cologne, the most important Roman town on the Rhine, the Romans stationed part of a legion there. Several western Roman emperors made Trier their capital, as did Constantine the Great during the fourth century (306–331). Diocletian made it the capital of the Diocese of Gaul.

Frankish incursions in the third and fourth centuries led the Romans to fortify the town, and it remained a walled city throughout later Roman times and the Middle Ages. Sections of the Roman wall are still standing, including the famous Porta Nigra. A Roman basilica, later converted into a Christian church, the remains of extensive Roman baths, a Roman amphitheater, and a stadium are also still standing. The museum at Trier has an important collection of Roman artifacts.

The fall of Trier to the FRANKS in A.D. 455 marked the end of Roman rule in northeast Gaul. (Trier had already been sacked by the HUNS in A.D. 451.) The Franks did not destroy the town, however, and it remained important throughout the Middle Ages, especially after it was raised to the status of an archbishopric during the ninth century. The archbishop of Trier became one of the most important ecclesiastical princes of the HOLY ROMAN EMPIRE. (*See also* GOLDEN BULL OF 1356)

The founder of Luxembourg, SIGEFROI was attorney for the ABBEY OF ST. MAXIMIN IN TRIER, from which he acquired, in 963, the land upon which he built his castle, beneath whose walls the town of Luxembourg grew up. Sigefroi's successors maintained good relations with the archbishop of Trier, although there were occasional quarrels. Baldwin of

Luxembourg, brother of the emperor HENRY VII, became archbishop of Trier in 1308.

St. Jerome, whose translation of the Bible into Latin, the Vulgate, became the authorized version of the scriptures in the Catholic Church, lived and studied in Trier some time between 366 and 370.

Trier is the closest German city to the borders of the Grand Duchy today. Since branches of some of the largest German department stores are located in Trier, many Luxembourgers do some of their shopping there.

VALLEY OF THE SEVEN CASTLES (VALLEE DES SEPT CHA-TEAUX). (1.) The valley of the Eisch River from the Belgian border to MERSCH. Castles or ruins of castles are located in Koerich, SEPTFONTAINES, Ansembourg (two), Hollenfels, and Mersch. The seventh castle is located at SCHÖNFELS, south of Mersch. This is not strictly speaking in the valley of the Eisch, but in the valley of the Mamer River, which joins the Eisch at Mersch.

(2.) A folklore group which keeps alive the costumes, dances, and songs of old Luxembourg. Its headquarters are in Mersch. An international folklore festival with groups from as far away as Turkey and Bulgaria took place in Mersch several years ago, with the Group Folklorique de la Vallée des Sept Chateaux serving as hosts.

VAUBAN, MARSHAL SEBASTIEN DE. The celebrated French military engineer who designed the fortifications of many of the major French cities during the reign of LOUIS XIV. Vauban took part in the French siege of the city of Luxembourg under the MARSHAL DE CREQUI in 1648. Soldiers and workmen under his command dug trenches, blew up the palisades and the city walls on the northwest side of the city, and undermined the walls on the eastern side.

The fortifications of Luxembourg had been strengthened by the Burgundians and Spanish, but during the French occupation of 1684–1697 Vauban improved and extended the fortifications, using the most advanced principles of European military architecture of the nineteenth century, turning the city into the "Gibraltar of the North." Vauban built new fortifications on the BOCK, the site of SIGEFROI's original castle, which had been destroyed in 1544 during the war between CHARLES V and Francis I, and incorporated them into the city's defenses. He also added star-shaped bastions and redoubts in the outlying areas beyond the city, including the PLATEAU DU RHAM.

Most of Vauban's military works disappeared when the fortifications of the city were demolished after 1867, under the terms of the SECOND TREATY OF LONDON. Some of the buildings he constructed as barracks are still standing, although they have been put to other uses; some of them house government offices.

VIADUCT. A bridge composed of twenty-five arches that curves over the valley of the PETRUSSE, built in 1861 to connect the upper city with the new railroad station. It was supplemented later by the PONT ADOLF, built between 1899 and 1903.

A wooden pedestrian passage called the "Passerelle" was built while the Viaduct was under construction, and for a time the Viaduct was known as the Passerelle.

VIANDEN. A town on the Our River in the northeastern part of the Grand Duchy, dominated by an eleventh century feudal castle, formerly the seat of the COUNTS OF VIANDEN. (*See also* CASTLE OF VIANDEN) The town is located on both banks of the river, not far from the German border. A large dam built since WORLD WAR II blocks the Our a short distance above Vianden, forming an artifical lake. The hydro-electric power generated by this dam supplies power not only to Luxembourg but also to the German electricity grid.

Vianden is on the edge of the ARDENNES and attracts many tourists during the summer. A chairlift carries visitors from the east bank across the river and up the hillside to a café on the Belvédère, a hill 1440-feet-high overlooking the town and the castle. Wild boar abound in the forests and may be hunted in season. VICTOR HUGO, who paid several visits to Luxembourg during his exile from France, lived in Vianden for a time, and the house that he lived in has been turned into a museum.

Vianden, with fewer than two thousand inhabitants, is the chief town of one of the twelve cantons into which the Grand Duchy is divided. It has one of the oldest churches in the country, which formerly served as the chapel of a Trinitarian monastery. In the year 1270 the defenses of the town included a wall with thirty-three turrets and five gates. Sections of the wall and some of the turrets are still standing. During the thirteenth century the Knights Templar had a commandery at Roth on the east bank of the Our, which included a basilica donated to them by Count Philip of Vianden in 1228. When the order was dissolved, their property was taken over by the Knights of St. John.

Vianden holds an annual nut fair in the fall. During the winter, some cross country skiing is done in the locality.

VIEUX LUXEMBOURG (OLD LUXEMBOURG). A society formed to carry on the work of restoring the buildings of the oldest part of the city, the GRUND. Twenty-five percent of the funding for this enterprise comes from the national government, twenty-five percent from the city of Luxembourg, and fifty percent from private contributions. A leading spirit in this enterprise is George M. Lentz, Jr., an active member of the AMERICAN LUXEMBOURG SOCIETY.

VOCATIONAL SCHOOLS. There are vocational schools in various towns. The one in Luxembourg, formerly known as the Ecole Professionel, is now called the Lyceé Technique des Arts et Metiers." This school, located in LIMPERTSBERG in a fine new set of buildings, attracts many pupils. The school offers four- to six-year programs in various trades and occupations. The first two years, equivalent to the American seventh and eighth grades, comprise a prevocational course, after which the students begin to specialize. Those following a four-year program finish at the age of sixteen, but are obliged by law to keep attending part-time classes until they are eighteen. During this two-year period most of them are apprentices or trainees in their trades, and their employers are required to give them time off to attend classes.

WALL OF WENCESLAS. A line of fortifications built across the PLATEAU DU RHAM during the reign of WENZEL I, duke of Luxembourg 1346–1383. (Wenceslas is the Latin form of his name.) The original wall was 13 meters (42 feet) high and, along with its three watchtowers, is still standing, following a modern restoration. The wall incorporates the Porte du Trêves, through which the Roman road to TRIER once ran. The Roman gate was destroyed, and it is the medieval gate, built at the same time as the rest of the wall, that has been restored.

WAR OF THE LEAGUE OF AUGSBURG (1689–1697). As stadholder of the Netherlands, William III of Orange had resisted as best he could French invasions of the Dutch Netherlands in the war of 1672–1678 and attempts by the French to conquer the Spanish Netherlands and Luxembourg in that and subsequent wars. When he became king of England in 1689 as WILLIAM III, he added England to the League of Augsburg, created between Austria, Brandenburg, and several smaller German states to oppose LOUIS XIV's expansionist aims, and formed a Grand Alliance which included Austria, England, Holland (the Dutch Netherlands), Spain, Sweden, and various smaller states. The war which followed was ended by the TREATY OF RYSWICK in 1697. The French were forced to give up the Duchy of Luxembourg and the other provinces in the Spanish Netherlands they had occupied. Dutch troops commanded by Count Frédérick d'Autel took possession of the fortress of Luxembourg in the name of Spain in 1698.

WAR OF THE SPANISH SUCCESSION (1702–1713). When Charles II, the last of Spain's Hapsburg rulers, died in 1700, he left his throne to Philip of Anjou, second grandson of LOUIS XIV of France. This raised at once the prospect of a Spanish-French alliance that would give Louis XIV everything he had been fighting for during the previous half-century. Emperor Leopold I of Austria, head of the German Hapsburgs, had hoped to place his son CHARLES VI on the Spanish throne, and he immediately asserted his son's right to rule. When Louis XIV put French troops into the forts along the border between France and the Spanish Netherlands, including Luxembourg, the Austrians were joined by England, Holland, and various other powers in a new grand alliance that carried on the War of the Spanish Succession against Louis XIV for the next eleven years. The English and the Dutch armies were commanded by England's best general, John Churchill, ancestor of Winston Churchill, and the Austrian armies by Prince Eugene of Savoy. Churchill was made duke of Marlborough as a reward for the victories his armies won in this war.

Many of the battles of this war were fought in the Spanish Netherlands. Luxembourg was involved only indirectly, although her fortress was occupied again by French troops. Marlborough captured TRIER in 1704, occupied the MOSELLE Valley, and his troops pillaged both Grevenmacher and ECHTERNACH, but he left without laying siege to the fortress. The armies of Louis XIV overran the Duchy in 1704, however, and the Luxembourgers were taxed heavily by both the Spanish and their enemies to help pay the costs of the war. A heavy freeze, with the temperature dropping to 30 degrees below zero Celsius, struck the country during the winter of

1709, and a famine followed the next summer because of the failure of the crops. The times were so bad that many Luxembourgers emigrated to England and Holland.

The TREATY OF UTRECHT ended the War of the Spanish Succession in 1713. By the terms of the treaty, the Spanish Netherlands, including the Duchy of Luxembourg, were awarded to Charles VI, who had succeeded Leopold I as Holy Roman Emperor. A Dutch garrison manned the fortress of Luxembourg from 1713 to 1715, when the Austrians finally took over.

WEBER, BATTY (1861–1940). Novelist, playwright, and author of newspaper serials. Although he wrote in German, his writings express a strong patriotic fervor, stressing Luxembourg's right to political and cultural independence.

WEIS, SOSTHENE (1872–1941). Postimpressionist Luxembourg painter who painted over four thousand watercolors, mostly views of the city of Luxembourg and its suburbs. He was a master at depicting the variations of light and atmosphere.

WELTER, NIKOLAUS (1871–1951). Luxembourg poet, a native of MERSCH, who wrote mostly in German but also wrote some poems in LETZEBUERGESCH. One of his patriotic poems in Letzebuergesch is inscribed on the base of the monument to national independence in Mersch.

WENZEL (WENCESLAS) I. Count, then duke of Luxembourg from 1353 to 1383. Wenzel was the son of JOHN THE BLIND by his second marriage, and was left Luxembourg in his father's will. When John died at the BATTLE OF CRECY in 1346, however, Wenzel was only nine, and his elder half-brother CHARLES IV usurped his titles, lands, and revenues for the next seven years. In compensation, Charles, now firmly established in his kingdom of Bohemia, raised Luxembourg to the status of a Duchy in 1354, so that Wenzel became the first duke of Luxembourg.

By his marriage to Jeanne of Brabant in 1352, Wenzel I acquired title to Brabant, greatly expanding the lands he ruled. During Wenzel's reign, Luxembourg reached its largest extent, four times the size of the present Grand Duchy. Wenzel made Brussels his capital and ruled his domains from there, rather than from the former capital of Luxembourg city.

Wenzel continued the work of extending the fortifications of

Luxembourg begun by his father John the Blind. He completed the third wall begun by John and built further defenses in the city's suburbs. The remains of the famous WALL OF WENCESLAS he constructed on the PLATEAU DU RHAM can still be seen.

Wenzel I succeeded in paying off the colossal debts run up by his father and older brother. He also purchased additional territories, including the County of Chiny, and greatly increased the number of his vassals. During his reign he had to fight several wars against his neighbors, in which he was not always successful. In 1341 he was captured by robber knights against whom he was waging a campaign. His brother, Charles IV, ransomed him and secured his release. Careful diplomacy repaired the losses he had suffered, however, and his realm increased in wealth and importance.

Wenzel I's death in 1383 without a male heir began the decline of Luxembourg. The Duchy of Brabant, held in his wife's name, passed into the hands of Anthony of Burgundy. Luxembourg reverted to the ownership of WENZEL II, son of Charles IV, who had been elected Holy Roman Emperor to succeed Charles the same year. Wenzel pawned the Duchy to Josse of Moravia, who pawned it in turn to Louis of Orleans. When Louis died, Wenzel II gave the pawned Duchy as a wedding present to his niece, ELIZABETH OF GOERLITZ.

Wenzel I and Wenzel II, especially the latter, are frequently referred to by the Latinized version of their name, Wenceslas.

WENZEL II (WENCESLAS). Son of Emperor CHARLES IV and king of Bohemia as Wenceslas IV, Wenzel II was elected Holy Roman Emperor upon the death of his father in 1376 and served as such until 1400. Both as Holy Roman Emperor and as king of Bohemia, Wenzel II is more commonly known as Wenceslas.

Wenzel II inherited the Duchy of Luxembourg upon the death of his uncle, WENZEL I, in 1383, but took little interest in it, visiting it only twice during his reign, in 1384 and 1388. He appointed John of Goerlitz as his lieutenant in Luxembourg in 1386, but mortgaged the entire duchy to Josse of Moravia in 1388. In 1402 Josse pawned Luxembourg in turn to Louis of Orleans for the sum of 100,000 gold ducats. Louis was assassinated in 1409, whereupon Josse took over Luxembourg again. In 1411, Wenzel II turned Luxembourg over to his niece, ELIZABETH OF GOERLITZ, in place of the dowry he had promised her when she married Anthony of Burgundy in 1409, but was unable to pay.

With Luxembourg, Elizabeth inherited the debt her uncle had incurred when he pawned it. Anthony died at the battle of Agincourt in 1415, whereupon Elizabeth married John of Bavaria, who died in 1425.

Wenzel's reign over Bohemia and the Holy Roman Empire was no more successful than his management of the Duchy of Luxembourg. He was deposed as Holy Roman Emperor for incompetence in 1400, although he continued to assert his right to the title until his death in 1419. His principal faults were, apparently, laziness and drunkenness. His brother SIGIS-MUND inherited the Duchy of Luxembourg upon his death.

The Great Schism in the Catholic Church took place during Wenzel's reign as emperor, with rival popes ruling at Avignon and Rome from 1389 to 1417. In 1407, the Council of Pisa deposed both popes and elected a new one, John XXIII. Neither of the other two popes would resign, however, so for nine years there were three rival popes. Finally, in 1417, all three popes were deposed by the Council of Constance, and an entirely new pope, Martin V, elected.

The Great Schism had an important effect on European politics. Wenzel sided with the Roman popes, but rival claimants to the imperial throne could appeal to the popes at Avignon in opposing him.

WERNER, PIERRE. Finance minister of the Grand Duchy from 1953 to 1974, and prime minister from 1959 to 1974 and from 1979 to 1984, continuing to serve as finance minister during his tenure as prime minister. More than any other political leader, Werner was responsible for the changes that made Luxembourg into a major world financial center, encouraging the development of banking and other financial services. He exerted great influence over other European finance ministers and heads of state and helped develop many of the financial policies adopted by the EUROPEAN UNION while it was still the European Economic Community.

Werner was leader of the CHRISTIAN SOCIAL PEOPLE'S PARTY. Although he retired as party leader and prime minister in 1984 in favor of JACQUES SANTER, he continues to enjoy great prestige as an elder statesman.

WIGERIC. Count of the Ardennes and count palatine of LO-THARINGIA (Lorraine). Father of SIGEFROI, the founder of

Luxembourg. As count palatine, he exercised power in the king's name, holding courts of law, coining money, and collecting taxes. From 900 to 925 he was nominally vasssal to both the king of France and the king of Germany, but after 925, he was vassal only to the German king.

Wigeric was married to a niece of Charles the Simple, king of the West Franks. He was the most powerful ruler in Lorraine and able to provide amply for his several sons, one of whom became bishop of Metz, one duke of Upper Lorraine, one duke of Lower Lorraine, and still another count of the Ardennes. Sigefroi, his youngest son, did not inherit any of his father's titles, but was given a considerable amount of property in the Saarland, in the BON PAYS, the ARDENNES, and the part of Germany centered on BITBURG.

WILLIAM I. King of the Netherlands and grand duke of Luxembourg, 1815–1840, and a lineal descendant of the COUNTS OF VIANDEN. William was the prince of Orange who went into exile after NAPOLEON I conquered the Netherlands. Just before the final defeat of Napoleon at Waterloo, the CONGRESS OF VIENNA joined both the former United Provinces and Belgium into a single kingdom and made William king. He was also awarded the Duchy of Luxembourg, which was raised to the rank of Grand Duchy, to be ruled by William and his successors of the House of Orange-Nassau as a separate state. At the same time, Luxembourg was made a member of the GERMAN CONFEDERATION and a Prussian garrison was installed in its fortress to defend it against possible future attacks by the French.

William I made himself unpopular in both Belgium and Luxembourg by trying to bring them under direct Dutch rule and by staffing their governments principally with Dutchmen. He made the use of the Dutch language compulsory in the law courts and in both the civil and military administrations and thus closed most public offices to the French-speaking Walloons of southern Belgium and the Luxembourgers. He closed the Catholic schools and ecclesiastical colleges and set up a separate college in the University of Louvain through which all aspirants to the Catholic priesthood had to pass, thus turning the Catholic clergy against him. He also imposed new taxes upon both Belgium and Luxembourg, which brought about great financial distress, especially in Luxembourg, the poorest of his provinces.

For these and other reasons, the Belgians rose in revolt

against William I in 1830 and established their own independent government, choosing Leopold of Saxe-Coburg-Gotha as their king. Although Luxembourg, particularly the capital city with its Prussian garrison, remained fairly quiescent, it did send delegates to the Belgian National Congress, and the provisional government in Brussels declared the Grand Duchy to be an integral part of Belgium.

The five great powers (Austria, France, Great Britain, Prussia, and Russia), appealed to by William I, sent representatives to a conference in London in 1830 that agreed to the separation of Belgium and Holland but confirmed William's personal rule over Luxembourg. Modifying their original position the following year, the London conference left the possession of Luxembourg to be decided by personal negotiations between Belgium and Holland, with Belgium being given the right to acquire Luxembourg. (*See* FIRST TREATY OF LONDON)

William I rejected the decisions of the London conference and refused to recognize Leopold as king of the Belgians. A Dutch army under his eldest son, the prince of Orange, was sent into Belgium to force it to submit to his rule. This army might have succeeded, but the French government intervened, sending fifty thousand soldiers into Belgium to support the new Belgian government. The London conference then agreed to the division of both Limburg and Luxembourg between Belgium and Holland. The Belgians accepted the compromise in 1831, but William I refused to accept it until 1839. Luxembourg remained in an anomalous position during these eight years, partly under Belgian and partly under Dutch rule. (*See* JOINT RULE, 1830–1839)

When William I finally agreed to the terms of the FIRST TREATY OF LONDON in 1839, the Grand Duchy was partitioned between Belgium and Holland. The five primarily French-speaking districts of Arlon, Bastogne, Marche, Neufchâteau, and Virton, comprising more than half its territory, were joined to Belgium, becoming the Belgian province of Luxembourg. The Grand Duchy was reduced to the three LETZEBUERGESCH-speaking districts which comprise the present Grand Duchy. (*See also* THREE PARTITIONS OF LUXEMBOURG)

William I abdicated as king and grand duke in 1840, in favor of his eldest son, the prince of Orange, who became WILLIAM II. Despite the shortcomings of his reign, William I had accomplished some good. The old Jesuit college in Luxembourg, which the French had turned into a municipal college in

1795, was renamed the ATHENEE GRAND-DUCAL in 1817 and William took many other measures to encourage education. He also conceived the project of joining the Meuse to the MOSELLE with a grand canal to cross Luxembourg from southeast to northwest, which would have done a great deal for the Grand Duchy had it been carried to completion. (Work on this canal was begun and a few sections completed, but it was never finished.)

WILLIAM II. King of the Netherlands and grand duke of Luxembourg (1840–1849). William II was the prince of Orange who commanded the Belgian and Dutch forces serving under the duke of Wellington at the Battle of Waterloo (1815) at which NAPOLEON I met his final defeat. An equestrian statue to William II stands on the PLACE GUILLAUME facing the GRAND DUCAL PALACE.

William II succeeded to the thrones of the Netherlands and Luxembourg upon the abdication of his father, WILLIAM I. William II was the most popular sovereign of the House of Orange–Nassau which ruled the Grand Duchy from 1815 to 1890. He dismissed most of the Dutch functionaries who had governed Luxembourg during the reign of his father and separated the administration of Luxembourg from that of the Netherlands. He created a Council of Government for the Grand Duchy, and with the assistance of a commission of eight prominent Luxembourgers he drew up a new constitution which went into effect in 1841. Luxembourg was divided into the three districts, twelve cantons, and numerous communes that make up the country today. By a treaty signed in 1842, he agreed to the accession of Luxembourg to the ZOLLVEREIN, the German Customs Union, membership in which brought prosperity to Luxembourg during the second half of the nineteenth century. He created a system of universal primary education modeled on the Belgian system, which allowed the teaching of the Catholic religion in the schools, a measure which did a great deal to conciliate the clergy. The ATHENEE GRAND-DUCAL was enlarged, and higher courses (cours supérieurs) were added to its curriculum. He also set up a vocational school and a normal school for the education of teachers.

The reconciliation with the church was confirmed by Pope Gregory XVI, who elevated the Grand Duchy into an apostolic vicarate. An episcopal seminary was established in Luxembourg in 1845 at which candidates for the priesthood were to be educated.

A more liberal constitution was promulgated under William II in 1848, creating a single-chamber legislature. This constitution, considered to be too liberal by the German Diet, was modified in 1856 during the reign of WILLIAM III but was restored in 1868.

WILLIAM III. King of the Netherlands and grand duke of Luxembourg (1849–1890). During the reign of William III, the Grand Duchy began the process by which it was transformed from a land of small farms and forests with most of its people living in rural poverty into a prosperous country with a major industrial, commercial, and financial base. The first railroads were built during his reign, iron and steel production was begun on a large scale in the southwestern part of the country, and the first major banks in the country were established. Luxembourg became an independent bishopric, and, largely through the efforts of the church, both primary and secondary education were strengthened and enhanced. (*See* BANKING, IRON AND STEEL MANUFACTURE, and RAILROAD SYSTEM)

Despite the many changes for the better that took place during his reign, William III was not a popular monarch. In 1856, over the objections of the CHAMBER OF DEPUTIES, he replaced the liberal constitution granted in 1848 by his father, WILLIAM II, with a reactionary constitution, which strengthened the powers of the monarchy, increased the financial qualifications for voting, abolished the Chamber of Deputies, and replaced it with an Assembly of Estates, dominated by a few wealthy and powerful people. He also set up a COUNCIL OF STATE, its members to be appointed by the monarch, with veto power over the Assembly.

More than that, William III showed his lack of interest in Luxembourg by agreeing to sell it to NAPOLEON III of France for five million Dutch florins. In a series of secret negotiations, Bismarck, the Prussian chancellor, agreed to the French purchase of the Grand Duchy, but public opinion in Germany, when it became aware of the proposed annexation, forced him to oppose it publicly. (*See also* CRISIS OF 1866–67) This almost led to war between France and Germany, but a conference of the various European powers in London worked out a compromise, set forth in the SECOND TREATY OF LONDON, by which the Grand Duchy would remain independent under the rule of William III and would become permanently neutral. The Prussian garrison would be withdrawn from Luxembourg, and the city's fortifications demolished. Later William III tried to sell the Grand Duchy to Belgium, with the price increased to seven million florins, but the attempted sale fell through.

The wisest and most popular thing William III did was to appoint his younger brother HENRY prince lieutenant of Luxembourg at the beginning of his reign. Henry governed the Grand Duchy from 1850 to 1879 in his brother's name, quietly opposed some of his brother's worst measures, and tried his best to advance and defend the interests of his adopted country.

William III died in 1890 and was succeeded by his daughter Wilhelmina on the Dutch throne. By the terms of the Nassau family compact of 1793, however, he was succeeded as grand duke of Luxembourg by ADOLF OF NASSAU-WEILBURG.

WILLIAM III, king of England (1689–1702). William, prince of Orange and hereditary stadholder of the Netherlands from 1650 to 1702, married Mary, older daughter of James II of England. When the English parliament deposed James II in the Glorious Revolution of 1688, they invited William and Mary to rule England. Parliament's original idea was to have Mary rule alone, but William refused to be merely the prince consort, so Parliament gave in and crowned them both in 1689 as William III and Mary II. They ruled jointly until Mary's death in 1694, after which William ruled alone until his own death in 1702.

William III was important in Luxembourg history because he added England to the alliance that had been formed against LOUIS XIV of France, whose armies were attempting to conquer the Spanish Netherlands. Louis's armies had already laid siege to and captured the fortress of Luxembourg in 1683–84 after occupying the rest of the Duchy. They had also conquered much of the rest of the Spanish Netherlands (modern Belgium) and their steady advance worried the Dutch, who had already been invaded by French armies during the war of 1672–1678.

William III added England to the alliance between Austria, Brandenburg, the Netherlands, Spain, Sweden, and other powers known as the League of Augsburg. In the WAR OF THE LEAGUE OF AUGSBURG that followed neither side won a decisive victory, but in the end Louis was forced to give up his conquests in the Spanish Netherlands, including the Duchy of Luxembourg. (*See* TREATY OF RYSWICK, 1697.)

Among the other titles he held, William III, as prince of Orange-Nassau, was hereditary count of Vianden, although his estates in the Grand Duchy along with his title had been given by Louis to someone else during the French occupation. (*See also* COUNTS OF VIANDEN)

WILLIAM IV. Grand duke of Luxembourg, 1905–1912. Second ruler of the present dynasty. Like his father, GRAND DUKE ADOLF, William was born in Germany. He ruled Luxembourg during the period of extensive economic development that took place before WORLD WAR I.

William IV's chief dynastic success was to persuade the CHAMBER OF DEPUTIES to change the law of succession to allow his daughters to succeed him. William had six daughters but no son, and if the Nassau family compact had been adhered to, the Grand Duchy would have passed into the hands of the nearest male relative of one of the other branches of the Nassau family. With the succession changed, William IV was succeeded in 1912 by his eldest daughter, MARIE-ADELAIDE, and in 1919 by his second daughter, CHARLOTTE.

William IV, like his father, was a German Protestant, and was buried on the grounds of the family castle at Weilburg rather than in the vault of the cathedral in Luxembourg.

WILLIAM THE SILENT (WILLIAM OF ORANGE). As prince of Orange and stadholder of Holland, Utrecht, and Zealand, William became the leader of the opposition to Spanish rule in the Netherlands between 1566 and 1584, when he was assassinated. His opposition began in defense of the rights of the "grandees," the leading members of the Council of State, who had been accustomed to playing a leading part in the government of the Netherlands as advisors to the king and his regents. CHARLES V had relied heavily upon the Council of State to maintain his rule in the Netherlands.

PHILIP II, son of Charles V, ruled the Netherlands personally from his capital at Brussels between 1555 and 1559. He spoke neither Dutch nor French, had little sympathy for the rights and privileges of the people he ruled, and excluded the grandees from his government. When Philip left for Spain in 1559, he appointed his half sister, Margaret of Parma, regent of the Netherlands in his place and left her a small council of servants loyal to the Spanish crown under the leadership of Antoine de Granvelle to advise her. In 1561, Granvelle was made a cardinal.

Between 1559 and 1566 the grandees, led by William the Silent and the counts of Egmont and Horn, led a movement to weaken the power of the inner council and restore their own authority. They succeeded in having Cardinal Granvelle removed from office and sent back to Spain.

The grandees, restored to power, pressed Margaret to relax the laws against heresy in the Netherlands, under which the small Protestant minority had been persecuted. Margaret gave in to their demands and petitioned Philip to give his consent to the measures granting religious toleration she had been forced to adopt.

This promising beginning to a policy of religious toleration came to a swift end in 1566 when the Iconoclastic Fury broke out. Protestant mobs throughout the Netherlands broke into Catholic churches, destroying images of the saints, statues, and paintings. The grandees rallied to Margaret's aid and helped her restore order, but the attack on the churches infuriated Philip, and he sent an army under the duke of ALVA to the Netherlands in 1567 to punish the heretics and restore Spanish rule. By the time the army arrived in the Netherlands it was no longer needed, because order had already been restored by Margaret and the grandees.

The leaders of the nobility in the Netherlands believed that they had acted as loyal subjects of the king, attempting to defend their traditional rights and liberties, but Philip regarded them as traitors. Alva hanged Egmont and Horn. William the Silent, wiser and warned in time, fled to Germany. From his place of exile, he became the leader of the revolt against Spanish rule. He invaded the Netherlands twice with an army. His first invasion, initially successful, failed, but the second succeeded, with the help of popular uprisings and the Sea Beggars, Dutch seamen who had been operating as privateers out of French and English ports. In the end, William the Silent failed to unite the Netherlands as an independent state free of Spanish rule, but he was responsible for the establishment of the Dutch Republic (the United Netherlands) in the seven northern provinces, which joined together in the Union of Utrecht in 1579 and declared their independence from Spain in 1581.

William the Silent had only a peripheral connection with the Duchy of Luxembourg, which remained loyal to the king of

Spain during the long struggle against Spanish rule in the rest of the Netherlands, but he had an important influence on Luxembourg history. He began the process which divided the Netherlands into two separate nations, Belgium and Holland, and the eventual reestablishment of Luxembourg as an independent state.

WILLIBRORD. First archbishop of Utrecht and first abbot of ECHTERNACH. Willibrord was one of twelve Anglo-Saxon monks who were sent to the Netherlands in 690 to begin the work of converting the Frisians to Christianity. He was befriended by PEPIN OF HERSTAL, who sent him to Rome, where he was consecrated archbishop of Utrecht in 696.

Willibrord extended his missionary work into other lands under Frankish rule. In 698 he was given land and buildings near Echternach by Irmina of Oeren, abbess of a nearby convent, where he founded a small monastery that became a center for the spread of Christianity in northern Europe.

Willibrord was born in Northumbria in 657 but spent twelve years in Ireland (c. 677–89), where he was strongly influenced by the Irish monastic tradition, which did not at that time separate the work of regular clergy distinctly from that of the secular clergy.

Willibrord, in the Irish tradition, divided the Frankish lands in the vicinity of Echternach into parishes and appointed parish priests. He smashed pagan altars and acquired a reputation for working miracles in fighting the plague that broke out in 718. Although he did his principal missionary work among the Frisians, he paid frequent visits to the abbey he had founded in Echternach, which he came to consider his home. He died at the abbey in 739, and was buried in the crypt of the abbey church, in a Merovingian sarcophagus. He came to be venerated as a saint, and his tomb in Echternach became a place of pilgrimage during the Middle Ages, as it continues to be today.

ALCUIN OF YORK was Willibrord's first biographer, but his life and work were also referred to in the ecclesiastical history written by the Venerable Bede. (*See also* ABBEY OF ECHTERNACH, BASILICA OF ECHTERNACH, DANCING PROCESSION AT ECHTERNACH, and GOLDEN BOOK OF ECHTERNACH)

WILTZ. A small city in the northwest part of the Grand Duchy sometimes known as the capital of the ARDENNES. The name Wiltz is of Celtic origin and means "by the brook". The town is located on a river bearing the same name.

The feudal lords of Wiltz were first mentioned in the eighth century. They became vassals of the counts of Luxembourg at a later date, and one of them attended the wedding of the COUNTESS ERMESINDE in 1214. The town received a feudal charter from its lords during the thirteenth century. The original charter was burned in a fire towards the end of the fourteenth century, but a new charter was granted in 1437. The Custine family became counts of Wiltz in 1653, and held the title until 1793, when the last count, François de Custine, fled the town during the French revolution.

The first feudal castle in Wiltz was destroyed some time between the twelfth and fourteenth centuries. A new castle in late Renaissance style was built between 1631 and 1727 on a hill near the site of the present castle. After the last count fled in 1793, the castle became national property. A girls' boarding school was lodged in the castle from 1896 to 1940, when it was taken over by the Germans as a women's teacher training college.

The castle was badly damaged during the BATTLE OF THE BULGE, but it was restored by the government after the war and is still the most prominent building in Wiltz. It now contains a museum of ancient arts and crafts as well as a war museum and an open-air stage where the annual European Festival of Open-Air Theatre and Music has been held since 1953. Operas by Mozart, Gounod, and Verdi, have been performed at these festivals, as well as plays by Molière and Schiller. The programs have also included musical performances by great artists ranging from Duke Ellington to Mtislav Rostropovitch.

Wiltz has been an industrial center since the seventeenth century, when its first paper mill opened. It was a weaving center long before the first cloth factory opened in 1857, but tanning was its principal industry until recently. Leather was being produced in Wiltz four hundred years ago, but production reached its height during the nineteenth century. Oak bark from the surrounding forests provided the most important material needed for tanning. By 1867 there were twenty-seven tanneries in Wiltz, but new processes developed in other countries gradually made their operations uneconomical, and the last tannery closed in 1960–61. New industries have been established which produce, among other things, plastic bags, floor coverings, and copper foil.

At one time Wiltz had two important breweries, but one of them ceased operations in 1956. (A project has just begun to convert its former premises into a museum.) The Simon Brewery, established in 1824, still survives and produces some of the finest beer in Luxembourg.

Wiltz was first connected to the PRINCE HENRI RAILROAD in 1881, with a line extended from Kautenbach. At one time the line went as far as Bastogne, just across the Belgian border, but that section was shut down in 1967.

Wiltz has a history of resistance to oppression. The KLÖPPELKRIEG of 1798, a protest against the French occupation and the drafting of Luxembourgers to serve in the French army, was centered in Wiltz, and the GENERAL STRIKE OF 1942 in protest against the German annexation of the Grand Duchy and the conscription of Luxembourgers into the German army during WORLD WAR II also began there. Six citizens of Wiltz, including four school teachers, were among the twenty-one Luxembourgers executed by the Germans in reprisal.

Ninety-one of Wiltz's people were forcibly resettled in Germany, 15 of its men died in Nazi concentration camps, and 164 of its young men were conscripted into the German army, of whom 42 were killed, 15 were reported missing in action, and 21 came back badly mutilated. Wiltz did not suffer much physical damage during the German occupation (1940–1944), but it was directly in the path of the Rundstedt Offensive of December 1944 and in that offensive the castle and 80 percent of its houses were destroyed or damaged and fifty townspeople were killed. The town was rebuilt after the war, however, and there are few remaining signs of extensive war damage. (*See also* BATTLE OF THE BULGE)

Besides the annual Summer Festival, Wiltz also holds a Broom Festival each year during the Pentecost holiday. At this time the golden broom plant (known as *Gênet* in French) blooms throughout the region. The festival features a parade of decorated floats, and thousands of visitors flock to Wiltz to watch it.

Wiltz is also the principal center of European Scouting, with eleven chalets and thirteen camping sites. Each year, as many as 36,000 scouts from all over Europe camp in Wiltz. The town also has a small airfield.

WINE MAKING. Most of the vineyards in Luxembourg are located on the sunny southward-facing slopes of the MO-

SELLE River. Viticulture was introduced by the Romans, perhaps as early as the third century A.D., and has continued to be an important industry ever since.

During the nineteenth century, Luxembourg wines were considered somewhat dry and sour and were blended with heavier, richer German wines for the general market. During the years 1925 through1940, however, a new policy was introduced by the Luxembourg government, by which vineyards on poorer soils that received less sunlight were abandoned, and new disease-resistant types of grapes such as the Auxerrois, Gewürztraminer, Pinot, and Riesling were introduced. The quality of Luxembourg wines was greatly improved, and they found a larger market outside the Grand Duchy.

White wines are the chief product of Luxembourg vineyards, but small quantities of an excellent rosé wine, a Pinot Noir, are produced. As a minimum sign of quality, wines must receive the Marque Nationale. Better wines made from selected grapes may receive the designation premier cru or grand premier cru. The Rieslings, Auxerrois, Pinot Blancs, Pinot Gris, and Gewürztraminers are considered the best wines. The Eblings and Rivaners form the bulk of the ordinary table wines.

Today, the better Luxembourg wines are considered superior to most of the German white wines and command a higher price. Luxembourg law limits the use of most additives, whereas German law permits the addition of sugar and other additives to their wines, so that Luxembourg wines are more acceptable to an educated palate.

Luxembourg vintners also produce good quality sparkling wines, by a méthode champenoise. (Luxembourg and EUROPEAN UNION law prevent them from being referred to as "champagne", because that designation is restricted to wine produced in the Champagne region of France.) The sparkling Moselles produced in Luxembourg have one great advantage over the French champagnes—they cost a great deal less. A superior type of sparkling Moselle, Crémant de Luxembourg, has recently been developed by Luxembourg vintners that matches many French champagnes in quality and has the added advantage of being cheaper.

Most Luxembourg vintners are organized into cooperatives, although there are still a few independent vintners and the Luxembourg government itself owns a vineyard or two.

Each village along the Moselle holds an annual wine festival, an occasion of great rejoicing. Decorated floats are prepared and a parade held, followed by an evening of drinking and dancing. Onlookers may purchase a small glass for ten francs which is refilled as often as they wish.

WORLD WAR I. Despite having signed the SECOND TREATY OF LONDON, under which the major European powers had agreed to respect the Grand Duchy's neutrality, Germany invaded Luxembourg during World War I at the same time it invaded Belgium, another country whose neutrality Germany had agreed to respect. On 1 August 1914 a German detachment seized the railroad station at Troisvierges, and the following day German troops occupied the entire Grand Duchy. They continued to occupy the country throughout the entire war, until after the armistice of 11 November 1918.

During the war, Germany took over the Luxembourg railroads, using them to transport troops and munitions to the western front. The Luxembourg iron and steel industry, the fifth largest in Europe (*See* IRON AND STEEL INDUSTRY), was put under German direction and its entire production diverted to meet the needs of the German war effort. A large part of Luxembourg's agricultural production was requisitioned and sent to Germany, producing severe food shortages in the Grand Duchy and making rationing necessary. Although the Luxembourg government continued to function, its measures were subject to the approval of the German military authorities, and the Grand Duchy was prevented from maintaining normal diplomatic relations with other countries, even those not directly involved in the war.

One important difference distinguishes the German occupation of Luxembourg during World War I from that during WORLD WAR II. In the First World War, the Grand Duchy was not annexed to Germany and remained under German military rather than civil government. The German Chancellor, Bethman-Hollweg, admitted that Germany's violation of the neutrality of both Belgium and Luxembourg was morally wrong and could be justified only by military necessity. The occupation was to be only temporary, and the independence of both nations was to be restored as soon as the fighting was over. As the war went on, however, and the sacrifices of the German people mounted, sentiment grew among the Germans for annexation of both Belgium and Luxembourg after a German victory as some compensation for these sacrifices. The German government seriously considered the possibility in 1917, and if the Germans had won the war, the Grand Duchy and a large part of Belgium might have been incorporated into the German empire.

The German occupation did accomplish one thing for Luxembourg. It helped unite people of all social classes and political parties against the Germans. The close economic ties which existed under the ZOLLVEREIN and the general prosperity it helped create in Luxembourg, as well as the immigration of large numbers of Germans to work in the iron and steel industry, had helped create a certain amount of pro-German sentiment in Luxembourg, and it is possible that the Grand Duchy might eventually have been absorbed into the German empire. The German occupation put an end to pro-German sentiment. Although the sort of atrocities visited on Luxembourgers by the Nazis during World War II were not committed during World War I, the military occupation was severe enough. When a strike, caused by low wages, high prices, poor working conditions, and food shortages, broke out in the iron and steel industry in May 1917, it was put down by the Germans with great severity. Some of the strikers were arrested and imprisoned in Germany, others were evicted from company houses and barred from company canteens, and some were blacklisted from further employment in the factories. By the end of the war, Luxembourgers had grown to dislike the Germans intensely.

The German occupation also almost brought about the fall of the ruling dynasty. Although her government had protested against many of the German actions, including the occupation itself, the GRAND DUCHESS MARIE-ADELAIDE came to be considered pro-German. When the German emperor, Wilhelm II, paid a state visit to Luxembourg during the war, the grand duchess received him, and she continued to visit her relatives in Germany. She kept her German advisors and entertained officers of the German garrison and visiting members of the German nobility. By the time the war ended, a considerable amount of republican sentiment had grown up in the Grand Duchy, which was not entirely ended by Marie-Adelaide's abdication and the accession of her sister CHARLOTTE to the grand-ducal throne.

Citizens of the Grand Duchy played another part in the First World War. When war broke out, thousands of Luxembourgers were working or studying abroad, the majority in France. Three thousand of them enlisted in the French army, most of them in the Foreign Legion, and two thousand lost their lives during the war. After the war, a monument was erected to the

Luxembourgers who died fighting on the Allied side (*See* GOLDEN LADY). The Germans demolished the monument during World War II, but it was reerected after that war.

WORLD WAR II. Despite Germany's failure to respect the neutrality of the Grand Duchy during WORLD WAR I, the Luxembourg government clung to its posture of neutrality during the period leading up to the Second World War, hoping that this time the Germans would keep their word. The Germans continued to promise to respect Luxembourg's neutrality in the event of another war; as late as 26 August 1939 the German minister to Luxembourg declared his government's intention to respect the inviolability of Luxembourg territory. Even on the day before the actual German invasion, the German government issued a memorandum declaring its intention not to impair the integrity and independence of the Grand Duchy either then or in the future.

Nevertheless, on 10 May 1940 the German armies invaded Luxembourg at the same time they invaded Belgium and the Netherlands. Fortunately, the Luxembourg government had anticipated the invasion. Between 3:00 and 5:00 A.M. the grand ducal family and most of the members of the government crossed the French border ahead of the German army and made their way to England by way of France, Spain, and Portugal. Upon reaching England, they repudiated the policy of neutrality that had been violated twice by the Germans and declared war on Germany. Over fifty thousand other Luxembourgers crossed the border into France at the same time, and another fifty thousand took refuge in the ARDENNES.

While the German army, the Wehrmacht, was in control of the Grand Duchy during the short period from 10 May until 21 July 1940, it behaved correctly and Luxembourg was not subjected to any great degree of persecution, although bands of German fifth columnists living in Luxembourg, with their few Luxembourg sympathizers, came out into the open and carried out an unsystematic persecution of their opponents. On 1 August 1940, however, the Grand Duchy was placed under the civil administration of Gauleiter Gustav Simon of Koblenz, and the full apparatus of Nazi terror went into operation. Jews were rounded up and deported to death camps, and thousands of other Luxembourg citizens were deported to Germany and forced to work in factories and on the roads. Some of them, known opponents of the Nazis, were shut up in concentration camps. The goods of Jews, emigrants, and deportees were confiscated. The Reichsmark was made the official currency and Luxembourgers were forced to trade their francs for Reichsmarks at an unfavorable rate of exchange. The Gestapo and the S.S. took over convents and government buildings, some of which were turned into schools for Hitler Youth and Mädchen. The GRAND DUCAL PALACE in Luxembourg was turned into a German officers' club. Policemen were forced to join the Nazi party; if they refused they lost their jobs and were deported. Listening to foreign radio stations, especially the BBC, was forbidden.

The Germans stopped the teaching of French in the schools and forebade the use of French expressions in ordinary conversation. The avenue de la Liberté was renamed Adolf Hitler Strasse, and Luxembourgers with French names were forced to adopt their German equivalents. The monument to the two thousand Luxembourgers who died fighting on the Allied side during World War I was destroyed.

On 30 April 1941 the conscription of Luxembourg youth into the Arbeitsdienst, the German labor force, began. On 10 October the same year, a survey was distributed to all Luxembourgers requiring them to list their nationality, ethnic roots, and native language. Only German and French were given as choices—the citizens were not given the opportunity to declare themselves Luxembourgers in any of these respects. This turned into a fiasco for the Nazi government. "Dreimal Letzebuergesch" became the slogan of all those opposed to the Nazi occupation, and 97 percent of the citizens surveyed crossed out the German and French options and wrote in "LETZEBUERGESCH" as their answer to all three questions.

The Luxembourgers resisted their oppressors by all means possible. At least five separate resistance organizations were formed, which published underground newspapers, forged identification papers, smuggled draft resisters and escaped Allied prisoners of war into France, committed acts of sabotage, and spied for the Allied powers. Links were established with the Belgian and French resistance, and some Luxembourgers joined the French resistance in the Auvergne and the Belgian resistance in the Ardennes.

On 30 August 1942 the Grand Duchy was officially annexed to the German Reich and military conscription was introduced. Over twelve thousand Luxembourgers were called up for service in the German army, although about 30 percent never

reported but hid themselves or escaped into neighboring coun-
tries. Many of those who were actually inducted into the
Wehrmacht deserted. In spite of this almost three thousand
Luxembourgers lost their lives serving in the German army.

In opposition to annexation and military conscription, a
general strike was called throughout the Grand Duchy. It began
in WILTZ in the north, but spread rapidly throughout the
country, reaching the steel mills in the south, the railway and
postal workers, printers, teachers, and school children. The
strike was put down with great brutality. Hostages were taken
and shot, thousand of individuals and families were deported
to Germany, and a reign of terror spread throughout the
country. The strike was broken and any illusions the Luxembourgers had about German respect for law or German sympathy for the people of Luxembourg disappeared. (*See* GEN-
ERAL STRIKE OF 1942)

Throughout the period of Nazi occupation, the Luxembourg
steel mills were forced to work day and night for the Nazi war
effort. A large part of the country's agricultural production
was confiscated and shipped to Germany, and Luxembourg's
forests were stripped to meet German needs. After the Allied
breakout from Normandy in 1944, plans were made by the
Germans to destroy factories, railroads, and bridges in Luxembourg, but the Allied advance was too rapid to allow them to
do this. Gauleiter Simon escaped to TRIER on 1 September
1944 but was forced by a German general to return to his post
in shame three days later.

The four years of Nazi occupation came to an end on
9 September 1944 when American troops, accompanied by
PRINCE FELIX, entered the Grand Duchy. Within days they
had pushed the retreating Germans out of all but a narrow strip
of territory in the east. The German army reoccupied the
northern part of the Grand Duchy three months later when
they launched their last major offensive in the west, the Rundstedt Offensive, also known as the BATTLE OF THE
BULGE. During this last attack the villages and towns in the
north suffered greater damage than they had during the entire
war up to that point. (*See also* PATTON, GENERAL
GEORGE S., JR.)

WURTH-POLFER, LYDIE. Mayor of Luxembourg city since
1982 and a leading vote-getter for the DEMOCRATIC PARTY
(DP). Mrs. Wurth-Polfer heads a city council made up of
a coalition between the DP and the CHRISTIAN SOCIAL

PEOPLE'S PARTY (CSV), In October 1994 she was chosen to be leader of the Democratic Party.

YOLANDE OF VIANDEN. When Yolande, daughter of a thirteenth century count of Vianden, wanted to become a nun in 1238, her family shut her up in one of the towers of the castle. She escaped by knotting her bedclothes together and climbing down the outside of the tower, and made her way to the convent at MARIENTHAL founded in 1235 by COUNTESS ERMESINDE as a refuge for ladies of noble birth. She was admitted to the convent and spent the rest of her life there, eventually becoming abbess. Her skull, preserved in a blue satin-lined box, was still being shown to visitors in 1955. She died in 1283.

ZOLLVEREIN. A customs union established in 1834 among the states of the GERMAN CONFEDERATION. Luxembourg adhered to the Zollverein from 1842 to 1918, despite having left the German Confederation in 1867. (*See the* SECOND TREATY OF LONDON)

Membership in the Zollverein was on the whole beneficial to the Grand Duchy, since it gave it a protected market for many of its products, including iron and steel. Germans helped develop the Luxembourg steel industry and German tariffs protected Luxembourg farm products as well as manufactured products from French and Belgian competition.

Close economic ties were built with the new German empire after 1871. Luxembourg imported high-grade coking coal from the Ruhr district and exported both iron ore and iron and steel products to Germany. With German support, Luxembourg developed one of the largest steel industries in Europe. It is possible that, had it not been for WORLD WAR I, membership in the Zollverein might eventually have led to Luxembourg becoming a part of the German empire, like the other possessions of the Nassau-Weilburg family. The German occupation of the Grand Duchy from 1914 to 1918 turned public sentiment against the Germans, however, and Germany's defeat forced Luxembourg to seek new economic relationships. (*See* CUSTOMS AND MONETARY UNION WITH BELGIUM)

Appendix A
Rulers of Luxembourg

Counts of Luxembourg

963–998	Sigefroi
998–1026	Henry I
1026–1047	Henry II
1047–1059	Giselbert
1059–1086	Conrad I
1086–1096	Henry III
1096–1129	William
1129–1136	Conrad II
1136–1196	Henry IV, count of Namur
1196–1247	Ermesinde
1247–1281	Henry V
1281–1288	Henry VI
1288–1310	Henry VII, Holy Roman Emperor (1310–1313)
1310–1346	John the Blind, king of Bohemia (1312–1346)
1346–1353	Charles, king of Bohemia and Holy Roman Emperor (as Charles IV) (1346–1383)
1353–1354	Wenzel I (became duke in 1354)

Dukes of Luxembourg

1354–1383	Wenzel I
1383–1419	Wenzel II, king of Bohemia as Wenceslas IV (1383–1419) and Holy Roman Emperor (1383–1410)
1419–1437	Sigismund, king of Hungary (1387–1437), king of Bohemia (1419–1437), and Holy Roman Emperor (1410–1437)
1437–1439	Elizabeth, daughter of Sigismund. Never exercised rule over Luxembourg, which had been in pawn to Elizabeth of Goerlitz since 1410. Sold rights to William of Saxony in 1439.
1439–1443	William, duke of Saxony

Burgundian Rulers

1443–1467 Philip the Good. Purchased Duchy of Luxembourg from Elizabeth of Goerlitz in 1441, captured fortress of Luxembourg in 1443.
1467–1477 Charles the Bold
1477–1482 Mary, daughter of Charles the Bold, married Maximilian of Austria in 1477.
1482–1506 Philip the Fair. Under regency of his father Maximilian until 1494.
1506–1555 Charles of Ghent, son of Philip the Fair. King of Spain as Charles I (1516–1556), Holy Roman Emperor as Charles V (1519–1558).

Spanish Rulers

1555–1598 Philip II, king of Spain (1556–1598)
1598–1621 Albert and Isabella
1621–1665 Philip IV
1665–1700 Charles II (except for 1684–1697 when French troops occupied the Duchy)
1700–1713 Philip V

Austrian Rulers

1713–1740 Charles VI, Holy Roman Emperor (1711–1740)
1740–1780 Maria Theresa, archduchess of Austria
1780–1790 Joseph II, Holy Roman Emperor (1765–1790)
1790–1792 Leopold II, Holy Roman Emperor (1790–1792)
1792–1796 Francis II, Holy Roman Emperor (1792—1806)

French Rulers

1795–1799 French Republic and Directory
1799–1815 Napoleon I, first consul (1799–1804) and emperor of the French (1804–1815)

House of Orange-Nassau
(kings of the Netherlands and grand dukes of Luxembourg)

1815–1840 William I
1840–1849 William II
1849–1890 William III

House of Nassau-Weilburg

1890–1905	Adolf I
1905–1912	William IV
1912–1919	Marie-Adelaide
1919–1964	Charlotte
1964–	Jean

Appendix B
Ministers of State (Prime Ministers) since 1848

1848–1853	Jean-Jacques Willmar (President of the Government)
1853–1860	Charles-Matthias Simons
1860–1867	Baron Victor de Tornaco
1867–1874	Emmanuel Servais
1874–1885	Felix de Blochausen
1885–1888	Edward Thilges
1888–1915	Paul Eyschen
1915–1916	Hubert Loutsch
1916–1917	Victor Thorn
1917–1918	Léon Kauffmann
1918–1925	Emile Reuter
1925–1937	Joseph Bech
1937–1953	Pierre Dupong
1953–1958	Joseph Bech
1959–1974	Pierre Werner
1974–1979	Gaston Thorn
1979–1984	Pierre Werner
1984–1995	Jacques Santer
1995–	Jean-Claude Juncker

Appendix C
American Units Stationed in the Grand Duchy

During World War I (1918–19)
5th Division
33rd Division

During World War II (1944–45)
5th Armored Division
90th Infantry (Texas-Oklahoma) Division
4th Infantry (Ivy) Division
28th Infantry (Keystone) Division
9th Armored (Phantom) Division
76th Infantry Division
50th Infantry (Red Diamond) Division
6th Cavalry Group
5th Infantry Division
17th Airborne Division
26th Infantry (Yankee) Division
80th Infantry (Blue Ridge) Division
10th Armored Division
4th Armored Division
35th Infantry (Santa Fe) Division
83rd Infantry (Thunderbolt) Division
6th Armored Division
2nd Cavalry Group
28th Infantry Division
87th Infantry Division

Appendix D
The Luxembourg National Hymn

ONS HÉMECHT (OUR HOMELAND)

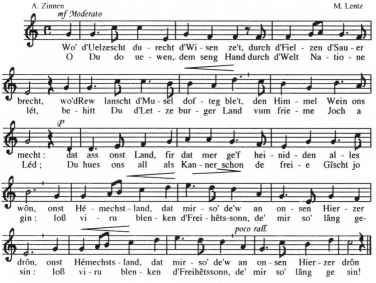

A. Zinnen *mf Moderato* M. Lentz

Wo' d'Uelzescht du - recht d'Wi - sen ze't, durch d'Fiel - zen d'Sau - er
O Du do ue - wen,. dem seng Hand durch d'Welt Na - tio - ne

brecht, wo'dRew lanscht d'Mu - sel dof - teg ble't, den Him - mel Wein ons
lét, be - hitt Du d'Let - ze bur - ger Land vum frie - me Joch a

mecht: dat ass onst Land, fir dat mer ge'f hei - nid - den al - les
Léd; Du hues ons all als Kan - ner_schon de frei - e Gîscht jo

wôn, onst Hé - mechst - land, dat mir - so' de'w an on - sen Hier - zer
gin: loß vi - ru blen - ken d'Frei - hêts-sonn, de' mir so' lâng ge-

poco raff.

drôn, onst Hémechts - land, dat mir - so' de'w an on - sen Hier - zer drôn
sin: loß vi - ru blen - ken d'Freihêtssonn, de' mir so' lâng ge sin!

French Translation by M. Tresch	English Version by N. E. Weydert
Ou s'en va par les vertes plaines l'Alzette aux bords fleuris, où par les monts boisés de chênes la Sûre creuse son lit, la Moselle en ses flots dorés mire la vigne en fleur c'est là mon pays adoré. aimé du fond du coeur.	Where you see the slow Alzette flow, the Sura play wild pranks, where lovely vineyards amply grow on the Moselle's banks, there lies the land for which our thanks are owed to God above, our own, our native land which ranks well foremost in our love.
O Seigneur, dont la main puissante gouverne les humains, à ma patrie indépendante donne d'heureux destins! De notre enfance qu'animait l'antique fierté fais luire, radieux à jamais, le soleil Liberté!	Our Father in Heaven Whose powerful hand makes states or lays them low, protect Thy Luxembourger Land from foreign foe or woe. God's golden liberty bestow On us now as of yore. Let freedom's sun in glory glow for now and evermore.

219

Bibliography

Introduction

Compiling a bibliography about Luxembourg for the average American or British reader is a difficult task, largely because few books about Luxembourg have been written in English. James Newcomer, a veteran of Patton's Third Army, published a history of Luxembourg from 963 to1983 in English a few years ago, and plans to bring his book up to date in the near future. Apart from that, there have been a few accounts by travelers, a few works published by the Luxembourg government for the tourist trade or to influence opinion in other countries at critical moments, and sections of other works written about times when Luxembourg played a major part in larger European affairs, such as the Burgundian attempt to establish a kingdom in the Netherlands, or the revolt of the Netherlands against Spanish rule in the sixteenth and seventeenth centuries.

Many works have been written about Luxembourg in French or German, of course, since these are the two foreign languages in which most Luxembourg writers are fluent. Their own language is Letzebuergesch, not commonly spoken or read outside the boundaries of the Grand Duchy. Luxembourgers have written a great deal about their own country, but little of their work is accessible to readers in England or the United States. There is a large and growing school of historians in Luxembourg, of whom the current dean is Christian Calmes, who has written extensively about the Grand Duchy during the nineteenth and twentieth centuries, but only one of his works has been translated into English so far.

There is ample source material available for a scholarly history of Luxembourg. There are, to begin with, the Luxembourg State Archives and the archives of the city of Luxembourg. In addition, there are the collection of the Luxembourg National Library and the resources of the National Museum of History and Art. The Royal Library in Brussels, to which Charles V moved many of Luxembourg's state records during the sixteenth century, and the National Museum in Paris also contain large collections of material about Luxembourg. The researcher must, of course, be able to read French and German well, and if possible, Latin, in which many of the earlier documents were written.

Why a scholarly history about Luxembourg? First, because the country has had a long, interesting history, and second because at various times it has played an important role in European history. There is the further advantage that the American or British researcher would be working in a largely virgin field, in which he or she would find few predecessors. There is some doubt whether we need yet another book about the American or British civil wars, but little doubt that we need to know a great deal more about Europe. A Fulbright grant, or a grant from some other source, to sustain a historian while he compiled a scholarly history of Luxembourg would seem to be in order.

Contents

1. Accounts by Travelers and Visitors

Casey, Robert J. *The Land of Haunted Castles*, New York, Century Co., 1921. The author spent several months wandering about Luxembourg in 1920, and his work is a mine of information about the Grand Duchy and its history.

Miles, Beryl. *Attic in Luxembourg*, London, John Murray, 1956. This may be the best book about Luxembourg written by a foreigner. The author spent several months in Luxembourg in 1955, meeting people in all walks of life. She traveled everywhere in the country by automobile, bicycle, and train. She paints an excellent picture of the country, its people, and its institutions at a particular point in their history, and supplies a good deal of information about the art, buildings, culture, customs, history, literature, towns, and regions of the country.

Passmore, T. H. *In Further Ardenne: A Study of the Grand Duchy of Luxembourg*, New York, E. P. Dutton and Co., 1905. An older book, depicting the Grand Duchy as it was during the early years of the twentieth century, during the reign of Grand Duke Adolf.

Pilkington, Roger. *Small Boat to Luxembourg*, London, Macmillan, 1967. Pilkington traced Robert Louis Stevenson's journey down the Belgian and French canals in *The Inland Journey*, then crossed to the Moselle and followed that river down to Luxembourg.

Renwick, George. *Luxembourg: The Grand Duchy and Its People*, London, Unwin, 1913. Published just before the First World War, this book contains many facts about Luxembourg history, some not available in more recent publications, as well as some interesting sidelights.

Saint-Hilaire, Paul de. *L'Ardenne Mysterieuse*, Brussels, Ressel, 1976.

Schroen, Michael. *Das Grossherztum Luxembourg: Portrait einer Kleinem Demokratie*, Bochum, Studienverlag N. Brockmeyer, 1986.

Taylor-Whitehead, W. J. *Luxembourg: Land of Legends*, New York, Garden Press, 1976 (also London, Constable, 1951).

2. Archaeology

Bronze Figures de l'Epoque Romaine (2me edition), Luxembourg, Musée d'Histoire et d'Art, 1975.

Bulletin trimestriel de l'institut archéologique, Arlon, Imp. G. Everling, 1924–present.

Cartes archéoligiques du Grand Duché de Luxembourg, Luxembourg, Musée d'Histoire et d'Art, 1975.

Krier, J. et R. Wagner, "Das römische Theater in Dalheim," *Hémecht* 37, 1985.

Reding, Lucien. *Les monnaies gauloises de Titelberg*, Luxembourg, Ministère des Arts et Sciences, 1972.

Rink, E. "Ricciacus-Dalheim," *T' Hémecht* 5, 1952.

Stillwell, Richard. *The Princeton Encyclopedia of Classical Sites*, Princeton, N.J., Princeton University Press, 1976.

Ternes, Charles, M., ed. *Bulletin des antiquités luxembourgeo-*

ises, Luxembourg, Société des Antiquités Luxembourgeoises, issued annually 1969–present.

Ternes, Charles M. *Etudes concernant l'histoire et l'archaeologié de la gaule belgique*, Luxembourg, Centre Universitaire, 1990.

———. *Le Grand-Duché de Luxembourg à l'epoque romaine*, Mersch, Impr. Fr. Faber, 1991.

———. *Répertoire archéologique du Grand-Duché de Luxembourg*, Bruxelles, Centre national des recherches archéologiques au Belgique, 1970.

———. *Das Romische Luxemburg*, Zurich, Roggi-Verlag, 1971.

Wagner, Robert. *Archäeologischer Rundgang um Dalheim*, Luxembourg, Musée National d'Histoire et d'Art, 1991.

Weiller, Raymond. *Monnaies antiques découvertes du Grand-Duché de Luxembourg*, Berlin, Mann, 1972.

———. "Neuere Münzfunde aus Dalheim" *Hémecht* 30, 1978.

3. Art and Architecture

L'Art au Luxembourg, Luxembourg, Ministère des Arts et Sciences, 1966.

Brown-Manrique, Gerarde. *Preservation and Architectural Continuity in Luxembourg: Proposals*, Oxford, Ohio, Miami University Press, 1985.

Clement, Raymond. *Oesling: Lichtspiel*, Luxembourg, Eds. Sams-Pfaffenthal, 1994.

Engels, Michel, et Matthias Huss. *Le Luxembourg pittoresque: das romantische Luxembourg*, Luxembourg, E. Kutter, 1973. Reprint of 1901 edition. Contains color drawings and sketches by noted artists.

Entringer, Henri. *Le monde et le marche de l'art au Luxembourg*, Luxembourg, Impr. Saint-Paul, 1991.

Fresez, Jean-Baptiste. *Album pittoresque du Grand-Duché de Luxembourg*, Luxembourg, E. Kutter, 1968. Reprint of 1857 edition. Fresez was one of Luxembourg's best-known artists.

Goergen, Edmond. "Les peintures murales du moyen age et de la Renaissance," in *L'Art au Luxembourg*, Luxembourg, Ministère des Arts et Sciences, 1966.

Hemmer, Carlo. *Aspects du Luxembourg*, Luxembourg, Impr. Bourg-Bourger, 1958.

———. *Images du Luxembourg*, Luxembourg, Impr. Bourg-Bourger, 1972. In three languages. English translation by Franz Reuter and R. Warren-Davis.

Hubert, Jean. *L'art pre-romain*, Chartres, Librairie des Arts et Metiers, 1994.

Meyers, Joseph. "La prehistoire et les temps des romains," in *L'Art au Luxembourg*, Luxembourg, Ministère des Arts et Sciences, 1966.

Muller, Joseph-Emile. *L'Art au vingtième siècle*, Paris, Larousse, 1967.

————. *Joseph Kutter*, Luxembourg, Eds. Pierre Linden, 1946.

————. "Les miniatures d'Echternach," in *L'Art au Luxembourg*, Luxembourg, Ministère des Arts et Sciences, 1966.

Northumb, Albert. "L'architecture religieuse aux temps gothique," in *L'Art au Luxembourg*, Luxembourg, Ministère des Arts et Sciences, 1966.

————. "L'Art au Luxembourg," in *Le Luxembourg: Livre du Centenaire*, ed. Albert Northumb, Luxembourg, Gouvernement Grand-Ducal, 1948.

150 Ans d'Art Luxembourg Au Musée Nationale d'Histoire et d'Art: Peinture et Sculpture depuis 1837 (2e edition), Luxembourg, Musée Nationale, 1991.

Raus, M. *Nico Klopp: Das Licht, der Schätten*, Schwebsange, Les publications mosellanes, 1974.

Schmitt, Georges. *Gustave Trémont*, Luxembourg, Impr. Saint-Paul, 1980.

————. "Les scupltures romane et la sculpture gothique," in *L'Art au Luxembourg*, Luxembourg, Ministère des Arts et Sciences, 1966.

Sitwell, Sacheverell, and Roger Madol. *Album de Redouté: with 25 facsimile colour prints from the edition of 1824 and a new Redouté bibliography*, London, Collins, 1954.

Spang, Paul. "L'epoque franque," in *L'Art au Luxembourg*, Luxembourg, Ministère des Arts et Sciences, 1966.

Sprunck, Alphonse. *Le palais grand-ducal à travers les âges*, Luxembourg, Eds. du Centre, 1957. English text by Marcel Schiltz.

Staub, Richard M. "L'architecture religieuse preromaine et romain," in *L'Art au Luxembourg*, Luxembourg, Ministère des Arts et Sciences, 1966.

Turner, Joseph M. W. *Vues pittoresques de Luxembourg: dessins et aquarelles*, Luxembourg, E. Kutter, 1977. Drawings and watercolors of Luxembourg made by the celebrated English painter during his trips to Luxembourg in 1825 and 1834.

Weicherding-Goergen, Blanche. *Les manuscripts à peintures de la bibliothèque nationale de Luxembourg*, Luxembourg, Impr. Joseph Beffort, 1968.

4. Banking, Finance, and the Economy

Adam, Ferdy, ed. *L'economie luxembourgeoise en 1993*, Luxembourg, STATEC, 1994.

Als, George. *Luxembourg: Historical, Geographic, and Economic Profile*, Luxembourg, Service Information et Presse, 1980.

———. *Le Luxembourg: Profil historique, geographique, et economique*, Pau, Eds. Bonneton Christine, 1984.

Businessman's Guide to Luxembourg (2nd ed.), Luxembourg, Group Presse Consultant International, 1991.

Cahiers d'economie, Luxembourg, Centre Universitaire, 1993.

Calmes, Albert. "Aperçu de l'histoire economique de 1859 a 1939," in *Le Luxembourg: Livre du Centenaire*, ed. Albert Northumb, Luxembourg, Gouvernement Grand-Ducal, 1948.

Calmes, Christian. *Une banque raconte son histoire: histoire de la Banque Internationale, 1856–1981*, Luxembourg, Impr. Saint-Paul, 1981. Vol. V in *Histoire Contemporaine du Grand-Duché de Luxembourg*.

Dargent, Jean. *Luxembourg: An International Finance Center* (translated from the French by Fernand Rau), Luxembourg, Service Information et Presse, 1972.

Hemmer, Carlo. *L'economie du Grand-Duché de Luxembourg*, Luxembourg, Eds. Joseph Beffort, 1948.

The International Review. *Destination: The Grand Duchy of Luxembourg*, Jersey, Channel Islands, Review Publishing Company, 1990. Recent publication providing an economic survey of the Grand Duchy.

Kieffer, Elizabeth. "Le Luxembourg dans l'Union economique belge-luxembourgeoise," in *Benelux, revue trimestrielle*, Bruxelles, no. 24, 1987, pp. 27–31.

Margue, Paul et Marie-Paule Jungblut. *Le Luxembourg et sa Monnaie*, Luxembourg, Eds. Guy Binsfeld, 1990.

Nash, Nathaniel C. "German Tax Revolt in Luxembourg." in *International Herald Tribune*, Saturday-Sunday, 26–27 November 1994.

Rollman, N. *Le marché financier luxembourgeoise face à la conversion industrielle*, Luxembourg, Impr. Saint-Paul, 1963.

Schuller, Guy. *Le commerce exterieur du Luxembourg, 1973–1992*, Luxembourg, STATEC, 1994.

Treinen, J. *L'economie luxembourgeoise sous la régime de l'union douanière belgo-luxembourgeoise*, Luxembourg, J. Beffort, 1974.

Weber, Paul. *Histoire de l'economie luxembourgeoise*, Luxembourg, Chamber of Commerce, 1980.

5. Bibliography

Bibliographie luxembourgeoise, Luxembourg, Bibliothèque Nationale, 1944–90. Published annually. The 1990 edition was published in 1993.
Christophory, Jul. *150 manuscrits precieux du 9e au 16e siècle conserves à la bibliotheque nationale de Luxembourg*, Luxembourg, Bibliothèque Nationale, 1989.
Hury, Carlo, and Jules Christophory. *Luxembourg*, Oxford and Santa Barbara, Clio Press World Bibliographical Series, 1981.
Hury, Carlo. *Luxemburgensia: Eine Bibliographie des Bibliographies*, Luxembourg, Impr. Saint-Paul, 1964.
Vekene, Emil van der. *Les acquisitions du Département de la Réserve précieuse en 1971*, Luxembourg, Bibliothèque Nationale, 1972.
———. *Katalog der Inkunabeln der National-bibliothek Luxemburg*, Luxembourg, Impr. Saint-Paul, 1970.
———. *Repertoire de bibliothèques scientifiques ou populaires au Grand-Duché de Luxembourg*, Luxembourg, Impr. Saint-Paul, 1971.
Yonte, Jean-Marie. *Sources pour l'histoire contemporaine du Grand-Duché de Luxembourg*, Bruxelle, Archives Générales du Royaume, 1992.

6. Biography

Mersch, Jules, ed. *Biographie Nationale*, Luxembourg, Impr. Victor Buck (11 vols.), 1974–75.
Neyen, Auguste: *Biographie luxembourgeoise: histoire des hommes distingués originaire de ce pays* (3 vols.), New York, Olms, 1972–73.

7. Castles in Luxembourg

Casey, Robert L. *The Land of Haunted Castles*, New York, The Century Company, 1921.
Friedrich, Evy. *Luxembourg: Châteaux et châteaux-forts*, Luxembourg, Eds. Guy Binsfeld, 1984.

Koltz, Jean-Pierre. *Les chateaux historiques de Luxembourg* (with photographs by Tony Krier), Luxembourg, Impr. Saint-Paul, 1975.

Northumb, Albert. "Chateaux forts et enceintes urbaines," in *L'Art au Luxembourg*, Luxembourg, Ministère des Arts et Sciences, 1966.

Valenne, Roger. *Les chateaux forts du Grand-Duché de Luxembourg*, Luxembourg, Helmsange, 1989.

8. Cities and Towns

A. Luxembourg, City and Fortress

A Brief Survey of the City of Luxembourg, Luxembourg, Syndicat d'Initiative et du Tourisme, 1982.

Burns, André. "Die Bundesfestung Luxemburg," in *Luxemburg und die Festungen des Deutsche Bundes, 1815–1866*, Luxembourg, Frënn vun der Festungsgeschicht Lëtzebuerg, 1994.

Burns, André et al. *Das Leben in der Bundesfestung Luxemburg (1815–1867)*, Luxembourg, Musée nationale d'histoire et de l'art, 1993.

Conly, Robert L. "Luxembourg, the quiet fortess," in *National Geographic*, vol. 138, no. 1, 1970.

Englehardt, Friedrich W. *Geschichte der Stadt und Festung Luxemburg*, Luxembourg, Verlag S.D. Krippler-Muller, 1979.

Feitler, Edouard. *Luxemburg Deine Heimatstadt*, Luxembourg, Impr. Saint-Paul, 1967.

Jacquemin, Albert. *Die Festung Luxemburg von 1654 bis 1867*, Luxembourg, Eds. Saint-Paul, 1994.

Kartheiser, Josiane. *Luxembourg City*, Luxembourg, Eds. Guy Binsfeld, 1989. Parallel texts in German and French, English translation by Simon Gray.

Koltz, Jean-Pierre. *Baugeschichte der Stadt und Festung Luxemburg*, 3 vols., Luxembourg, Impr. Saint-Paul, 1970.

Lascombes, François. *Chronik der Stadt Luxemburg*, Luxembourg, Impr. Saint-Paul, 1976.

Pauly, Joseph et Paul Spang. *Luxembourg, la forteresse éclatée*, Luxembourg, RTL Edition, 1984.

Rousseau, Paul. Luxembourg: La Forteresse, Luxembourg, Eds. Guy Binsfeld, 1984.

Soldeville, Alain et Michel Raus. *Luxembourg: capitale*, Luxembourg, Eds. Saint-Paul, 1990.

Trausch, Gilbert, et al. *La Ville de Luxembourg: Du chateau des*

comtes à la métropole européenne, Antwerp, Fonds Mercator Paribas, 1994.
Ville de Luxembourg, Guide de l'Administré, Luxembourg, Impr. Saint-Paul, 1987.

B. Other Cities and Towns

Aperçu historique et touristique illustré de la commune et de la ville de Differdange, Differdange, Syndicat d'Initiative, 1937.
Chronik der Stadt Vianden, Vianden, Veiner Geschichts frënn, 1976.
Clervaux en Ardenne (2nd ed.), Clervaux, Syndicat d'Initiative, 1993.
Echternach Notre Ville, Echternach, Société d'Embellissement et du Tourisme, 1972.
Livre du Centenaire de la ville d'Esch-sur-Alzette, Esch-sur-Alzette, Imprimerie Cooperative, 1956.
Massard, Joseph A. *Echternach und die Cholera*, Luxembourg, Centre Universitaire, 1988.
Mersch, Grand-Duché de Luxembourg, Mersch, Syndicat d'Initiative et du Tourisme, 1985.
Molitor, Ben. *Diekirch, A Short History*, Diekirch, Syndicat d'Initiative, 1983.
Rousseau, Paul. *Echternach, Cité Abbatiale* (ill.), Luxembourg, Eds. Guy Binsfeld, 1985.
Schritz, P. und A. Hoffman. *Echternach: Abteistadt*, Luxembourg, Impr. Saint-Paul, 1981.
Spang, Paul. *Echternach: Geschichte einer Stadt*, Luxembourg, RTL Edition, 1983.
Steinmetz, Al. *Rosport: die Geschichte eines Dorfes*, Luxembourg, Impr. Saint-Paul, 1973.
Wiltz: Portrait of a Town, Wiltz, Syndicat d'Initiative, 1987. A brief history of the "Capital of the Ardennes."

9. Constitution and Government

Als, Nicholas et Robert L. Philipport. *La Chambre des Deputés: Histoire et Lieux de Travail*, Luxembourg, Eds. Guy Binsfeld, 1994.
Arendt, Ernest. "Le silence de l'Administration en Droit Luxembourgeois," in *Le Conseil d'Etat du Grand-Duché de Luxembourg*, ed. Raymon Mehlen, Luxembourg, Eds. Bourg-Bourger, 1957.

Biever, Tony. "De l'irresponsibilité de l'Etat legislateur: Esquise de droit luxembourgeois," in *Le Conseil d'Etat du Grand-Duché de Luxembourg*, ed. Raymon Mehlen, Luxembourg, Eds. Bourg-Bourger, 1957.

Bonn, Alex. *La constitution oubliée*, Luxembourg, Impr. Centrale, 1968.

———. "L'examen du fait par le Conseil d'Etat: Etude de jurisprudence luxembourgeoise," in *Le Conseil d'Etat du Grand-Duché de Luxembourg*, ed. Raymon Mehlen, Luxembourg, Eds. Bourg-Bourger, 1957.

Flesch, Colette. *The Luxembourg Chamber of Deputies*, Luxembourg, European Parliament, 1974.

Hammes, Charles-Léon. "Le gouvernment du Grand-Duché: Essai sur son évolution," in *Le Conseil d'Etat du Grand-Duché de Luxembourg*, ed. Raymon Mehlen, Luxembourg, Eds. Bourg-Bourger, 1957.

Loesch, Alfred. "Le Conseil d'Etat, Comité de Contentieux," in *Le Conseil d'Etat du Grand-Duché de Luxembourg*, ed. Raymon Mehlen, Luxembourg, Eds. Bourg-Bourger, 1957.

Majerus, Nicolas. "L'Evolution de la justice et de droit," in *Le Luxembourg: Livre du centenaire*, ed. Albert Northumb, Luxembourg, Gouvernement Grand-Ducal, 1948.

Majerus, Pierre. *L'Etat Luxembourgeois, Manual de Droit Constitutionel et de Droit Administrif* (6e edition), Esch-sur-Alzette, Impr. Editpress, 1990. A guide to the constitution and government of the Grand Duchy, brought up to date by the author's son, Marcel Majerus.

———. *Les institutions de l'état luxembourgeoise*, Luxembourg, Ministère d'Etat, 1989. Brought up to date by J. M. Goerens.

———. *The Institutions of the Grand Duchy*, Luxembourg, Service information et Presse, 1970. Brief guide in English to the institutions and government of the Grand Duchy.

Maul, Roger. "Le conseil d'Etat et les tendences actuelles du régime de sécurité sociale," in *Le Conseil d'Etat du Grand-Duché de Luxembourg*, ed. Raymon Mehlen, Luxembourg, Eds. Bourg-Bourger, 1957.

Mehlen, Raymon, ed. *Le Conseil d'Etat du Grand-Duché de Luxembourg*, Luxembourg, Eds. Bourg-Bourger, 1957.

Pescatore, Pierre. "Essai sur la notion de la loi," in *Le Conseil d'Etat du Grand-Duché de Luxembourg*, ed. Raymon Mehlen, Luxembourg, Eds. Bourg-Bourger, 1957.

Ruppert, Pierre. *La gouvernement, le Conseil d'Etat, et la Chambre législative*, Luxembourg, Victor Buck, 1889.

Schaeffer, N. *Les forces politique au Grand-Duché de Luxembourg, 1919–1960*, Paris, memoire non publié, 1961.

Schaus, Lambert. "Les fundaments du statut international du Luxemboug, 1944–1957," in *Le Conseil d'Etat du Grand-Duché de Luxembourg*, ed. Rayman Mehlen, Luxembourg, Eds. Bourg- Bourger, 1957.

Waline, Marcel. "Le principe 'Audi alterum partem'," in *Le Conseil d'Etat du Grand-Duché de Luxembourg*, ed. Raymon Mehlen, Luxembourg, Eds. Bourg-Bourger, 1957.

Weber, Paul. "La constitution," in *Le Luxembourg, Livre du centenaire*, ed. Albert Northumb, Luxembourg, Gouvernement Grand-Ducal, 1948.

———. "Les constitutions du 19e siècle," in *Le Conseil d'Etat du Grand-Duché de Luxembourg*, ed. Raymon Mehlen, Luxembourg, Eds. Bourg-Bourger, 1957.

Wehrer, Albert. "Le statut international du Grand-Duché de Luxembourg," in *Le Luxembourg: Livre du centenaire*, ed. Albert Northumb, Luxembourg, Gouvernement Grand-Ducal, 1948.

10. Ecology and Land Use

Bodry, Alex, et al. *Quel Luxembourg pour demain?: esquisse structurelle d'amenagement du territoire*, Luxembourg, Ministère de l'amenagement du territoire, 1994.

Christians, Charles. *L'agriculture*, Liège, Seminaire de Géographie de l'Université de Liège, 1977.

La Forêt du Grand-Duché de Luxembourg, Luxembourg, Administration des Eaux et Forêts, 1971.

Hemmer, Carlo. *Quelques problèmes de l'amenagement du territoire au Grand-Duché de Luxembourg*, Luxembourg, Université Internationale de Sciences Comparées, 1973.

Lucius, Michel. "La Terre Luxembourgeoise," in *Livre du Centenaire*, Luxembourg, Impr. Saint-Paul, 1948.

Muhlen, Ernest. *Politique de structure et amenagement du territoire au Grand-Duché de Luxembourg*, Luxembourg, Université Internationale de Sciences Comparés, 1971.

Programme directeur de l'amenagement du territoire, Luxembourg, Ministère des Finances, 1978.

Rousseau, Paul, *La forêt luxembourgeoise du XVIe au XIXe siècle*, Walferdange, P. Rousseau, 1991.

Vögel Luxemburgs: Bilderatlas der hemischen Vogelwelt (5th ed.), Bern, Switzerland, Hallweg, 1979.

11. Education

Aperçu sur le system d'enseignment luxembourgeois, Luxembourg, Ministère de l'Education Nationale, 1993.

Braunshausen, N. "Les langues et l'enseignment," *Le Luxembourg: Livre du Centenaire*, ed. Albert Northumb, Luxembourg, Gouvernement Grand-Ducal, 1948.

Bray, Mark, and Stephen Packer. *Education in Small States; Concepts, Challenges, and Strategies*, Oxford & New York, Pergamon Press, 1993.

Centre de Psychologie et d'Orientation Scolaire, *Was tun nach dem 6. Schuljahr?* Luxembourg, Ministère de l'Education Nationale, 1994.

Le Centre Universitaire de Luxembourg, Luxembourg, Service Information et Presse, 1976.

Christophory, Jules. "Education in Luxembourg," in *Luxembourg Weekly Review*, nos. 33 and 34, August 1975.

Decker, Robert. "Das Luxemburger Schulsystem," in *Leibesübungen in Europa I: die Europäische Gemeinschaft*, London, Arena Publications, 1985.

Diederich, Victor, *Notre loi scolaire*, Luxembourg, Association des Instituteurs Réunis, 1973.

Education at a Glance, Paris, Organization for Economic Cooperation and Development (OECD), 1993.

Eis Spillschoul: brochure d'information pour l'education préscolaire, Luxembourg, Ministère de l'Education Nationale, 1993.

Goedert, Pierre et al., eds. *Lycée Michel-Rodange*, Luxembourg, Impr. RERA, 1993.

Kaiser, Ley "La gestion du système éducatif, pour qui? pourquoi?," in *d'Letzebuerger Land*, 31, 1984.

Krieps, Roger, "Jungendzentrum Hollenfels: die Schule der Natur," in *d'Letzebuerger Land*, 24, 1979.

Ministère de l'Education Nationale, *L'enseignement primaire au Grand-Duché de Luxembourg*, Luxembourg, Courrier de l'Education Nationale, 1990.

Organisation scolaire, 1994–1995, Luxembourg, Impr. Joseph Beffort, 1994.

Rapport d'Activité, 1986–1987, Luxembourg, Ministère de l'Education Nationale, 1988.

Simmer, L., ed. *Athenée grand-ducal de Luxembourg: trois cent cinquantième anniversaire de sa fondation*, Luxembourg, Impr. Bourg-Bourger, 1955.

Unité Nationale d'Eurydice, *Education in the Grand Duchy of*

Luxembourg, Luxembourg, Ministère de l'Education Nationale, 1992.

Weber, Josianne. "Ein Weilburger in Luxembourger," in *Lycée Michel Rodange: 1968–1993*, Luxembourg, 1993

12. Geography and Geology

A. General Geographies

Connors, Noel. *Luxembourg*, New York, Chelsea House, 1988. For young people.

Edwards, K. C. and E. J. Markhouse. *Luxembourg*, Cambridge, Naval Intelligence Division of the British Admiralty, Geographic Section, September 1944.

Faber, Robert. *Climatology du Grand-Duché de Luxembourg*, Luxembourg, Musée d'Histoire Naturelle, 1971.

Kieffer, Paul, ed. *Luxembourg: The Grand Duchy* (ill.), Luxembourg, Eds. Guy Binsfeld, 1985. English text by David Quinlan.

Lehr, Eugène. *Temps et climat au Grand-Duché de Luxembourg*, Luxembourg, Ministère de l'Agriculture, Service Météorologique et Hydrographique, 1964.

Lucius, Michel. *Beitrage zur Geologie von Luxembourg*, Luxembourg, Service Géologique de Luxembourg, 1955.

Petit, Joseph. *Luxembourg: Yesterday and Today* (ill.), Luxembourg, P. Linden, 1964.

Schmithüsen, Josef. *Das Luxemburger Land: Landesnatur, Volkstum, und Bauerliche Wirtschaft*, Leipzig, S. Hercel, 1940.

Veit, Manfred. *Luxembourg*, Heroldsburg (BRD), Glock & Lutz, 1979.

B. Regional Geographies

Aperçu sommaire sur la Moselle luxembourgeoise, Luxembourg, Impr. Saint-Paul, 1966.

Friedrich, Evy. *Le Lac de la Haute-Sûre* (ill.), Luxembourg, Eds. Guy Binsfeld, 1985. English text by David Quinlan.

———. *Moselle Sacra*, Wormer, Lëtzebuerger Guides a Scouten, 1988.

———. *La Petit Suisse Luxembourgeoise*, Luxembourg, Eds. Guy Binsfeld, 1985. English text by David Quinlan.

Kieffer, Paul. *Musel: La Moselle Luxembourgeoise* (ill.), Luxembourg, Eds. Guy Binsfeld, 1984 (?).

Ries, Adrien. *Oesling: les Ardennes luxembourgeoises*, Luxembourg, Eds. Guy Binsfeld, 1984.
Waterlot, Gérard et al. *Ardenne, Luxembourg*, Paris, Masson, 1973.

13. The Grand Ducal Family and the Nobility

Evan, Pierre, und Wolfgang Podehl. *Adolph, Herzog zu Nassau, Grossherzog von Luxembourg, 1817–1905*, Wiesbaden, Hessichen Landsbibliothek, 1992.
Ludovicy, Ernest. "La famille souveraine," in *Le Luxembourg: Livre du Centenaire*, ed. Albert Northumb, Luxembourg, Gouvernement Grand-Ducal, 1948.
Meyer, Joseph. *Deux maisons souveraines, 1890–1955*, Luxembourg, Eds. du Centre, 1955.
O'Shaugnessy, Edith. *Marie-Adelaide: Grand Duchess of Luxembourg, Duchess of Nassau*, New York, Harrison Smith, 1932.
Press and Information Service. *The Luxembourg Grand-Ducal Family*, Luxembourg, Impr. Saint-Paul, 1991.
Reuter, Raymond. *Charlotte: Portrait d'une grande dame, Luxembourg-Bridel, Eds. Luxnews, 1982.*
———. *Marie-Astrid*, Luxembourg, Eds. Luxnews, 1982.
Reuter, Raymond et Christian Calmes. *Jean: Grossherzog von Luxembourg*, Luxembourg, Eds. Luxnews, 1986.
Schleich de Bosse, Jean Robert. *La noblesse au Grand Duché de Luxembourg* (2 vols.), Luxembourg, Eds. du Centre, Vol. I 1954, Vol. II, 1957.
Schoos, Jean. *Thron und Dynastie: Aufsatze aus drei Jahrzeiten*, Luxembourg, Impr. Saint-Paul, 1978.

14. Guidebooks

Bour, Roger. *Taschenführer durch die Burgen und Schlösser in Luxembourg* (2 vols.), Luxembourg, Impr. Saint-Paul, Vol. I 1982; Vol. II 1983.
Cosyn, Paul. *Grand Duchy of Luxembourg*, Brussels, Cosyn's Guides, 1973.
Echternach, Passau (BRD), Kunstverlag-Peda, 1993.
Entdeckungsfahrten zu den Burgen, Schlossen, Kirchen, und Stadten des Grossherzogstum Luxembourg, Köln, Du Mont Buchverlag, 1989.

Focus on Luxembourg, Young Visitor's Guide, Luxembourg, Centre Information Jeunes, 1988.

Foder, Eugene. *Belgium and Luxembourg, 1978–79*, London, Hodder & Stoughton, 1978.

Friedrich, Evy. *Wandern in Luxemburg*, Luxembourg, Eds. Guy Binsfeld, 1983. Describes fifty journeys, with maps, that may be made on foot through the Grand Duchy.

The Grand Duchy of Luxembourg, Luxembourg, Press and Information Service, 1992.

Hausemer, Georges, ed. *The Grand Duchy of Luxembourg: Tourist Guide*, Luxembourg, Eds. Guy Binsfeld, 1994. English text by Robert West.

Leipold, L. E. *Come Along to Luxembourg*, Minneapolis, Dewison, 1973.

Luxembourg: Promenade à Travers le coeur historique de la capitale (3e edition), Luxembourg, Syndicate d'Initiative et du Tourisme, 1983. Parallel text in French and German.

Muirhead, Litellus. *Belgium and Luxembourg* (4th edition), London, Benn, 1963.

Nelson, Nina. *Belgium and Luxembourg*, London, Batsford, 1975.

15. Historiography

Kellen, T. *Die Luxemburgische Geschichtschreibung: Ein Ruckblick und ein Ausblick* (2 vols.), Luxembourg, G. Soupert, 1933 and 1937.

Medernach, Paul. "Table genérale des Publications de la Section historique de l'Institut grand-ducal," in *Publications de la section historique de l'institut grand-ducal*, vol. 97, 1983.

Publications de la section historiques de l'institut grand-ducal, vols. 1–108 (1846–1992), Luxembourg, Jos. Beffort, 1933–1992. Earlier volumes published by various publishers.

16. History of Luxembourg

A. General Histories

Barteau, Harry C. The *Grand Duchy of Luxembourg*, Luxembourg, Imp. J. P. Meyer, 1994. An introduction to the Grand Duchy with a short historical survey.

British Foreign Office, Historical Section. *Luxembourg and Limburg*, London, H. M. Stationery Office, 1920.

Cooper-Pritchard, A. H. *History of the Grand Duchy of Luxembourg*, Luxembourg, Imp. P. Linden, 1950. A translation of the fifth edition of Arthur Herschen's *Manuel d'Histoire Nationale*. (See below.)

Edwards, Kenneth C. *Luxembourg: The Survival of a Small Nation*, Nottingham, The University, 1967.

Glesener, Jean-Pierre. *Le Grand Duché de Luxembourg: historique et pittoresque*, Esch-sur-Alzette, Eds. Reliures Schortgen, 1985.

Herschen, Arthur. *Manuel d'Histoire Nationale* (9e edition), Luxembourg, Imp. P. Linden, 1972. The latest edition of the standard text on the history of the Grand Duchy, brought up to date by N. Margue and J. Meyers. Contains an excellent genealogy of the rulers of Luxembourg.

Margue, Nicolas. "Apercu Historique," in *Le Luxembourg, Livre du Centenaire*, ed. Albert Northumb, Luxembourg, Gouvernement Grand-Ducal, 1948.

Margue, Paul. *Histoire Sommaire de Luxembourg*, Luxembourg, Eds. Beffort, 1985.

Meyers, J. *Geschichte Luxemburgs*, Luxembourg, Impr. Linden et Hansen, 1953.

Muller, Pierre J. *Tatsachen als der Geschichte des Luxemburger Landes* (4e ed.), Luxembourg, Eds. Bourg-Bourger, 1968.

Newcomer, James. *The Grand Duchy of Luxembourg: The Evolution of Nationhood, 963 A.D. to 1983*, Lanham, Md., University Press of America, 1984. The only full-length history of Luxembourg in English. The author served as an officer in Patton's Third Army, and took part in the two liberations of Luxembourg.

Northumb, Albert ed. *Le Luxembourg: Livre du Centenaire*, Luxembourg, Gouvernement Grand-Ducal, 1948. This book was prepared to celebrate the centennial of Luxembourg independence in 1939, and was actually on the presses when the Germans invaded on 10 May 1940. They destroyed that edition, but it was reconstructed after the war and finally published in 1948.

Petit, Joseph. *Luxembourg: Yesterday and Today*, Luxembourg, Imp. P. Linden, 1964. Contains a brief history of the Grand Duchy to 1950. The author was a professor at the Athenée Grand-Ducal, who later became director of the government's Service of Information and the Press.

Schaak, Raymond. *Le Luxembourg*, Saint-Cloud, Eds. Romain Pages, 1991.

Trausch, Gilbert. *Histoire du Luxembourg*, Paris, Hatier, 1992

————. *Le Luxembourg: Emergence d'un Etat et d'une Nation*, Antwerp, Fonds Mercator, 1989. Reprinted in 1993.

Weber, Paul. *Geschichte des Luxemburger Landes*, Luxembourg, Eds. Victor Buck, 1948.

————. *Histoire du Grand-Duché de Luxembourg*, Bruxelles, Office de Publicité, 1961.

Wehrer, Albert. "L'histoire du Luxembourg dans une Europe divisée, 963–1945," in *Le Conseil d'Etat du Grand Duché de Luxembourg*, ed. Raymon Mehlen, Luxembourg, Eds. Bourg-Bourger, 1957.

B. Prehistory and Gallo-Roman Times

Balsdon, J. P. V. D. *Romans and Aliens*, Chapel Hill, University of North Carolina Press, 1979.

Brogan, Olwen. *Roman Gaul*, London, Bell, 1953.

Burns, C. D. *The First Europe*, London, Allen and Unwin, 1947.

Dillon, Myles. *The Celtic Realms*, New York, New American Library, 1967.

Hatt, Jean-Jacques. *Les celts et les gallo-romains*, Paris, Nagel, 1970.

Herm, Gerhard. *The Celts*, New York, St. Martin's Press, 1976.

James, Simon. *The World of the Celts*, London, Thames and Hudson, 1993.

King, Anthony. *Roman Gaul and Germany*, Berkeley, University of California Press, 1990. Contains references to Roman sites in Trier, Arlon, Echternach, Dalheim, and the Titelberg, as well as a history of northeastern Gaul.

Lamesch, Marcel. *Contributions à la préhistoire du Grand-Duché de Luxembourg*, Luxembourg, J. Beffort, 1975.

McKay, Alexander G. *Houses, Villas and Palaces in the Roman World*, London, Thames and Hudson, 1977.

Meyers, Joseph. *Aus der Vor-und Frühgeschichte Luxemburgs*, Luxembourg, Krippler, 1976.

————. *Studien zur Siedlungsgeschichte Luxemburgs*,, Luxembourg, Krippler, 1976.

Piggott, Stuart. *Ancient Europe from the Beginnings of Agriculture to Classical Antiquity*, Chicago, Aldine Press, 1965.

————. *The Druids*, London, Thames and Hudson, 1968.

Powell, T. G. E. *The Celts*, London, Thames and Hudson, 1958.

Rousseau, Paul. *La romaine inconnue de Dalheim*, in *Lëtzebuerger Almanac, 1987*, Luxembourg, Eds. Guy Binsfeld, 1986.

Thill, Gérard. *Vor-und Frühgeschichte Luxemburgs* (2e ed.), Luxembourg, Impr. Bourg-Bourger, 1977.

Thompson, E. A. *Romans and Barbarians: The Decline of the Western Empire*, Madison, University of Wisconsin Press, 1982.

C. Early Middle Ages (A.D. 400–950)

Asimov, Isaac. *The Dark Ages*, Boston, Houghton Mifflin, 1968.

Bachrach, B. S. *Merovingian Military Organization, 481–751*, Minneapolis, University of Minnesota Press, 1972.

Cantor, Norman F. *Medieval History* (2nd edition), New York, Macmillan, 1969.

Goffert, W. *Barbarians and Romans, A.D. 418–585: The techniques of accommodation*, Princeton, N.J., Princeton University Press, 1980.

Gordon, C. D. *The Age of Attila*, Ann Arbor, University of Michigan Press, 1960.

Halphen, L. *Charlemagne et l'empire carolingien*, Paris, A. Michel, 1949.

Hilgarth, Jocelyn N. *Christianity and Paganism: The Conversion of Western Europe* (2nd edition), Philadelphia, University of Pennsylvania Press, 1986.

Hubert, Jean, J. Porcher, and F. Volbach. *Europe in the Dark Ages*, London, 1969.

———. *L'empire carolingien*, Paris, Gallimard, 1968.

———. *L'europe des invasions*, Paris, Gallimard, 1967.

James, Edward. *The Franks*, Oxford, Basil Blackwell, 1988.

Maenchen-Helfen, Otto J. *The World of the Huns*, Berkeley, University of California Press, 1973.

Musset, Lucien. *The Germanic Invasions: The Making of Europe, A.D, 400–600*, University Park, Penn., Pennsylvania State University Press, 1975,

Schaaf, Holger. *Die Altertümer der Merowingerzeit im Grossherzogtum Luxemburg*, Luxembourg, Musée nationale d'histoire et d'art, 1993.

Southern, R. W. *The Making of the Middle Ages*, London, Pimlico, 1993.

Thill, Gérard. *Vor-und Frügeschichte Luxemburgs*, Luxembourg, Bourg-Bourger, 1974.

Wallace-Hadrill, J. M. *The Barbarian West*, New York, Harper and Row, 1952

———. *The Frankish Church*, Oxford, Clarendon Press, 1983.

———. *The Long-Haired Kings and Other Studies in Frankish History*, Toronto, Toronto University Press, 1982.

D. Later Middle Ages, A.D. 950–1450

Bronsted, J. *The Vikings*, Baltimore, Penguin, 1973.

Cantor, Norman. *Medieval History* (2nd edition), New York, Macmillan, 1969.

Cazelles, Raymond. *Jean L'Aveugle, comte de Luxembourg et roi de Bohême*, Bourges, Tardy, 1947.

Dollar, Jacques. *Jean l'Aveugle à Crécy*, Luxembourg, Impr. Centrale, 1991.

Gade, John Allyne. *Luxembourg in the Middle Ages*, Leiden, Brill, 1951.

Goedert, Joseph. *La formation territorial du pays de Luxembourg depuis ses origines jusqu'au milieu du XVe siècle*, Luxembourg, Imp. Centrale, 1963.

Heimen, Hans-Dieter. *Zwischen Bohmen und Burgund: zum Ost-Westverhaltnis innerhalb des Territorialsystems des Deutsches Reiches im 15 Jahrhundert*, Köln, Bohlau, 1982.

Heyen, Franz-Josef. *Kaiser Heinrichs Romfahrt: die Bilderchronik von Kaiser Heinrich VII und Kurfürst Baldwin von Luxemburg*, Boppard (BRD), Boldt, 1965.

Holmes, George. *Europe: Hierarchy and Revolt, 1386–1450*, London, Fontana Press, 1988.

Joset, C. J. *Ermesinde (1186–1247): fondatrice du pays*, Arlon, Les Amis de Clairfontaine, 1947.

Margue, Paul. *Le Luxembourg en Lotharingie*, Luxembourg, Editions Saint-Paul, 1993.

———. *Luxembourg in Mittelalter und Neuzeit*, Luxembourg, Editions Bourg-Bourger, 1974.

Pauly, Michel. *Luxemburg in späten Mittelalter, vol. CIX, Publications de l'Institut Grand-Ducal de Luxembourg*, Luxembourg, Impr. Rapidpress, 1994.

Schneider, Friedrich. *Kaiser Heinrich VII: Dante's Kaiser*, Hildesheim (BRD), Olms, 1973.

Schoos, J. *Le developpement politique et territoriale du pays de Luxembourg dans le première moitié du XIII siècle*, Luxembourg, Imp. Joseph Beffort, 1950.

Schramm, D. E. *Kaiser, Rom, und Renovatie*, Berlin, Taubner, 1929.

Seibt, Ferdinand. *Kaiser Karl IV: ein Kaiser in Europa*, Munich, Süddeutscher Verlag, 1978.

———. *Kaiser Karl IV: Staatsman und Mäzen*, Munich, Prestel, 1978.

E. Luxembourg and the Netherlands under Burgundian Rule, 1443–1559

Alvarez, M. Fernandez. *Charles V, Elected Emperor and Hereditary Ruler*, London, Thames and Hudson, 1975.

Bartier, John. *Charles le Téméraire*, Bruxelles, Arcade, 1970.

Braudi, Karl. *The Emperor Charles V*, London, Jonathan Cape, 1939.

Calmette, J. *The Golden Age of Burgundy*, New York, Norton, 1973.

Colin, Paul. *Les ducs de Bourgogne*, Bruxelles, Nouvelle Societé d'Editions, 1941.

Elton, G. R. *Reformation Europe, 1517–1559*, London, Fontana, 1963.

Kalsky, René. *Charles le Téméraire*, Bruxelles, J. Antoine, 1984.

Lotherington, John, ed. *Years of Renewal: European History, 1470–1600*, London, Hodder & Stoughton, 1988.

MacDonald, Stewart. *Charles V: Ruler, Dynast, and Defender of the Faith*, London, Hodder & Stoughton, 1992.

Prevenier, Walter and W. M. Blockmans. *Burgundian Netherlands*, Cambridge, Cambridge University Press, 1986.

Putnam, Ruth. *Charles the Bold, Last Duke of Burgundy*, New York & London, G. P. Putnam's Sons, 1908.

Rady, Martyn C. *Emperor Charles V*, London, Longmans, 1988.

Rowen, Herbert. *The Low Countries in Early Modern Times*, London, Macmillan, 1972.

Schelle, Klaus. *Charles le Téméraire: La Bourgogne entre les lys de France et l'aigle de l'Empire* (translated from the German by Denise Meunier), Paris, A. Fayard, 1979.

Thoss, Dagmar. *Das Epos des Burgunderreiches*, Graz, Akademisches Druck, 1989.

Vaughan, Richard. *Charles the Bold, the Last Valois Duke of Burgundy*, London, Longmans, 1973.

———. *John the Fearless: the Growth of Burgundian Power*, London, Longmans, 1979.

———. *Philip the Good: the Apogee of Burgundy*, Harlow, Longmans, 1970.

———. *Valois Burgundy*, London, Allen Lane, 1975.

F. Luxembourg and the Netherlands under Spanish Rule, 1555–1714.

Elliott, J. H. *Imperial Spain, 1469–1716*, London, Edward Arnold, 1963.

Grierson, E. *King of Two Worlds, Philip II of Spain*, London, Collins, 1974.

Harpes, Jean. *La peste du pays de Luxembourg: essai historique et medical*, Luxembourg, P. Linden, 1952.

Harrison, Frederic. *William the Silent*, London, Macmillan, 1897.

Kamen, Henry. *Spain, 1469–1716: A Society of Conflict*, London, Longman, 1983.

Killsby, Jill. *Spain, Rise and Decline, 1473–1643*, London, Hodder & Stoughton, 1989.

Lotherington, John, ed. *Years of Renewal: European History, 1470–1600*, London, Hodder & Stoughton, 1988.

Lovett, A. W. *Early Habsburg Spain, 1517–1598*, Oxford, Oxford University Press, 1986.

Maltby, W. S. *Alba: A Biography of Fernando Alvarez de Toledo, 1509–1582*, Berkeley, University of California Press, 1983.

Mattingly, Garrett. *The Armada*, Boston, Houghton Mifflin, 1959. Shows the connection between the ill-fated attempt of Philip II to invade England in 1588 and the Spanish failure to reconquer the northern Netherlands.

Parker, Geoffrey. *The Army of Flanders and the Spanish Road*, Cambridge, Cambridge University Press, 1972.

———. *The Dutch Revolt* (2nd edition), Harmondsworth, Penguin, 1985.

———. *Philip II*, London, Cardinal Sphere Books, 1986.

———. *Spain and the Netherlands, 1559–1659*, London, Collins, 1979.

Pierson, P. *Philip II of Spain*, London, Thames and Hudson, 1975.

Putnam, Ruth. *William the Silent, Prince of Orange, 1533–1584, and the Revolt of the Netherlands*, New York & London, G. P. Putnam's Sons, 1911.

Rady, Martyn C. *From Revolt to Independence, the Netherlands, 1550–1650*, London, Hodder & Stoughton, 1990.

Rowen, Herbert. *The Low Countries in Early Modern Times*, London, Macmillan, 1972.

Salgado, M. J. *The Changing Face of Empire: Charles V, Philip II, and Habsburg Authority, 1551–1559*, Cambridge, Cambridge University Press, 1988.

Wedgwood, C. V. *William the Silent*, London, Jonathan Cape, 1944.

Wirion, Lewis. "Le comte-gouvernour Jean-Frédérick d'Autel, 1645-1716," in *Biographie Nationale, Vol. I*, ed. Jules Mersch, Luxembourg, Impr. Pierre Bruck, 1860.

Woodward, Geoffrey. *Philip II*, London, Longmans, 1992

G. Luxembourg during the Age of Louis XIV (1659–1715)

Campbell, Peter R. *Louis XIV, 1661–1715*, London, Longman, 1993.

Dollar, Jacques. *Vauban à Luxembourg*, Luxembourg, RTL Edition, 1983.

Donneau de Vise, Jean. *A Diary of the Siege of Luxembourg by the French King's Forces under the Command of the Mareschal de Créqui*, London, D. Brown, 1684.

———. *The Impartial Account of the Taking of Luxembourg by the French*, London, for A. Bancks, 1684.

Friedrich, Evy. "Pestjahre," in *Luxembourg Revue*, no. 6, 1987.

Luxembourg et Vauban: exhibition organisée à la Villa Vauban du 27 novembre à 23 decembre, 1984, Luxembourg, J. Beffort, 1984. Catalog.

Pujo, Bernard. *Vauban*, Paris, A. Michel, 1991.

Trausch, Gilbert. *Le Luxembourg sous l'Ancien Regime*, Luxembourg, Eds. Bourg-Bourger, 1986.

H. Luxembourg under Austrian Rule (1715–95)

Davis, Walter W. *Joseph II: An Imperial Reformer for the Austrian Netherlands*, The Hague, Nijhof, 1974.

Friedrich, Evy. "Joseph II in Luxembourg," in *Luxembourg Review*, no. 19, 1987.

Sprunck, Alphonse. *Le Duché de Luxembourg pendant la guerre de succession d'Autriche de 1744–1748*, Luxembourg, Buck, 1945.

———. "Le Duché de Luxembourg et la révolution brabanconne: première partie," in *Publications de la Section Historique de l'institut grand-ducal de Luxembourg*, vol. 73, 1953.

———. "Les etats du Luxembourg et le gouvernement de Bruxelles sous la règne du Marie-Thérèse," in *Annales de l'Institut archéologique du Luxembourg*, no. 80, Arlon, 1958.

———. *Etudes sur la vie économique et sociale dans le luxembourg au 18e siècle* (2 vols.), Luxembourg, Eds. du Centre, 1956 and 1963.

Trausch, Gilbert. *Le Luxembourg sous L'Ancien Regime*, Luxembourg, Eds. Bourg-Bourger, 1986.

Wirion, Louis. "Quelques episodes de l'epoque autrichienne," in *Jonghemecht*, no. 13, 1939.

I. Luxembourg during the French Revolution and the Napoleonic Era (1789–1815)

Calmes, Albert, et Christian Calmes. *Au fil de l'histoire, vol. I, 1794–1858*, Luxembourg, Impr. Saint-Paul, 1968.

Decker, François. *La conscription militaire au Départment des Forêts: Premier volume: de 1798 à 1808*, Luxembourg, Impr. Saint-Paul, 1980.

———. *Lettres de soldats luxembourgeois au service de la France, 1798–1814*, Luxembourg, Mersch, 1971.

Dollar, Jacques. *Le démystification du "Klöppelkrich,"* Luxembourg, Impr. Saint-Paul, 1981.

———. *Napoleon et le Luxembourg*, Luxembourg, Impr. Saint-Paul, 1979.

———. *La Prise du Luxembourg par l'armée républicaine*, Luxembourg, Impr. Centrale, 1984.

Friedrich, Evy. "Napoleon," in *Luxembourg Review* , no. 41, 1987.

Lefort, Alfred. *Histoire du départment des forêts, le duché de Luxembourg de 1795 à 1814*, Paris, A. Picard et fils, 1905.

Schaak, Charles. *Les Luxembourgeois, soldats de la France, 1792–1815*, Diekirch, Impr. J. Schroell, 1910.

Trausch, Gilbert. "La répression des soulèvements paysans de 1798 dans le Départment des Forêts," in *Publications de la Section Historique de l'Institut Grand-Ducal, de Luxembourg*, vol. 82, 1967.

J. Luxembourg from the Congress of Vienna to 1918

Angebourg, Comte d'. *Le Congrès de Vienne et les traités de 1815*, Vols. 1–4, Paris, Aymond, 1864.

Bac, Ferdinand. *Le secret de Talleyrand*, Paris, Hachette, 1939.

Busch, Moritz. *Bismarck—Some secret pages of his history*, vol. I, London, Macmillan, 1898.

———. *Bismarck und seine Leute, Nach den Tagebuch-blättern von Dr. Moritz Busch*, Berlin, Freundberg-Verlag, 1940.

Calmes, Albert. *Au Fils de l'Histoire*, Vol. I, Luxembourg, Impr. Saint-Paul, 1968.

———. *Au Fils de l'Histoire*, Vol. II (3e edition), Luxembourg, Impr. Saint-Paul, 1988.

———. *La création d'un Etat, 1841–1847* (2e edition), Luxembourg, Impr. Saint-Paul, 1983. Vol. IV in *Histoire contemporaine du Grand-Duché de Luxembourg*.

———. *La Grande-Duché de Luxembourg dans la Revolution belge, 1830–1839* (2e edition), Luxembourg, Impr. Saint-Paul, 1982. Vol. II in *Histoire contemporaine de Grand-Duché de Luxembourg*.

———.*Naissance et débuts du Grand-Duché, 1814–1830: Le Grand-Duché dans le royaume des Pays-Bas* (2e edition), Luxembourg, Impr. Saint-Paul, 1971. Vol. I in *Histoire contemporaine du Grand-Duché de Luxembourg*.

———. *Le restauration de Guilliaume Ier, roi des Pays-Bas, 1839–1840*, Luxembourg, Impr. Saint-Paul, 1947. Vol. III in *Histoire contemporaine de Grand-Duché de Luxembourg*.

———. *La revolution de 1848 au Luxembourg* (2e edition), Luxembourg, Impr. Saint-Paul, 1982. Vol. V in *Histoire contemporaine du Grand-Duché de Luxembourg*.

———. *Zollenschluss des Grossherzogtums Luxemburg an Deutschland, Vol. I, 1842–1819, Vol. II, 1919*, Luxembourg, Joseph Beffort, 1919.

Calmes, Albert et Christian Calmes. *Au fils de l'histoire*, Vol. III (2e edition), Luxembourg, Impr. Saint-Paul, 1988.

———. *Ouvrages en préparation pourtant sur la période de 1872–1913*, Luxembourg, Impr. Saint-Paul, 1985. Vol. VI in *Histoire contemporaine du Grand-Duché de Luxembourg*.

Calmes, Christian. *Au fils de l'histoire*, Vol. IV, Luxembourg, Impr. Saint-Paul, 1977.

———. *Au fils de l'histoire*, Vol. VI, Luxembourg, Impr. Saint-Paul, 1986.

———. *Au fils de l'histoire*, Vol. VIII, Luxembourg, Impr. J. H. Watgen, 1990.

———. *Creation et Formation d'un pays, 1815 à nos jours*, Luxembourg, Impr. Saint-Paul, 1989. Vol. XII in *Histoire Contemporaine du Grand-Duché de Luxembourg*. Translated into English by John Hargreaves as *The Making of a Nation, from 1815 to the present day*, Luxembourg, Impr. Saint-Paul.

———. *1867: L'Affaire au Luxembourg* (3e edition), Luxembourg, Impr. Saint-Paul, 1982. Vol. VII in *Histoire Contemporaine du Grand-Duché de Luxembourg*.

———. *Le Luxembourg dans la guerre de 1870*, Luxembourg, Impr. Saint-Paul, 1970. Vol. VIII in *Histoire Contemporaine du Grand-Duché de Luxembourg*.

Friedrich, Evy. "Rosen von Limpertsberg," in *Ons Stadt*, No. 18, April 1985.

Hubert, Ernst Rudolf. *Deutsche Verfassungs seit 1789*, Stuttgart, Kohlhammerverlag, 1975.

Jacoby, L., et R. Trauffler. *Histoire de la force armée luxembourgeoise*, Luxembourg, Impr. Saint-Paul, 1980.

Jungblut, M. *Die Luxemburgische Frage 1867 im Spiegel der Luxemburgischen Presse*, Göttingen, Staatsexamensarbeit, 1967.

Melchers, E. T. *Kriegschauplatz Luxembourg, August, 1914–Mai, 1940*, (4 ed.), Luxembourg, Impr. Saint-Paul, 1979.

Mersch, François et Jean-Pierre Koltz. *Luxembourg: forteresse et belle époque*, Luxembourg, F. Mersch, 1976.

Millman, Richard. *British Foreign Policy and the Coming of the Franco-Prussian War*, Oxford, Clarendon Press, 1965.

Muellendorff, Prosper. *Das Grossherzogtum Luxemburg unter Wilhelm I, 1815–1840*, Luxembourg, Impr. Victor Buck, 1921.

————. *Luxemburg unter Wilhelm II und Wilhelm III*, Luxembourg, Impr. Victor Buck, 1944.

Oncken, Hermann. *Die Rheinpolitik Kaiser Napoleons III von 1863–1870, vol. 2, Juli 1866–Juli 1868*, Stuttgart, Deutsche Verlagsanstalt, 1926.

O'Shaughnessy, Edith. *Marie-Adelaide: Grand Duchess of Luxembourg, Duchess of Nassau*, New York, Harrison Smith, 1932.

Pirenne, Henri. *Histoire de la Belgique*, Vol. VI, Bruxelles, Lamertin, 1926.

Putnam, Ruth. *Luxembourg and Her Neighbors*, New York and London, G. P. Putnam's Sons, 1918.

Rie, Robert. *Der Wiener Kongress und das Völkerrecht*, Bonn, Röchrscheid, 1957.

Servais, Emmanuel. *Le Grand-Duché de Luxembourg et le Traité de Londres du 11 mai 1867*, Paris, Pion, 1879.

Sorel, Albert. *Le Traité de Paris du 29 novembre 1815*, Paris, Baillière, 1872.

Trausch, Gilbert. *Le Luxembourg à l'epoque contemporaine*, Luxembourg, Eds. Bourg-Bourger, 1975.

————. *La significance historique de la date 1839: Essai d'interpretation*, Luxembourg, Ministère de l'Etat, 1989.

Trausch, Gilbert, et al. *Le Luxembourg: émergence d'un Etat et d'une Nation*, Anvers, Fond Mercator, 1989.

Von Kalken, Frans. *Histoire du Royaume des Pays-Bas et de la révolution belge*, Bruxelles, 1910.

K. 1919: Year of Crisis

Calmes, Christian. *1914–1919: Le Luxembourg au Centre de l'Annexationnisme Belge*, Luxembourg, Impr. Saint-Paul, 1976. Vol. X in *Histoire Contemporaine du Grand-Duché de Luxembourg*.

————. *1919: L'Etrange Référendum du 28 Septembre*, Luxembourg, Impr. Saint-Paul, 1979. Vol. XI in *Histoire Contemporaine du Grand-Duché de Luxembourg*.

Lautsch, Hubert. *Pour la patrie, le grand-duché du luxembourg*, *son passé historique, sa situation internationale et economique d'aprés les traités*, Luxembourg, Impr. Saint-Paul, 1919.

O'Shaughnessy, Edith. *Marie-Adelaide: Grand Duchess of Luxembourg, Duchess of Nassau*, New York, Harrison Smith, 1932.

Pletschette, Nik. "Amerikanischen Truppen in Rumelingen, 1918–1919," in *Luxemburger Zeitung*, November, 1938.

Prum, Xavier. *The Problem of Luxembourg*, New York, Knickerbocker Press, 1919.

Trausch, Gilbert. *Le Luxembourg à l'époque contemporaine*, Luxembourg, Eds. Bourg-Bourger, 1975.

Welter, Nikolaus. *Im Dienste: Erinnerungen aus verworrener Zeit*, Luxembourg, Impr. Saint-Paul, 1925.

L. Luxembourg between the Wars (1919–40)

Calmes, Christian. *Création et Formation d'un pays, 1815 à nos jours*. Luxembourg, Impr. Saint-Paul, 1989. Vol. XII in *Histoire Contemporaine du Grand-Duché de Luxembourg*. Translated into English by John Hargreaves as *The Making of a Nation from 1815 to the Present Day*.

Fischer, Batty. *Luxembourg: album de souvenirs*, Luxembourg, E. Kutter, 1966.

Mersch, Carole. *Le national-socialism et la presse luxembourgeoise de 1933 à 1940*, Luxembourg, Impr. Saint-Paul, 1977.

Mersch, François. *Luxembourg: belle époque, guerre et paix*, Luxembourg, Fr. Mersch, 1978.

Trausch, Gilbert. *Joseph Bech: Un homme dans son siècle*, Luxembourg, Impr. Saint-Paul, 1978.

———. *Le Luxembourg à l'époque contemporaine*, Luxembourg, Eds. Bourg-Bourger, 1975.

M. Luxembourg during the Second World War (1940–45)

Amicale des Concentrationnaires et Prisonnières Politique Luxembourgeoises. *Le Livre de souvenir, 1940–1945*, Impr. Bourg-Bourger, 1965. The story of Luxembourgish women who were imprisoned for political reasons or sent to concentration camps during the German occupation of the Grand Duchy.

Barnes, Col. C. de Mars. "The Battle of Vianden," in the *Luxembourg News of America*, June 1944.

Basque, Fritz. *Das Oesling im Krieg*, Christnach, Eds. Emile Borschette, 1991.

Bech, Joseph, ed. *Luxembourg and the German Invasion, Before and After*, London, Hutchinson & Co., 1942.

Blan, Lucien. *La résistance au Grand-Duché de Luxembourg, 1940–1945*, Metz, University of Metz, 1984–85. Master's thesis.

Candidi, Gino. *La résistance du peuple luxembourgeoise*, Luxembourg, Editions du Rappel, 1977.

Cerf, Paul. *L'etoile juive en Luxembourg*, Luxembourg, RTL Edition, 1986.

———. *Longtemps j'aurai mémoire*, Luxembourg, Ed. Lëtzebuergerland, 1974.

Cole, Hugh M. *The Ardennes: Battle of the Bulge*, Washington, D.C., Office of the Chief of Military History, 1965.

Delvaux, Franc. *Luxemburg in Zweiten Weltkrieg, 1940–1944*, Christnach, Eds. Emile Borschette, 1989.

Dollar, Jacques. *L'exode des luxembourgeois sur les routes de France en mai, 1940*, Luxembourg, Impr. Centrale, 1990.

———. *Josy Goerges et les Pi-men dans la Résistance*, Luxembourg, Impr. Saint-Paul, 1986.

Erasme, Georges. *De Friedland in Blitzkrieg, 1807–1940: Histoires d'une famille luxembourgeoise*, Luxembourg, Christiane Mueller-Zarotti, 1991.

———. *Temoins des tourmentes, 1940–1948*, Luxembourg, Polyprint, 1992.

Essame, H. *Patton, the Commander*, London, Batsford, 1974.

Feil, Raymon. *Ich war der Executierte!*, Luxembourg, Saint-Paul, 1984.

Fletcher, W. A. "The German Administration in Luxembourg, 1940–1942," in *Historical Journal*, vol. 13, 1970.

Friedrich, Evy. *Als Luxembourg entvolkert werden sollte: Geschichte und Geschichten der Umsiedlung*, Luxembourg, Impr. Bourg-Bourger, 1969.

———. "Juden in Luxemburg," in *Luxembourg-Review*, no. 19, 1987.

Haag, Emile, et Emile Krier. *La Grand-Duchesse et son gouvernement pendant la deuxième guerre mondiale*, Luxembourg, Eds. RTL, 1987.

Jacoby, L., et R. Trauffler. *Freiwëllige Kompanie, 1940–1945*, Luxembourg, COPE, 1963.

Koch-Kent, Henri. *Années d'Exil (1940–1946)*, Luxembourg, Impr. Centrale, 1986.

———. *Putsch à Luxembourg?*, Luxembourg. Impr. Hermann, 1979.

———. *Sie boten Trotz 1939–1945*, Luxembourg, Impr. Hermann, 1974.

———. *10 Mai 1940 en Luxembourg: témoinages et documents*, Mersch, Impr. Fr. Faber, 1971.

Koch-Kent, Henri et al. *Hitlertum in Luxemburg, 1933–1944* (2e edit.), Luxembourg, Impr. Hermann, 1972.

———. *Luxemburger als Freiwild* (2e ed.), Luxembourg, Impr. Herman, 1972.

———. *Luxemburg im SD-Spiegel: ein Bericht vom 12 Juli, 1940*, Luxembourg, Impr. Hermann, 1973.

Lorang, Fernand. "Quand les horloges s'arretant à Rumelange," in *Luxemburger Wort*, Janvier à Mars, 1984.

———. *Das Vermächtis einer Jugend*, Luxembourg, Impr. Saint-Paul, 1982.

Maertz, Jos. *Luxemburg in der Rundstedt Offensive*, Luxembourg, Impr. Saint-Paul, 1948.

May, Guy. *Memorial de l'Histoire*, Luxembourg, RTL edition, 1983.

Melchers, E. T. *Befreiung und Ardennen Offensive, 1944–1945*, Luxembourg, Impr. Saint-Paul, 1981.

———. *Bombenangriffe auf Luxemburg in zwei Weltkriegen*, Luxembourg, Impr. Saint-Paul, 1984.

———. *Les deux liberations du Luxembourg, 1944–1945*, Luxembourg, Eds. du Centre, 1959.

Reichelt, Walter E. *Phantom Nine, The Ninth Armored (Remagen) Division, 1942–1945*, Austin, Presidial Press, 1987.

Schiltges, Marie-Madeleine. *La deportation au Luxembourg, 1942–1945*, Luxembourg, Impr. Saint-Paul, 1992.

———. "17 Septembre 1942: Tag der Umsiedlung in Luxembourg," in *Luxemburger Wort*, 17 Septembre 1987

Spang, Paul. *10 Mai, 1940, en Luxembourg*, Mersch, Impr. Fr. Faber, 1991.

———. *Von der Zauberflöte zum Standgericht*, Luxembourg, Impr. Saint-Paul, 1982.

Starr, Marcel. *Waffenträger wider Willen*, Luxembourg, Impr. Saint-Paul, 1987.

Steffen, Francis. *Die geopferte Generation: die Geschichte der Luxemburger Jugend wahrend des zweiten Weltkrieges* (2e edit.), Luxembourg, Föderation der Luxemburger zwangsrekruiteren Naziopfer, 1977.

Union des Movements de Resistance. *L'épopée des sous uniforme*, Luxembourg, U.M.R., 1979.

Weber, Paul. *Geschichte Luxemburgs in zweiten Weltkrieg*, Luxembourg, Victor Buck, 1948.

N. Postwar Luxembourg (1945–1996)

Cerf, Paul. *De l'epuration au Grand-Duché de Luxembourg apres le seconde guerre mondiale*, Luxembourg, Impr. Saint-Paul, 1980.

———. *Le Luxembourg et son armée: le service militaire obligatoire au Grand-Duché du Luxembourg de 1945 à 1967*, Luxembourg, RTL Edition, 1984.

Dolibois, John. *Pattern of Circles: An Ambassador's Story*, Kent, Ohio, Kent State University Press, 1989.

Fally, Vincent. *Le Grand-Duché de Luxembourg et la construction européenne*, Luxembourg, Eds. Saint-Paul, 1992.

Kill, Jean. *1000 jahriges Luxembourg, Woher? Wohin?*, Luxembourg, Impr. C.O.P.E., 1963.

Pauly, Michel. *De l'état à la nation, 1839–1989*, Luxembourg, Impr. Saint-Paul, 1984.

Poos, Jacques. "From Marshall Plan to the Creation of Europe," in *Present at the Creation*, New York, Harper & Row, 1980.

———. *Le Luxembourg dans le marché commun*, Luxembourg, Impr. Bourg-Bourger, 1961.

Poos, Jacques, et Henri Rieben. *Jean Monnet et le Luxembourg dans la construction de l'Europe*, Lausanne, Centre de recherches européennes, 1989.

Poos, Jacques, et al. "Luxemburg: Daten, Informationen, Analysen," in *Handelsblatt*, Düsseldorf, 1984. pp. 2–17

Robert Schuman: Les racines et l'oeuvre d'un grand Européen, Luxembourg, Impr. Victor Buck, 1986. Guide to an exposition organized for the centenary of Robert Schuman.

Schmit, Mars. *Charnière d'Europe*, Luxembourg, Schortgen, 1990.

Sion, Georges. *Six villes: une Europe*, Brussels, Union des Capitales de la Communauté Européenne, 1968.

Spang, Paul. "Les sources pour l'histoire de l'unification européenne au Grand-Duché de Luxembourg," in *Sources de l'histoire de l'integration européenne*, Bruxelles, 1980.

Stoffels, Jules. *La canalisation de la Moselle*, Luxembourg, Eds. Banque Generale du Luxembourg, 1984.

Trausch, Gilbert. *Joseph Bech: Un homme dans son siècle*, Luxembourg, Impr. Saint-Paul, 1978.

———. *Le Luxembourg à l'époque contemporaine*, Luxembourg, Eds. Bourg-Bourger, 1975.

Wiese, Ernst. *Le Grand-Duché de Luxembourg: carrefour européen*, Namur, Ed. du Soleil Levant, 1953.

17. Humor

Erasmus, George. *How to Remain What You Are*, Luxembourg, Editpress, 1989. A light-hearted spoof of Luxembourg history in the vein of *1066 and All That*.

18. Industry

Chomé, Felix. *Un demi-siècle d'histoire industrielle, 1911–1964*, Luxembourg, ARBED, 1972.

Mousset, Jean-Luc. *L'Industrialisation du Luxembourg de 1800 à 1914* (2e edition), Luxembourg, Musée National d'Histoire et d'Art, 1994.

Quasten, Heinz. *Die Wirtschaftsformation des Schwerindustrie im Luxemburger Minette*, Saarbrucken, Universität des Saarlandes, 1970.

Simon, Francois. "L'outillage national," in *Le Luxembourg: Livre du Centenaire*, ed. Albert Northumb, Luxembourg, Gouvernement Grand-Ducal, 1948.

Spang, Paul. *Un siècle de hauts-fourneaux à Rodange, 1872–1972*, Rodange, Minière et Métallurgique de Rodange, 1972.

Statistiques de l'artisanat, 1993, Luxembourg, Chambre des Metiers, Center de Promotion et de Recherche, 1994.

Steffes, Michel, et Guy Steffes. *Les industries minière et sidérurgique du Luxembourg au fil des années*, Luxembourg, Impr. Bourg-Bourger, 1962.

19. Letzebuergesch: Dictionaries, Grammars, and Vocabularies

Actioun Lëtzebuergesch. *Eis Sprooch, Kommt mir léiere lëtzebuergesch*, Luxembourg, Impr. P. Linden, 1983.

Bruch, Robert. *Précis populaire de grammaire luxembourgeoise* (3e edition), Section de Linguistique de l'Institut grand-ducal, 1973.

Christophory, Jul, *The Luxembourgers in their own words*, Luxembourg, Eds. Bourg-Bourger, 1978.

————. *Mir schwatze lëtzebuergesch*, Luxembourg, Impr. Saint-Paul, 1974.

————. *Sot et op lëtzebuergesch*, Luxembourg, Impr. Saint-Paul, 1973.

Hess, J. *Der sprache der Luxemburger*, Luxembourg, Paul Bruck, 1946.

Krings, Sandra. "Language Problems in Luxembourg," in *Luxembourg Weekly*, 29 July 1977.

Leyers, Pierre. "Die sprache des Landes Luxemburg und seiner Beudiner ist seit jeher Deutsch," in *Tageblatt*, Esch-sur-Alzette, 26 April 1990.

Luxembourger Wörterbuch, Luxembourg, Impr. P. Linden, 5 vols., 1950–1977.

Zimmer, Jacqui. *6000 Wierder op Lëtzebuergesch*, Luxembourg, Eds. Saint-Paul, 1993.

20. Literature, Science, and Culture

Ausonius, Decimus Magnus. *Mosella*, Paris, Universitaires de France, 1972.

Bibliographie courante de la litterature luxembourgeoise, 1990, Luxembourg, Archives Nationales, 1991.

Bourg, Tony, et Frank Wilhelm. *Le Grand-Duché de Luxembourg dans les cahiers de Victor Hugo*, Luxembourg, RTL Edition, 1985.

Les cahiers luxembourgeois: Revue libre des lettres, des science et des arts, published annually, first series, Luxembourg, Impr. P. Schroell, 1922–1939, second series, Luxembourg, Impr. Bourg-Bourger, 1946–1964.

Christophory, Jul. *A Short History of Literature in Luxembourgish*, Luxembourg, Bibliothéque Nationale, 1994. Includes English translations.

Cultural Life in the Grand Duchy of Luxembourg, Luxembourg, Ministry of Cultural Affairs, 1977.

Hoffman, Fernand. *Geschichte der Luxemburger Mundartdichtung* (2 vols.), Luxembourg, Ministère des Arts et des Sciences, Vol. I, 1964, Vol. II, 1965.

Kieffer, Rosemarie, ed. *Litterature Luxembourgeoise de Langue Française*, Quebec, Eds. Nauman, 1980

————. "Luxembourg Literature Today," in *Books Abroad: Literary Quarterly*, Summer 1974.

Meyers, Joseph, "La Vie Musicale," in *Luxembourg: Livre du Centenaire*, Luxembourg, Impr. Saint-Paul, 1948.

Nichols, Richard. *Radio Luxembourg: The Station of the Stars: History of Fifty Years of Broadcasting*, London, W. H. Allen & Co., 1983.

Nopenny, Marcel. *Victor Hugo dans le Grand-Duché du Luxembourg* (2e ed.), Luxembourg, Impr. Pierre Linden, 1948.

Rapport d'Activité 1992, Luxembourg, Ministère des Affaires Culturelles, 1992.

Revue Luxembourgeoise de litterature génerale & comparée, Vols. 1–7, Luxembourg, Rapidpress, 1987–1994. Annual.

Ries, Nicolas. "La vie litteraire," in *Le Luxembourg: Livre du Centenaire*, ed. Albert Northumb, Luxembourg, Gouvernement Grand-Ducal, 1948.

Rodange, Michel. *Renert,* Luxembourg, Edi-Centre, 1968.

Sprunck, Alphonse. "L'Activité Scientifique," in *Luxembourg: Livre du Centenaire*, Luxembourg, Impr. Saint-Paul, 1948.

21. Luxembourg and the Low Countries: Early Times to Benelux

Bernard, Henri. *Terre commune: histoire du pays de Benelux, microcosme de l'Europe*, Brussels, Brepols, 1961.

Clement, L. "Luxembourg," in *Portrait of the Regions, Vol. I: Germany, Benelux, Denmark*, Luxembourg, Office for Official Publications of the European Communities, 1993.

Eyck, F. Gunther. *The Benelux Countries, an Historical Survey*, Princeton, Van Nostrand, 1959. In two sections, the first a short history of the Low Countries from Roman times to the creation of Benelux, the second a number of documents relating to that history.

Gay, François, et P. Wagnet. *Le Benelux*, Paris, Presse universitaires de France, 1960.

George, Pierre, et Robert Severin. *Belgique, Pays-Bays, Luxembourg*, Paris, Presses universitaires de France, 1967. Historical geography.

Hamblock, Herman. *Die Beneluxstaaten: eine geographie Länderkunde*, Darmstadt, Wissenschaftliche Buchgesellschaft, 1977.

International Review. *Destination Benelux*, Jersey, Channel Islands, Review Publishing Company, 1994.

Kunitzki, N. von. *Le Luxembourg dans l'U.E.B.L.*, Luxembourg, Eds. d'Letzebuerger Land, 1972.

Majerus, Emile. *Das Wirtschaftbündnis des Grossherzogtums Luxemburg mit Belgien*, Luxembourg, P. Hausmer, 1928.

Mansfield, Anthony J., and P. J. Powrie. *France and Benelux*, London, Harrap, 1972.

Mast, André. *Les pays de Benelux*, Paris, Pichon, 1960.

Ormond, George W. T. *Belgium and Luxembourg*, London, Hodder & Stoughton, 1923.

Riley, Raymond C. et al. *Benelux: An Economic Geography of Belgium, the Netherlands, and Luxembourg*, London, Chatto & Windus, 1975.

Rowen, Harry H., ed. "The Low Countries in Early Modern Times," in *Documentary History of Western Civilization*, ed. Harry H. Rowen, New York, Walker, 1972.

Tamse, Coenrad, et Gilbert Trausch, eds. *The relations between The Netherlands and Luxembourg in the 19th & 20th Centuries*, la Haye, SDU Uitgeverij, 1991.

Weil, Gordon L. *The Benelux Nations: The Policies of Small-Country Democracies*, New York, Holt, Rinehart, and Winston, 1970.

Wickman, Stephen B. *Belgium: A Country Study*, Washington, The American University, 1985. Contains a section on Luxembourg.

22. Maps, Charts, and Atlases

Atlas du Luxembourg, Luxembourg, Ministère de l'Education Nationale, 1971.

Ferraris, Joseph de. *Carte du Cabinet des Pay-Bays autrichienne: Grand Duchy of Luxembourg* (3 vols.), Brussels, Pro Civitate, 1970.

Grand-Duché de Luxembourg: carte topographique et touristique, echelle 1:100,000, Luxembourg, L'Administration du Cadastre et de la Topographie, 1980.

Vekene, Emile van der. *Les Cartes Géographiques du Duché de Luxembourg* (2e ed.), Luxembourg, Eds. J.-P. Krippler-Muller, 1980.

———. *Les Plans de la Ville et Forteresse de Luxembourg*, Luxembourg, Impr. Saint-Paul, 1976.

23. Personal Names

STATEC. *Die Luxemburger und ihre Vorname, Luxembourg*, RTL Edition, 1987.

24. Periodicals

A. Newspapers

The European. A weekly newspaper published in London with excellent coverage of the continent. Runs an occasional article or story about Luxembourg.

International Herald Tribune. Daily newspaper published in Paris and simultaneously in various other cities. Infrequent articles or stories about Luxembourg, generally on the financial pages or in supplements on money and banking.

Lëtzebuerger Journal. Daily newspaper that supports and is supported by the Democratic Party. Good news coverage.

d'Lëtzebuerger Land. German-language weekly with thoughtful articles on various topics.

Luxembourg News. Weekly newspaper in magazine format that keeps the English-speaking community informed about what is going on in Luxembourg. Formerly known as the *News Digest*, it is still frequently referred to by that name.

Luxembourg News of America. Monthly published in Skokie, Illinois, which keeps the Luxembourg community in the United States informed about the activities of various associations and clubs in the United States with some news about what is going on in Luxembourg.

Luxemburger Wort. Luxembourg's leading newspaper with a daily circulation of over 80,000 copies. Editorially, it represents the viewpoint of the Catholic Church and the Christian Social People's Party, but its news columns are generally unbiased. Most of its articles are written in German, but there is an occasional article in French or, nowadays, Portuguese.

Lux-Post. Advertising "throw away" in German with an occasional article in Lëtzebuergesch. It does contain information about what is going on in Luxembourg and some interesting articles.

Le Républicain Lorraine. French regional daily that publishes a Luxembourg edition. Read fairly widely by that portion of the population that cannot read German easily.

Tageblatt. German-language daily that represents the viewpoint of the Luxembourg Socialist Workers Party (LSAP). Tabloid in form, but not in style. Its circulation is about a quarter that of the *Luxemburger Wort.*

B. Magazines

Bulletin d'Information et de Documentation, Governement du Grand-Duché de Luxembourg, Service Information et Presse.

Facts, figures, articles and speeches, mostly in French, about events in Luxembourg, state visits, etc. Published four times a year.

Hémecht (Homeland): *Revue d'histoire luxembourgeoise*, Luxembourg, Impr. Saint-Paul, 1948–present. Published annually in book format, with articles about various aspects of Luxembourg history. Successor to *Ons Hémecht*, which was suppressed by the Germans in 1940.

Luxembourg Business. Monthly newsmagazine that keeps English-speaking readers informed about what is going on in the Luxembourg business world.

Ons Hémecht (Our Homeland): *Organ des Vereins für Luxemburger Geschichte, Literature und Kunst*, Luxembourg, 1895–1939. Various publishers. The last few editions were published by the Imprimerie Saint-Paul.

Ons Stad. Published trimestrially by the city of Luxembourg. Contains articles and stories about the capital city in German and French. Notices about events and services are sometimes written in Italian and Portuguese.

Revue d'lëtzebuerger illustriert. Weekly illustrated news magazine written in German, with a good deal of advertising.

Voila Luxembourg. Monthly illustrated magazine with both French and English-language editions. Contains interesting articles on various aspects of Luxembourg life, culture, and history.

25. Politics, Politicians, and Political Parties

Fayot, Ben. *Sozialismus in Luxemburg: von der Anfängen bis 1940*, Luxembourg, Centre de Recherches et d'Etudes Socialistes, 1979.

Frank, Robert. *Pierre Werner: eine politische Karriere*, Luxembourg, Impr. Saint-Paul, 1988.

Hennicot-Schoepges, Erna. "Pierre Werner à la Chambre de Deputés," in *Innovation-Integration: Festschrift für Pierre Werner*, Luxembourg, Impr. Saint-Paul, 1993.

Krier, Antoine. *75 Jor Lëtzebuerger Socialismus: aus dem Parteilehen Luxemburger Arbeiter und Sozialisten*, Esch-sur-Alzette, Impr. Victor, 1977.

Schaus, Emile. *Ursprung und Leistung einer Partei: Rechtspartei und Christliche-Soziale Volkspartei 1914–1974*, Luxembourg, Impr. Saint-Paul, 1974.

Werner, Pierre. *Itineraire Luxembourgeois et Européen: Evolu-*

tions et Souvenirs (2e edition), Luxembourg, Impr. Saint-Paul, 1992.

26. Population, Immigration, and Emigration

Christophory, Jules. "Portrait of the Luxembourger," in *Les Luxembourgois par eux-mêmes*, Luxembourg, Impr. Bourg-Bourger, 1978.

Ensch, Jean et. al., eds. *Luxembourgers in the New World* (2 vols.), Esch-sur-Alzette, Eds. Relieures Schortgen, 1987.

Gonner, Nicholas. "Die Luxemburger in der Neuen Welt," Dubuque, Iowa, *Luxembourg Gazette*, 1889.

Hess, Joseph. "L'emigration luxembourgeoise," in *Le Luxembourg: Livre du Centenaire*, Luxembourg, Impr. Saint-Paul, 1948.

Krieps, R. *Luxemburger in Amerika*, Luxembourg, Impr. Bourg-Bourger, 1962.

Laby, Claude. *L'emploi et les migrations au Grand-Duché de Luxembourg*, Luxembourg, Université Internationale de Sciences Comparées, 1969.

Meyers, Joseph. "Le peuple luxembourgeois," in *Le Luxembourg: Livre du Centenaire*, Luxembourg, Impr. Saint-Paul, 1948.

Milles, Mary E. *Dann singen wir Victoria! Luxembourg immigration to America, 1848–1872: a selective bibliography*, Brussels, Center for American Studies, 1979.

———. *Rollingstone*, Luxembourg, Eds. Guy Binsfeld, 1983. Rollingstone is a Luxembourg settlement in Minnesota.

Pably, Michel. *L'immigration au Luxembourg*, Luxembourg, (s.n.) 1985.

———. *Lëtzebuerg de Lëtzebuerger? Le Luxembourg face à l'immigration*, Luxembourg, Eds. Guy Binsfeld, 1985.

Ries, Nicolas. *Le peuple luxembourgeois: essai de psychologie*, Diekirch, Eds. Schroell, 1920.

Stumper, Robert. *Luxemburger Wissenschaftler im Ausland*, Luxembourg, *Lëtzeburger Land*, 1962.

Trausch, Gérard. *La croissance démographique du Grand-Duché de Luxembourg du debut du XIX siècle à nos jours* (2e ed.), Esch-sur-Alzette, Impr. P. Victor, 1972.

27. Religion and the Church

Bertholet, R. P. Jean. *Histoire Ecclesiatique et Civile du Duché de Luxembourg et Comté de Chiny* (8 vols.), Bruxelles, Eds.

Culture et Civilisation, 1973. A reprint of a work by a noted Jesuit historian, originally published in 1743.

Donkel, E. *Die Kirche in Luxembourg von dem Anfangen bis sur Gegengwart*, Luxembourg, Impr. Saint-Paul, 1950.

Friedrich, Evy. "Juden in Luxembourg," in *Luxembourg-Review*, No. 19, 1987.

Hamer, Pierre. *Anselme d'Esch*, Luxembourg, Impr. Saint-Paul, 1977. Part of a three-volume *Histoire des Capucins de Luxembourg*.

———. *Raphael de Luxembourg: Une contribution luxembourgeoise à la colonisation de la Louisiane*, Luxembourg, Impr. Saint-Paul, 1966. Part of a three-volume *Histoire des Capucins de Luxembourg*.

Heiderscheid, André. *Aspects de Sociologie Religieuse du Diocese de Luxembourg*, Vol. I, Luxembourg, Impr. Saint-Paul, 1992.

Heilighausen, Georges, et Alex Langini. *Welcome!*, Luxembourg, Impr. Saint-Paul, 1991. Information about churches, religious ceremonies and processions, and places of pilgrimage in the Grand Duchy.

Hirsch, Joseph. *Die Wegkreuze des Cantons Mersch*, Luxembourg, Impr. Saint-Paul, 1992.

Krier, Tony, ed. *L'Octave de Notre Dame de Luxembourg*, Luxembourg, Impr. Saint-Paul, 1969.

Langini, Alex. *La procession dansante d'Echternach: son origine et son histoire*, Echternach, Société d'Embellissement et du Tourism, 1977.

Lehrmann, Ch. & Gr. *La communité juive du Luxembourg dans le passé et dans le présent*, Esch-sur-Alzette, Impr. Cooperative Luxembourgeoise, 1953.

Ludmann, P. et al. *Klosterkirche Sankt Alfons Luxemburg*, Luxembourg, Impr. Fr. Faber, 1993.

Majerus, N. *L'erection de l'évêche de Luxembourg*, Luxembourg, Impr. Saint-Paul, 1951.

St. Willibrordus Basilika, Echternach, Munich und Zurich, Schnell & Steiner, 1965.

Wampach, Camille. *Sankt Willibrord: sein Leben und Lebenswerk*, Luxembourg, Impr. Saint-Paul, 1953.

28. Social Classes and Legislation

Bedos, François, et al. *Famille et structures sociales au Luxembourg*, Luxembourg, Ministère de la Famille, 1978.

Etienne, Emile. "Cent ans legislation sociale," in *Le Luxembourg: Livre du Centenaire*, ed. Albert Northumb, Luxembourg, Gouvernement Grand-Ducal, 1948.

Heiderscheid, André. *Les Luxembourgeois: un peuple épris de sécurité*, Luxembourg, Université Internationale de Sciences Comparées, 1970.

Schaack, Robert. *Prestations sociales au Grand-Duché de Luxembourg*, Luxembourg, Ministère de l'Education Nationale, 1969.

29. Statistics

Annuaire statistique Luxembourg 1992, Luxembourg, Statec, 1993.

Bulletin d'Information et de Documentation, Luxembourg, Service Information et Presse, 1945–1994. Published every three months.

Eurostat. *General Statistics Yearbook, 1993*, Luxembourg, Office des Publications Officielles des Communautés Européennes, 1993.

Luxembourg in Figures, Luxembourg, Service Central de la Statistique et des Etudes Economiques. Published annually.

Repertoire analytique des publications, Luxembourg, Service Central de la Statistique et des Études Economiques, 1970.

30. Transportation

Cermakian, Jean. *The Moselle River and Canal from the Roman Empire to the European Economic Community*, Toronto, University of Toronto Press, 1975.

Les chemins de fer au Grand-Duché de Luxembourg, Luxembourg, Féderation nationale des associations ferroviaires, 1985.

Etringer, Norbert. *Aus der Geschichte der Moselschiffart* (2e edition), Luxembourg, Krippler-Mulller, 1978.

Federmeyer, Edward. *Schmalspurbahnen in Luxemburg* (2 vols.), Luxembourg-Crauthein, Luxprint, 1992–1994.

Hamer, Pierre. *L'aviation luxembourgeoise: son passé, son avenir*, Luxembourg, Impr. Bourg-Bourger, 1978.

Majerus, Emile. *Les chemins de fer à section normale du Grand-Duché de Luxembourg*, Luxembourg, J. Beffort, 1933.

31. Viticulture

Georges, Martin. *Aus der Geschichte des Luxemburger Weinbaus*, Wiesbaden (BRD), Gesellschaft für die Geschichte des Weines, 1977.

The Luxembourg Moselle Wines, Luxembourg, Press and Information Service, 1973.

Ries, Adrienne. *L'agriculture et la viticulture luxembourgeoise dans le marché commun*, Luxembourg, Université Internationale de Sciences Comparées, 1973.

Werle, Otmar. *Die Bedeutung der Grenze im Weinbaugebiet der deutsch-luxemburgischen Obermosel*, Trier, Géographie Gesellschaft, 1972.

———. *Das Weinbaugebiet der Deutsch-Luxemburgischen Obermosel*, Trier, Géographie Gesellschaft, 1977.

About the Author

Harry C. Barteau (A.B., Northeastern University, M.A., Harvard University, and Ph.D., Miami University of Ohio) is a native of Fairhaven, Massachusetts. After teaching for several years in the United States, he entered the field of international education, and has held teaching and administrative positions in Taiwan, Singapore, Germany, the Dominican Republic, and the Grand Duchy of Luxembourg. He has recently retired after serving nineteen years as head of the American International School of Luxembourg, and is living in a small village in Luxembourg, where he and his wife, Maryann, have made their home.

Dr. Barteau has developed a keen interest in Luxembourg history, and a deep appreciation of the people and culture of the Grand Duchy. He is the author of a booklet on the Grand Duchy, developed to teach his students at the American International School about their host country, which has enjoyed a modest sale among English-speaking foreigners in Luxembourg and among people of Luxembourg descent living in the United States. He is currently working on a book about American education in the United States and overseas.

In 1994, Dr. Barteau was made an Officer in the Ordre Grand-Ducal de la Couronne de Chêne by His Royal Highness, Grand Duke Jean of Luxembourg.